THE IRISH WRITERS
HANDBOOK

'The *Handbook* is an essential tool for all Irish writers.'

John Banville

THE IRISH WRITERS
HANDBOOK

The
Books
IRELAND GUIDE

Edited by Ruth McKee

THE WORDWELL GROUP

First published 2024 by Books Ireland
Dublin, Ireland

www.booksirelandmagazine.com
www.wordwellbooks.com

First edition

Books Ireland
The Wordwell Group
Unit 9, 78 Furze Road
Sandyford
Dublin, Ireland

Individual pieces © the authors, 2024
Design, layout and selection © Wordwell Limited, 2024

ISBN: 978-1-916742-70-3 (paperback)
ISBN: 978-1-916742-71-0 (ebook)

'Storytelling and the Moon', by Yan Ge is published with the kind permission of Foyles, via agent Matthew Turner.

'Chop Wood, Carry Water', by Danielle McLaughlin is published with the kind permission of *The Stinging Fly*.

Illustration by Elina Braslina for *Bumpfizzle* by Patricia Forde (Little Island) reproduced by permission of the illustrator.

The publishers wish to thank the Royal Irish Academy and the PublishOA project for permission to reproduce publisher listings under licence CC-BY.

All information in this work is correct at the time of printing to the best knowledge of the publishers. All information is provided on a good-faith basis and the publisher disclaims any and all liability in relation to the usage of any information, commentary, analysis, opinions, advice and/or recommendations contained in this work.

British Library Cataloguing in Publication Data.
A catalogue record for this book is available from the National Library of Ireland and the British Library.

Typesetting and design by the Wordwell Group.
Printed in Ireland

www.booksirelandmagazine.com is generously supported by the Arts Council of Ireland.

CONTENTS

CRAFT – FICTION

CRAFT – NON-FICTION

PROPOSALS & PITCHES

The Publishing Experience

Facts & Figures

Opportunities & Resources

CHILDREN'S BOOKS

THIS WRITING LIFE

THE DIRECTORY

A Note from the Editor

Ruth McKee

Put your own writing first. This is Jan Carson's advice for surviving as a writer, and it's a good rule to keep close. From the blush of an idea to the first draft, from rewriting to editing, from querying a publisher to seeing your book as a real, living, thing – it always comes back to the work.

In the book you are holding, people from all parts of this writing life offer you their experience. If you write fiction, Donal Ryan explores reading as your window to empathy, Eoghan Smith discusses staying true to your vision, and Una Mannion touches on that blow to the heart in the genesis of a short story. Milena Williamson explores the evolution of a first poetry collection and Cristín Leach engages with writing that lies in the liminal, that music between fact and fiction. Hilary Fannin reaches for the truth in memoir, while commissioning editors from our major non-fiction publishers advise on your book proposal. There is useful practical advice and information here too, whether you're querying a newspaper or a festival, applying for funding, wondering whether self-publishing is for you, or figuring out copyright. Deirdre Nolan talks about that elusive animal – literary fiction which sells – while Ronan Colgan tackles the important question of why a book costs what it does, and how profits and royalties are distributed.

If you write or illustrate for children and young people, there are essential tips for building your career from Ashwin Chacko, words from our Laureate na nÓg, Patricia Forde, and Sarah Webb gives invaluable advice about giving workshops and events, while Ruth Ennis illuminates the joy and opportunities in children's books.

Then there is the view from the other side of the bridge, once your book is published. Olivia Fitzsimons gives guidance on how to manage the expectations of others – and of yourself, and Jessica Traynor discusses the slings and arrows of those second, third and fourth collections for a poet in the middle of their creative life. Paul Rouse brings an invigorating angle to sports writing and Paul Carroll explores Ireland's emerging comics scene.

You'll hear from the heart of our bookshops and literary organisations, along with suggestions on how to build community, and looking after your mental health. Perspectives on teaching and studying writing are here too, as are tips on setting up a writing group, and the pitfalls of defamation law.

And for those of you who are hesitant about whether this writing life is for you, if you belong, Kit de Waal speaks courage, asserting your place in our flourishing literary culture. In the end though, as Danielle McLaughlin concludes, it's about the practice – the hours, days, and years of writing that you will do regardless of that most slippery of concepts, 'success'. So I hope this guide will encourage you to prioritise your work: in the words of Maeve Brennan "you are all it has."

THE CONTRIBUTORS

CRAFT – FICTION

DONAL RYAN. Prize-winning author of novels including the Booker long-listed *The Spinning Heart* (Doubleday Ireland), *From a Low and Quiet Sea* (Doubleday) and *Heart, Be at Peace* (Penguin).

JAMIE O'CONNELL. Author of *Diving for Pearls* (Doubleday).

DAVID BUTLER. Poet, short-story writer, playwright, novelist. Books include *City of Dis* (New Island) and *Jabberwock* (Dedalus Books).

UNA MANNION. Author of *A Crooked Tree* and *Tell Me What I Am* (Faber).

NIALL MCARDLE. Short-story writer and contributor to Sunday Miscellany (RTÉ Radio 1).

MILENA WILLIAMSON. PhD in poetry from the Seamus Heaney Centre at Queen's University Belfast. Author of *Charm for Catching a Train* (Green Bottle Press) and *Into the Night that Flies So Fast* (Dedalus Press).

JESSICA TRAYNOR. Poet, essayist and poetry editor at Banshee. Author of *Liffey Swim*, *The Quick* (Dedalus Press) and *Pit Lullabies* (Bloodaxe Books) and winner of the Hennessy New Writer of the Year Award and the Lawrence O'Shaughnessy Award.

Yan Ge. Author of thirteen books in Chinese, including five novels. *Elsewhere* (Faber) is her debut English-language short-story collection.

Andrea O'Brien. An award-winning translator of fiction and non-fiction by authors such as Michelle Obama, Rónán Hession, Jessie Greengrass, Dana Spiotta and Claire Fuller.

Nuala O'Connor. Her fifth novel *Nora* (New Island), about Nora Barnacle and James Joyce, was a Top 10 historical novel in the *New York Times*. She won Irish Short Story of the Year at the 2022 Irish Book Awards and is editor at flash e-journal *Splonk*.

Paul Carroll. Writer and comic creator, editor of *Turning Roads*, *Down Below*, and *Fractured Realms*.

Eoghan Smith. Author of *The Failing Heart*, *A Provincial Death* and *A Mind of Winter* (Dedalus Books).

Craft – Non-Fiction

Kevin Power. Author of two novels, *Bad Day in Blackrock* (2008) and *White City* (2021), and a collection of criticism, *The Written World* (2022).

Christabel Scaife. Senior Commissioning Editor for Irish studies and literary studies at Liverpool University Press.

Paul Rouse. Historian, newspaper columnist and podcast host. Author of *Sport and Ireland: A History* (2015) and *author of Sport in Modern Irish Life,* shortlisted for the An Post Sports Book of the Year 2023

DONAL FALLON. Historian working with Dublin City Council Culture Company, and the presenter of the *Three Castles Burning* social history podcast.

CRISTÍN LEACH. Irish art critic and author of the memoir *Negative Space* (2022) and *From Ten till Dusk, A Portrait of the Royal Hibernian Academy of Arts in Twelve Stories* (2023).

HILARY FANNIN. Award-winning playwright, novelist, columnist and memoirist. Adapted Maxim Gorky's *Children of the Sun* for Rough Magic Theatre Company and The Abbey Theatre in 2024.

PROPOSALS & PITCHES

PATRICK O'DONOGHUE. Senior Commissioning Editor at Gill Books He has worked in the Irish publishing industry for over sixteen years.

MADELEINE KEANE. Literary editor of the *Sunday Independent*, lecturer with the School of English, UCD, and board member, Children's Books Ireland.

SARAH LIDDY. Publisher of the Gill Life imprint at Gill Books.

DEIRDRE NOLAN. Publishing director of Eriu, an imprint of Bonnier Books UK.

JULIANNE MOONEY SIRON. Festival Director of the Dublin Book Festival, one of Ireland's largest book festivals, which she has been programming since 2010.

CATHERINE HEARN. Co-founder and editor of *Tolka,* a biannual journal of formally promiscuous non-fiction.

The Publishing Experience

Ronan Colgan. Managing Director of the Wordwell Group, Chair of the Dublin Book Festival, past President of Publishing Ireland and former juror on the EU Prize for Literature for Ireland.

Mark Tighe. Joined the *Sunday Independent* in June 2022, having worked as a reporter with the *Sunday Times* for 16 years. As well as covering legal affairs, he specialises in investigative reporting, and is the co-author of *Champagne Football* with Paul Rowan (Penguin).

Kevin Curran. Author of *Beatsploitation* (Liberties Press), *Citizens* (Liberties Press), and *Youth* (The Lilliput Press).

Ruth Hallinan. Publishing professional for fifteen years, President of Publishing Ireland 2021-22, one of *The Bookseller* '150' 2021 and 2022, and *The Bookseller* Rising Star 2020.

Ivan O'Brien. Managing Director of O'Brien Press and past President of Publishing Ireland and the Dublin Book Festival.

Liz McSkeane. Founder and Director of Turas Press. Hennessy and Irish Writers Centre Novel Fair winner. Author of four poetry collections, a short story collection, and a novel.

Pamela G. Hobbs. Author of *The Fitzgerald Family Series*, five novels of romantic suspense set in Ireland (Poolbeg).

Patricia Gibney. Irish and international bestselling author of the Detective Lottie Parker series. Over two million sales and translated in multiple territories.

Facts & Figures

Belle Edelman. Marketing Content Manager for Nielsen Book-Data.

Samantha Holman. CEO of the Irish Copyright Licensing Agency and copyright expert for the text and image sector.

Opportunities & Resources

Claire Hennessy. Author of several YA novels, and a freelance editor and creative writing facilitator.

Jackie Lynam. Librarian and writer from Dublin. Her first collection *Traces: Poetry and Essays* was published in October 2023.

Peter Clarke. Poet, retired psychologist, published in 11 volumes of *Lifespan* anthologies, and 2 volumes of *Bealtaine Writers Anthologies*.

Gerard Beirne. Author of eight books of poetry and fiction, including his latest, *The Thickness of Ice* (Baraka Press 2024). He teaches on the BA Writing and Literature program at ATU Sligo.

Averill Buchanan. Editor and Publishing Consultant. Founder and member of the Editors' & Proofreaders' Alliance of Northern Ireland (EPANI)

Liz Quirke. Author of poetry collections *The Road Slowly*, and *How We Arrive in Winter* (Salmon).

Brian Langan. Freelance editor and founder of Storyline Literary Agency.

RUTH HEGARTY. Managing Editor of the Royal Irish Academy's publishing house.

FIONA MCKAY. Author of novella-in-flash *The Top Road* (AdHoc Fiction) and flash fiction collection *Drawn and Quartered* (Alien Buddha Press). SmokeLong Fiction Emerging Writer Fellow 2023.

CATHAL PÓIRTÉIR. Author of several books on the history of famine era Ireland, and Irish language book reviewer for *Books Ireland*. Author of *An Tiarna George Hill agus Pobal Ghaoth Dobhair* (Cló Iar-Chonnacht).

SINÉAD MACAODHA. A multi-lingual international arts executive with over twenty-five years' experience in literature policy formulation, strategy development and literature programme implementation. Executive Director of Literature Ireland.

VALERIE BISTANY. A professional arts manager and producer with over 30 years of international experience in Ireland, England and the USA. Former Director/CEO of the Irish Writers Centre 2013–2023.

JENNIFER MCMAHON. A winner of the IWC Novel Fair. Words in *Crannog*, the *Irish Independent* (New Irish Writing), the *Oxford Prize Anthology*, *Heimat Review*, *Empyrean*, *Books Ireland*, Loft Books.

VANESSA FOX O'LOUGHLIN. Founder of the award-winning website Writing.ie, board member of the Society of Authors and the Crime Writers Association. Vanessa writes crime as Sam Blake, and has been shortlisted for Irish Crime Novel of the Year three times.

AOIFE ROANTREE. Manager, The Book Centre, Kilkenny, and former Chair of Bookselling Ireland.

Children's Books

Ruth Ennis. M.Phil in Children's Literature and aspiring children's/young adult writer. Reviewer at Children's Books Ireland and *Books Ireland*.

Sarah Webb. Author of *Blazing a Trail: Irish Women who Changed the World* (illustrated by Lauren O'Neill), Co-editor of *I am the Wind: Irish Poems for Children Everywhere* (illustrated by Ashwin Chacko), and author of *The Weather Girls* (The O'Brien Press).

Lucinda Jacob. Award-winning children's writer and creative writing facilitator. Her books include *Hopscotch in the Sky* and *Climate SOS!* Co-editor of *I Am the Wind: Irish Poems for Children Everywhere*.

Lori Moriarty. Works for Laois Library Service, and is part of the YA social media team for the Discover Irish Kids' Books campaign. Reviews for Children's Books Ireland, where she is also a Book Doctor.

Siobhán Parkinson. Author, translator, editor. Inaugural Laureate na nÓg, founder of Little Island Books.

Patricia Forde. Ireland's seventh Laureate na nÓg. She writes in Irish and in English, and has published both picture books and novels, including *The Girl Who Fell to Earth* (Little Island 2023) and *An Mactíre Deireannach* (Futa Fata 2023).

Elina Braslina. An artist from Latvia who has illustrated more than thirty books, mostly for children. She also works in animation and creates feminist art.

PADDY DONNELLY. Award-winning author-illustrator of picture books such as *Fox & Son Tailers*, *The Vanishing Lake* and *Dodos Are Not Extinct* (O'Brien Press).

ASHWIN CHACKO. A positively playful author, illustrator and motivational speaker. His mission is to champion creativity and empower people to find their inner spark.

THIS WRITING LIFE

OLIVIA FITZSIMONS. Contributing editor, *The Stinging Fly*. Debut author, *The Quiet Whispers Never Stop* (John Murray), shortlisted for the Kate O'Brien and Butler Literary Awards, and an *Irish Examiner* Book of the Year.

JAN CARSON. Belfast-based author of three novels and five short-story collections including *The Fire Starters* (Doubleday Ireland) which won the EU Prize for Literature for Ireland 2019. She is a fellow of the Royal Society of Literature.

DARAGH FLEMING. Poet and essayist, author of *Lonely Boy* (BookHub Publishing) and founder of award-winning mental health blog, Thoughts Too Big.

ANNE TANNAM. Poet in Residence with Poetry Ireland (2023 - 2025). Author of four poetry collections, most recently *dismantle* (Salmon). Professional Certified Coach (PCC) who helps writers design and sustain flourishing writing practices.

CHANDRIKA NARAYANAN-MOHAN. A writer and consultant with a background in business development for the arts. Her writing has been published by Dedalus Press, *Banshee*, *Stinging Fly*, Poetry Ireland and others.

KIT DE WAAL. Author of several award-winning novels including Irish Book of the Year *My Name is Leon* (Viking 2016), *The Trick to Time* (Viking 2018) and a memoir, *Without Warning, and Only Sometimes* (Hachette 2022).

DANIELLE McLAUGHLIN. Author of a short-story collection, *Dinosaurs on Other Planets* (The Stinging Fly Press), and a novel, *The Art of Falling* (John Murray).

Craft

Fiction

Reading on the Frontline

Donal Ryan

I don't know what a good reader is, or a bad one, or if such a distinction can exist between people who have undertaken the very generous act of buying, or borrowing, or otherwise obtaining a book, and spending hours or days of their precious time travelling through the imaginings of a fellow human. A good reader must be a good listener, I think. Reading is an act of empathy, and of sympathy; like the writer, who must abandon their cold, critical, scientific faculties in the moment of creation, the reader must also, in the moment of bearing witness, shut off their objective analytical instincts, step outside of themselves almost completely, immerse themselves in the world that will rise from the words on the page, the new universe that can be wrought by the combinations of the tiny group of ciphers into which we have distilled the entirety of our armoury in our fight for understanding, of each other, of the world we share, of the struggles we face.

Ray Bradbury declared that the keyboard was no place for thinking. I agree. It's best that a writer should have their thinking done, their formulations worked out, their cold narrative equations balanced before they get to the act of making their story live in language. Emotion should be the overwhelming element that drives the moment of creation, so that it is embedded in the work and will remain latent there until the reader's eyes meet the page. The reader then becomes the most important part of the whole, the integral energy in the sublimation of imagination into art.

If our hearts and minds are open we will attune ourselves effortlessly to the writer's intent. If we readers are prepared to shuck off all prejudice about what a story *should* be, about what *should* happen, about how people *should* act, we will find ourselves forming in our imaginations beautifully detailed vistas peopled by characters who are no longer fictive beings but living, breathing creatures with actual lives, motivations, ambitions; they will have faults, sometimes grievous, they will sin, sometimes seemingly unforgivably, and still we'll hope for their triumph, their victory, their happy ending.

On a facile, surface level, the world seems to be divesting itself of nuance. Corporate media can seem one-note, trite, delivering news between bursts of advertising from whatever angle best suits the agendas of the people who control what we are told about the world we live in. Any doubt about the veracity or objectivity of the filtered, streamlined narratives that are foisted upon us 'ordinary' people, us 'consumers' of news, is too easily dismissed as stupidity, or paranoia, or a tendency towards extremism. We should be living through the most golden of ages for our frail and brilliant species; our various technological revolutions should have landed us at the apogee of human inquiry and expression. This age of almost total connection to a single network of communication, where every idea can be instantly published, every voice can be instantly heard, should be the age where we have our apotheosis, where we coalesce into a single loving family of gloriously disparate parts, tolerant of every idea except the ones that suggest that it's ever okay for one of us to harm another. But we seem in some ways to have regressed, coiled backwards on ourselves, restarted the hunt for heretics that has always been the dark corollary of the expression of ideas.

Readers are a powerful, silent army of opposition to this regression, to the burgeoning homogeneity of global platforms, to warmongering, greed, divisiveness, to the deleterious effects of unwavering certitude and intolerance. Books are still allowed to be blessedly transgressive, fiction is still occupied with the search for the truth of what it means to exist, to be human, to be contained within a prison of flesh and blood and bones while carrying in our minds, our imaginations, the power and potential of infinity.

There are still writers who ask themselves what it might feel like to be someone else, to believe something that is to them unbelievable, to do things that they themselves would not do. And there are still readers who will open themselves to these ideas, these possibilities, the unending variegations of shade of the human soul, the individual essence of each of us, the invisible, formless element of our being that is changed by each of our actions, thoughts, words, the part of us that comprises a ledger of the sum of our existence.

It is this part of us that is most moved when we read, most opened to change, to growth, to possibility, to difference. It sounds like a cliché, but it's true: reading is nourishment for the soul. And readers will save the world.

THE SEVEN STAGES OF
WRITING FICTION

Jamie O'Connell

I queue in my local supermarket, and it happens. I take
out my phone.
I am chatting with a friend while enjoying a glass of
wine and it happens. I find a napkin.
I run through the forest path, following The Beara Way,
and it happens. I make a voice note.

Here is where my stories begin. Inspiration is rarely discovered on a Monday morning as I sit at my desk with a coffee and contemplate my week. Quite often, the creative trail has gone cold over the weekend. What allows me to begin writing are these inspirations I have written into my phone, on a napkin or from listening to my voice notes.

Elizabeth Gilbert describes it best, certainly as I experience it. In *Big Magic* she writes that ideas and inspirations are 'disembodied, energetic life forms' out there in the wide world, driven by a single impulse, 'to be made manifest'. These ideas present themselves to each of us (often at inconvenient times) to either accept or ignore, in which case they move on. Over the years, I have learned to capture them, like a butterfly in a net, when they arrive. Because inspiration does not work to order. It does not concern itself with my needs on a Monday morning.

The second phase happens some months later. Each of the ideas I have saved seems to have potential, but Time weeds out the strong from the weak. Some become nothing more than that single stray thought, while others grow. One sentence leads to another, becoming a chain of inspiration. I create a Word document, usually called something generic like 'Ideas, Kenmare story', and I begin to place these inspirations into this file, not unlike a digital 'brainstorm'. Eventually, over many months, or even a year or more, the file becomes a few thousand words, and I read through them, trying to decipher what these 'disembodied energetic life forms' want me to write.

Stage three is figuring out where to begin. I put down the first few sentences, which I sense are no longer ideas, but words which will make up part of the actual story. This is not a chronological process, writing a story from A to B, but the piecing together of a puzzle, figuring out which captured idea goes where. Writing these early sections is one of the most enjoyable parts of the creative process, where the momentum and excitement grows. I find myself clumsy in everyday life, as my mind becomes obsessed with the new story and loses interest in the real world. I knock my elbows and graze my knuckles during this phase.

Then comes the hardest bit. The middle section is where the story is at its 'widest', where lots of characters are doing things simultaneously. I am often frustrated as the energy of the initial creative wave starts to wane, and the ending feels too far off to encourage me to push on. My daily word count drops. The project feels endless. I clock in my hours, like one of the proletariats in Fritz Lang's *Metropolis*. I do sums based on my current word count, trying to figure out when the first draft will likely be completed, and I get a depressing answer.

Then I get over the hump. Stage five begins. The story gets narrower as the chapters move towards the final section. Loose ends are tied up, subplots conclude, and the focus narrows to the climax, which has steered my writing since the beginning, though remaining distant, like the North Star guiding a ship. The momentum fires up again. My word count increases.

And then suddenly, when momentum is at its highest, the first draft is complete. I sit, dazed, examining the last few pages and immediately changing things, unsure if I can say I am 'finished', as there are already so many things that will need editing. And yet, it is complete in the sense that the narrative arc has concluded, even if the editing process will take significant time. In a way, it is only at the halfway point.

Stage seven. My editing process begins in earnest. I swing between excitement and despair. I fight feelings of wanting validation; it takes some restraint not to send it to anyone else. The manuscript word count drops as I read dialogue that is like real-life conversations and too wordy for that reason. My characters overthink, so I cut down their thoughts to the essential points. I wonder again and again: *is this boring?*

I work through draft after draft, saving each significant change, should I wish to return to a former version. This process continues until I feel that even though it may not be perfect (no doubt an editor's keen eyes will find countless mistakes), I am now blind to it. I have done all I can do, and it now needs a second pair of eyes. This is when I send the work to my agent, and the terrifying wait begins.

THE PRISM OF ACTION:

ON WRITING DRAMA

David Butler

In Ancient Greece, Aristotle distinguished between the two basic modes of relating a story: mimesis ($\mu\iota\mu\eta\sigma\iota\varsigma$, 'imitation'); and diegesis ($\delta\iota\eta\gamma\eta\sigma\iota\varsigma$, 'narration'). While mimesis shows, by means of actions performed as though 'in real time', diegesis tells, by means of a narrator speaking directly to their audience at an unspecified time after the event.

Although the latter has become something of a go-to on the recent Irish stage, the present article is limited to those plays in which the playwright chooses to dramatise rather than narrate their story – Friel's *Translations,* say, rather than his *Faith Healer.* This is not a value judgement *per se*; considerations of language and structure in the monologue play are more closely aligned to those of any first person narrative than to dramatic writing – a $\delta\rho\alpha\mu\alpha$ being a thing done or enacted, deriving from the verb $\delta\rho\alpha\omega$, I do or perform.

The American philosopher George Santayana observed that where the novelist gives us the protagonist's actions refracted through the prism of their mind, the dramatist gives us the protagonist's mind refracted through the prism of their actions. This is a good starting point. Where narration gives the audience direct access to interior thought and emotion, drama implies them (hence its challenge).

However, the language of the stage is by no means limited to the spoken word. It embraces mise-en-scène, lighting, soundscape, costume, gesture, action. Think how much information is relayed at the opening of Conor McPherson's *The Weir*: we watch a somewhat scruffy middle-aged character wearing a suit enter an empty country bar, go behind the counter, pour a pint of stout from a bottle, consult the list of prices and ring up the till, all this before a word is spoken.

DRAMATIC CONFLICT

Let us consider the opening scene – what the audience is presented with immediately the curtain rises. Here, the playwright must ask themselves 'why today?', and is best guided by the maxim 'in late, out early'. I'd argue that all effective plays begin at a moment when the status quo is either about to be overturned or has just been overturned. This crisis is the central question or problem of the play, and we are introduced to the protagonists *as they react to* this overturning of the status quo rather than in advance of it.

We don't see (or need to see) Lear before the abdication, or Macbeth before the weird sisters' prophecy, or Othello before the elopement, or Brutus and Cassius before the talk of conspiracy. In order to broach the question 'why today?', the playwright might ask themselves 'what has changed?' In such varied plays as *The Weir, The Playboy of the Western World, Translations, A Streetcar Named Desire* or *A View from the Bridge,* the answer, and the problem of the play, is an outsider's arrival.

The words protagonist and antagonist derive from the Greek term 'agon' ($\alpha\gamma\omega\nu$, a contest, conflict or dispute), and central to all drama is the idea of that which is contested. For any scene to be dramatically interesting, something needs to be in play or at stake. This truism holds both at the level of the overall play and the individual scene. It's worth reminding ourselves that conflict does not necessarily depend on dialogue – as Bryan Delaney who was reader for the Abbey usefully suggested several years ago, put two people in a room talking about water, you have dialogue; put two thirsty people in a room with just one glass of water, you have drama.

As an audience we are interested in dramatic conflict in the same way we are interested in a good tennis rally. Who is winning? Who are we supporting? Can a shot be pulled off to unexpectedly shift the dynamic? Two characters in agreement is dramatically uninteresting: no-one would watch a tennis match with both players on the same side of the net. That said, internal conflict can be of great interest, as when the protagonist is divided or uncertain about whether or how to accept the play's challenge.

STRUCTURE

So-called three act structure suggests that stories naturally fall into three movements: exposition, complication and resolution. Exposition, which typically lasts one quarter of the play's duration, sets out the what and then the who. It typically ends when the protagonist(s) decide how they will meet the challenge: Brutus will join the conspiracy; Hamlet will adopt an antic disposition; Romeo and Juliet will be secretly married.

In an undramatic world, the play would now move directly to resolution. It is up to the playwright to devise a series of obstacles, conflicts or reversals to prevent that from happening – the second movement, complication, typically lasting one half of the play's duration. A skilled dramatist will often place, at the centre of both this act and the play as a whole, a point of no return: Caesar is killed; Tybalt is murdered and Romeo exiled; Lt. Yolland is missing; Willy Loman is fired. The tone of the second half of the play, along with its point of interest, has altered irrevocably.

One aspect we expect from a good story is character arc – that the protagonist learn something in the course of their journey. Very often, this revelation or realisation is what carries the drama from complication to resolution, i.e., loosely three-quarters through the play's duration. This pattern holds true for film, too. Think when, precisely, Michael Corleone (a divided protagonist to begin with) discovers the family is being sold out in both the *Godfather I* and *II*, or when Ripley discovers the company deem her expendable in both *Alien* and *Aliens*. The plot of romantic comedy will often hinge upon a reassessment of each other by the two reluctant 'lovers' at this point, while realisation, or 'anagnorisis', is fundamental to any true tragedy – Othello would not be a tragic hero if he died believing Desdemona guilty.

Returning to the maxim 'in late, out early', once the question or problem set out by the inciting crisis has been answered, dramatic interest has gone. It is enough that the thwarted (or self-deluded) lovers are betrothed, there is no need for a wedding or epilogue. Once Hamlet or Macbeth or Richard III is dead, Shakespeare allows the remaining cast perhaps a single page before bringing down the curtain. As the Bard himself might put it, 'the rest is silence'.

SEEING THINGS

Una Mannion

———————

The morning of the full eclipse in March 2016, I passed a schoolyard full of children holding their handmade pinhole projectors, waiting for the sun to disappear, their excitement palpable in the fleeting seconds it took to pass them. Across the street, a woman sat alone in her parked car, watching. I saw her only momentarily on the periphery, but months later I could still see her alone in the car – and I could feel both the exuberant joy of the kids and her impending sense of despair, the sun about to vanish, the earth off kilter. Something was there but I didn't know what: it became a way into a story about a woman discovering her husband's infidelity the morning of the eclipse.

Claire Keegan describes a sense of a story choosing you, a picture lingering on the edge of consciousness: 'I have to write a story to make an image go away,' she says. 'It's like an elbow nudging you into examining something you don't quite understand, but need to.' In her introduction to *Selected Stories,* Alice Munro mentions something similar, a 'disturbance,' when she was young that she connects to her writing in the short-story form. She was maybe fifteen, standing in the window of the library waiting for a lift home. Outside the snow fell. She watched it as a team of horses drove on to the town weighing-scales, pulling a sleigh of grain.

> The patient horses with their nobly rounded rumps, the humped figure of the driver, the coarse fabric of the sacks. The snow conferring dignity and peace […]
> I saw it alive and potent, and it gave me something like a blow to the chest. What does this mean, what can be discovered about it, what is the rest of the story?

Munro captures that ineffable response we have to that fragment, that scene or image, that 'blow' – which is where a story often starts. How, she asks, 'can you get your finger on it, feel that life beating?' The image or scene may not be what the story is ultimately about, but it becomes a portal.

Some writers argue that the short story's fragmentary form and enigmatic ending bring it closer to how we experience life. In opting for the 'glancing view', the story form articulates that brush with human experience in a way that the novel cannot. The short story captures, Nadine Gordimer writes, 'the quality of human life, where contact is more like the flash of fire-flies, in and out, now here, now there, in darkness.' The writer as witness chooses to frame a moment, limiting it, but in such a way, Julio Cortázar says in *Some Aspects of the Short Story,* 'that this segment acts like an explosion which fully opens a much more ample reality.'

I am intrigued by other writers' processes, those moments they witnessed or imagined that illuminated something more beyond the small segment. Discussing 'Wolf Point', a devastating story about a man raising his daughter whose mother is debilitated by depression, Louise Kennedy describes two encounters that seeped into her consciousness, staying there until she wrote the story: one happened while shopping in Lidl, watching a middle-aged man with a young child in a trolley. He seemed old to be her father. Putting their shopping on the conveyor belt, his back turned, the child unzipped her cardigan. He rezipped it, his large hands clumsy with the fastenings. Separately, walking in Hazelwood, a lakeside trail along Lough Gill in Sligo, she heard the sea and rescue helicopter overhead and felt instant dread. Someone was missing. Something had gone wrong. 'Wolf Point' stitches these moments together. The man and his daughter are brought to the woods, the helicopter whir eliciting their particular apprehension and pain.

For me, these moments that I can't quite see begin to emerge or take shape as I start to write. The best analogy I can make is a process similar to photographic development. As I write and agitate the scene, the story latent within it starts to appear, characters and conflict become visible. Almost every short-story writer I know says they don't know what the story will be until they are writing it. For me, personally, this means writing to discover what it is I am trying to understand or reach; it also means overwriting, deleting, trying again, and trusting that this process will bring me closer to the mystery the image or scene has invoked.

Cortázar says the short-story form rejects 'that false realism which consists of believing that everything can be described and explained'. Instead, it embraces uncertainty, elision, the implied. I cut ruthlessly, and I encourage my students to try the same. What changes? What isn't essential? As I cut those stabilisers of exposition, description and causality, the story starts to lift; it has more possibilities and more tension because more has been left to the reader's imagination. James Lasdun describes it as 'a kind of force-field of negative space within the narrative'.

This negative or unsaid space of the story is critical to the form as is the story's instinctive open-endedness. In the short story, 'there are no solvent, tonic or consoling endings,' writes Sarah Hall. 'The reader is left to decide what everything might mean, and in this way the form is inordinately respectful.' Hall suggests that the reader experience is integral to the story's meaning. When I am completing a short story I am conscious that I am letting go more than ending the narrative; I try to resist the urge to pin everything down, to over explain: the story needs to offer the reader space – it's an art of restraint. Then, hopefully, the reader might also conjure that emerging picture, feel that blow to the chest.

ALIVE TO THE SENSES:

WRITING FOR RADIO

Niall McArdle

I was once at a reading where a woman collapsed, probably from having to listen to the appalling poetry coming from the stage.

She was a victim of the Curse of the Poet Voice. You know the Poet Voice when you hear it. The dreaded up and down, sober, sonorous, somnolent tone that you suffer through in open mic nights. Ponderous. Important. Boring.

We put so much effort into the look of a sentence on the page that we can forget how it sounds when read aloud. John McGahern said it best: 'there's verse and there's prose, and there's poetry in both.' A story needs to be alive to the senses. It is through our senses after all that we experience the world. All aspiring writers are told to always read their stories out loud, in part to catch artificial sounding dialogue: writing specifically for the radio requires a good ear.

SUNDAY MISCELLANY

I occasionally contribute essays to Sunday Miscellany on

RTÉ Radio – some humorous, some nostalgic, and I'm always aware of how they are going to sound when I record them. Listening to someone talking on the radio is an uncanny experience, both public and weirdly intimate. Sunday Miscellany goes out in the morning; I often listen to it in bed, my mind only just surfacing from the muddied depths of a confusing dream, cosy under the duvet and loath to draw the curtains on the morning outside.

On Sunday Miscellany, be it a memory of a beloved childhood toy, a strange encounter while travelling in some exotic locale, or a loving tribute to a deceased pet, it's the telling of the story that matters. Some can make me weep, others have me tumbling out of bed in laughter. The pieces that I enjoy are the ones where the voices that drift from the wireless are warm, comforting, quiet even when the story itself is not, a reminder that Sunday can be a day of rest.

TONE

Tone is everything in a story, perhaps the only thing that matters: everything else follows from it. We talk about a writer's style or a writer's voice – and what we mean is tone. It's difficult to get right on the page, and in any event every reader will often conjure up their own idea of what the words signify and what the mood is as they read. Reading allows you to go at your own pace, to linger over the writer's particular choice of word or a memorable turn of phrase.

Listening gives no such quarter. Listen to when your friend is telling you an anecdote or a joke. Listen for the rumble of their voice, the halt, the pause, the chuckle in their throat, the slight quiver if they're getting emotional. Notice how you are held rapt.

Listening to a story on the radio brings many of us back to the bedtime tales and campfire ghost stories of our childhood. Think of a scary story you were told; was it more frightening to read about a monster or to listen as the storyteller mimicked their unearthly grunts and groans? Our distant ancestors sat around the fire, huddled for warmth, wary of the darkness beyond the flames, the storyteller's voice filling the void. No wonder storytelling is such a powerful form. No wonder too the temptation when reading aloud to fall into the dreaded Poet Voice.

RHYTHM

Too often when we read a book, we read carelessly, and too often the same happens when we write. Writing for a listener should alert you to the rhythm of a sentence, to its rise and fall. Long sentence or short? Is there too much alliteration? Or just enough? Word choice is crucial. Should a character yell or holler, giggle or titter? Read the following aloud:

> 'The bird swooped down upon me from the branch above.'

I wrote 'branch' rather than 'tree' because I want to echo the b in 'bird'. Rereading it I realise that the 'down' is redundant and the line scans better without it. Without taking the time to read it aloud, I might not think about it. I'll rewrite that line several times before settling on 'from a branch above me, the bird swooped,' – which, when I say it, leaves the listener with an image of movement, rather than a now-empty branch. I might add something like 'in a bristling whoosh of feathers' which is admittedly a bit ripe but touches on both your sense of hearing and touch. You might think I'm being precious, and I probably am, but if you're not paying attention to the words you're writing, then why even bother?

FRANCIS MACMANUS

A couple of years ago I wrote a story, *Vena Amoris,* that was runner up in the Francis MacManus short-story contest on RTÉ Radio. This was the second time I had been in the competition, and in both cases I was blessed to have my story performed by an actor who got the tone right.

Vena Amoris is a story with a simple plot: a widower loses his wedding ring. I chose to tell it not from his perspective or from that of an omniscient narrator, but from the point of view of the ring itself. It's a risky move and somewhat gimmicky. On the page it possibly comes off a little pat and corny, but I had a sense it would work on the radio (I wrote it specifically with the contest in mind), and I was fortunate to have veteran actor Eamon Morrissey read it so brilliantly.

Critically, he caught the story's *tone*: exasperated, sad, befuddled. I'm conscious of repetition of phrases, both the power of it when done well and its weakness if done badly. Repetition is a writer's tic of mine. To avoid it in *Vena Amoris* I plundered the thesaurus. The ring in my story glimmered, shimmered, shone, glinted, gleamed.

It could also talk of course, but only to the listener sitting quietly in their kitchen or by the fire or tucked up in bed, hanging on every word, a child once again.

THE FIRST POETRY COLLECTION:

MICRO MANAGE, MACRO PLAN

Milena Williamson

Writing a book of poetry is a long, complex process and there are many ways to go about it. In 2024, my debut poetry collection *Into the Night that Flies So Fast* was published with Dedalus Press. I hope by reflecting on the collection both as a process and as a finished book, I will be able to offer some advice for other emerging poets.

In 2018, I applied for a grant from the Arts Council of Northern Ireland to research and write about Bridget Cleary. For context, Bridget Cleary was a young Irish woman who was burned to death by her family due to their suspicion that she may have been a fairy changeling. The external support from ACNI challenged me to think about what kind of book I was writing (and why I was committed to the idea) at the earliest stage. As strange as it is to pitch a project before you've written a single word of it (and as exhausting as funding applications sometimes are!), it was the first step for me and a good exercise.

There are some elements of what became my first collection that were present in its earliest versions. For example,

I wanted to (and did) write poems in the voice of Bridget Cleary as well as in the voices of other people whose lives intersected with hers in order to create a tapestry of conflicting narratives. This endeavour was always intended to be a research project, challenging me to write beyond my own experiences. By the end of 2018, I organised all the poems I had written to date (some would be cut, all would be majorly rewritten) into three acts. The three-act structure still remains. There is an important theatrical aspect to the story, since the judge at the trial of Bridget Cleary's family quotes *Macbeth,* while paradoxically insisting 'we are not here acting a play.' Therefore, my advice about early poems might echo the common mantra of killing your darlings, or to at least be critical of them. Conversely, my suggestion about structure and concept might be to trust your instinct.

That being said, the finished book of 2024 is dramatically different to what I envisioned in 2018. The title of the book changed many times. A few early runners were *The Tragedy of Bridget Cleary* and *Some Live Thing*: the former was too explanatory, the latter too abstract.

Writing a book of poetry—and finding the right publisher—takes a long time, so try not to stress about this. Use this time to your advantage. For example, when I received a rejection on the manuscript in process, I would come up with a 'bounce back list' of things I could try next (shout out to my partner Eoghan who taught me to do this!). The bounce back list means making room for serendipity in your work and reminding yourself that you are in control of the creative process.

In 2021, I received support from the Ireland Chair of Poetry Trust to take a road (and research) trip to County Tipperary. If I had published the manuscript earlier, I would have missed out on this opportunity and experience. I only began writing the poems that responded to *Buffy the Vampire Slayer* in 2022, towards the end of the project. I pushed myself to find new ways to channel the anger I felt about Bridget Cleary's death. Who better to speak to the everyday violence of womanhood than Buffy, with her chic 90s outfits and stake at the ready?

If you're still asking yourself, 'yes, but how do you actually *write* a poetry book?' then perhaps consider Zadie Smith's theory of 'Macro Planners and Micro Managers.' Smith writes: 'A Macro Planner makes notes, organises material, configures a plot and creates a structure—all before he writes the title page.' On the other hand, a Micro Manager 'starts at the first sentence…and finishes at the last.' Smith was describing the two types of writers in relation to prose but *both* approaches are valuable for poets. Generally, you write a book of poetry word by word, poem by poem like a Micro Manager but as time passes and the book's themes emerge, you may become a Macro Planner, particularly when it comes to (re-)ordering poems. I believe poets need to learn how to be both a Micro Manager and a Macro Planner at different stages in the long writing process.

This essay would be incomplete without some advice from writers who have guided me. Anne Lamott taught me how to embrace the 'shitty first draft' and 'quiet the voices in my head,' particularly those self-critical ones. Rainer Maria Rilke reminded me that 'a work of art is good if it has sprung from necessity.' Mary Oliver taught me to gracefully acknowledge the duality that a poem is 'a written document' and 'a mystical document.' We study craft—in universities, workshops, courses—in order to improve the written document. The mystical document is more elusive and personal.

If you're still feeling unsure or dejected, here's another piece of information. I checked my submission spreadsheet, and the manuscript that became my first book was rejected twenty-five times. And some of those rejections weren't actually rejections, but the painful non-rejection of silence. All those hours I spent wistfully staring at my inbox! That time I was rejected from one of my favorite presses and cried for hours, watching *The Princess Diaries* and eating a Magnum ice-cream in the middle of the afternoon. Maybe it's the rose-colored glasses as I look back, but perhaps it was all part of the long process of writing, revising, and submitting.

When in doubt, remember the motto of *The Little Engine That Could*. She says, 'I think I can, I think I can, I think I can.' I wrote my first book of poetry and so can you.

THE DIFFICULT SECOND
(THIRD, FOURTH...) COLLECTION

Jessica Traynor

A s emerging writers, we all have one goal in mind—
to hold that freshly printed debut book in our hands
and experience the excitement and validation that
comes from your hard work taking such a tangible form.
All those years of dreaming condensed into one slim volume that you hope will be read and enjoyed by thousands of
readers. You have arrived.

Of course, this destination—the first book—is not a destination at all. But we can't resist the urge to place shapes
on passages of time that allow us to understand and define
our own stories. The fact that writers suffer doubly from
this delusion, and make a metanarrative of the very act of
writing stories, makes me smile. But this tendency to try
and stick a 'happy ending' label on the delivery of a first
book can create difficulty for us when the question of next
steps emerges, or in those instances where the longed for
destination is not the sunlit uplands we might have hoped
for.

We live in a culture obsessed with youth and newness, and which abundantly rewards early success in a manner that can easily create the impression that the only real talent is the prodigy, that graft is for those who have no natural aptitude. I'm talking in extremes here, but the implication of all the praise and hysteria for those who seem to spring forth fully formed as writers worries me a little. It can create the sense—for others, whose debuts may not have set the world on fire—that there is no future for them. It can also be damaging for the subject of all this celebration, who may find that level of success hard to reproduce second time around. So here, in this essay, I'd like to take pause, and from the vantage point of making edits to my fourth collection talk a little about what I have observed on my own writing journey so far.

THE SECOND COLLECTION: BEGINNING AGAIN

Some of the most accomplished poets struggle with the pressures of a second collection. If your first collection was a formally coherent project, deftly exploring a theme or topic from different angles and perspectives, it can feel like you have to begin again and build an entire world anew. Poetry comes to us in different ways—sometimes in a way that speaks to a larger theme, and sometimes from our observations and engagement with a changing world. It's hard to force the alchemy of either of these approaches, and it takes time. But you simply don't have the same timescale with a second collection as you might have had with a debut: where the first might have come together over the course of a decade, most of us will want to publish a second within three to four years. This is a lot of pressure, and sometimes we try to publish again before we are ready. Ask yourself why you need to get that second book out there so quickly? Is it because you have work that you're excited to share? Or because you have a vague sense of anxiety that in the time it takes to write the next book, the world might move on and you might be forgotten? If the latter, then the good and bad news is that the world moves on no matter how quickly you produce that stunning sophomore collection. So, take your time. You cannot control the zeitgeist. Sometimes it works with you, and sometimes against you. But I've never read a second collection and thought 'I wish they'd taken less time over this.'

There are then, of course, the logistics of getting a second collection out there. Your publisher is most likely a busy small business with a large roster of poets, all of whom want to publish a collection every three or four years. There will be a queue. You cannot control the queue and you can't skip it, but you can communicate with your publisher about when the publication of that next collection might be possible, and hope that they might be able to give you a workable timeline, dependent of course on funding and the earth not falling off its axis in the interim. This might help avoid a situation where you approach your publisher with a nearly finished work to find they have no slots for the next two years. Having said that, a wait of a year or so is generally not a bad thing for a collection.

WHAT LIES BEYOND THE SECOND COLLECTION...

With my own second collection, I tried to give the slightly odder, more uncomfortable aspects of my poetry free reign, in spite of many gentle and well-meaning exhortations not to do so. For my third collection, I gave what I felt to be my worst self free reign. Is this an advisable career move? I'm not sure, but it became apparent to me sometime around the writing of my second collection that if I were to sustain my own interest in the work I was planning to continue to write for decades to come, I'd have to stay on my toes. Alongside trying to evolve my writing style by immersing myself in as much new and challenging poetry as I could get my hands on, I was actively trying to become a useful and supportive member of the poetry—that is, my—community. In order to thrive in the world of poetry, you need to work hard on both writing and relationship-building. Outside of your writing (which should be the product of your individual and intense reaction to the world around you) try to be as present for your community as you can—attending launches, buying books, amplifying the successes of others. Some may view these actions cynically and of course you shouldn't lie about work you don't like. But in my experience it is friendships with likeminded writers, who challenge and push themselves, that sustains us in our own creative pursuits. And like any freelancer, you have to work with a large number of people in arts organisations and county councils and libraries and universities. Be kind to them and each other. This part is not rocket science.

If you manage all this, I can't guarantee you will win prizes and publish a run of poetry bestsellers. But, you should be able to continue to write and publish poetry collections, which (if you recall) was that first dream all those years ago.

STORYTELLING AND THE MOON

Yan Ge

I n an interview, poet Natalie Diaz considered her relationship with language in the postcolonial context and
said: '… the real interaction I have with language is not
that a word means something but what I might do in relation to that word on my way toward it or in my misunder-
standing of it or in the way it was handed to me.'

My first words in Chinese were handed to me by my
mother. Yue, she said, which was the middle character of my
name, which meant moon. And now, many moons later, my
mother is long gone and I still cannot talk about her death
in my native language. Such subject matter seems to only
become viable in my acquired language, where every word
feels like a borrowed item and I a traveller from a distant
tribe who is setting up a shrine made of seashells, dandeli-
ons, and feathers.

My collage may or may not have meaning for you, or the
meanings I end up expressing might have been completely
altered after my long journey here – but it doesn't matter, what matters is that I am telling you a story. A story,
for various reasons, remained unattainable in my native
tongue and only begins to shimmer now as the peculiar

objects I gathered along the way finally converge on this page.

I brought up the notion of collage because I am a fervent believer of juxtaposition. Spacial correlations. It is through the spacial correlations of different strokes that the signifiers – characters – in my native language become distinctive and identifiable and are, through our collective knowledge as a community, linked to their designated signified, in the sense 月 means moon and 水 means water. It was also from such spacial correlation I began to make up stories, putting two actions side by side to form a plot. I should also mention that in Chinese there are no tenses. Therefore two neighboring sentences don't necessarily imply a temporal relationship, their narrative significance is manifested by their shared spacial structure. In Chinese, this is how I envision the drafting of a story: the characters, action, dialogue and images are invited into a room that is the story and propped up at different places. And then they are left alone, behind the closed door, to share the space and interact with each other. When they respectively entered the room/story is, although tangible, irrelevant. What matters is that they are all there and will coexist until the end of the time.

One of the biggest challenges I experienced, after beginning to write fiction in English, was the discovery of Time, time with a capital T, time as a principle of rationality that renders raw reality intelligible and defines fiction – fiction in English – as a predominately temporal structure. When I became a writer in English, I was coerced into adapting an obsession with time. Not at least because the language itself demands clear temporal treatment over each clause and sentence, but also because time has been seen, perhaps since

Aristotle's Poetics, as the device of justice and the process of rationalisation. Fiction, in the Western narrative tradition, is expected to construct, in Jacques Rancière's words, a specific time wherein the sequence of facts is identical to that of a chain of causes and effects. In other words, in typically western fiction, events are arranged by the compulsory process of causal rationalisation that manifests itself as a linear temporal structure.

What happens if, in fiction, we forget about time and treat the unfolding of the story as an articulation across the space on the page and we take such spacial correlation as a map of causes and effects? What if we go a step further and forget about time as the process of rationalisation, fabricated and enforced upon us by people from the power centre, and instead reinvent and restore a different type of time in fiction, a time whose meanings and structure are defined by people from the periphery?

I couldn't decide under which of the following scenarios I began to deliberately overlook time and focus instead on the spacial structure of my English stories: is it because I cannot completely rid myself of my old habit that comes from two decades of writing in Chinese? Was I too tempted by the possibility of another literary experiment? Or has there always been an uneasiness that halts me from submitting myself entirely, as a writer from elsewhere, to the Anglo-centric literary world and its language, literary values and narrative traditions?

It was in 1968 Ngugi wa Thiong'o authored his famous essay *On the Abolishment of the English Department*. In 2021, Cornell University officially renamed its English Department as The Department of Literatures in English. In the postcolonial context, the *final cause* – to borrow Aristotle's words – for a writer like me to write in English has to be more than just telling you stories from my tribe; I am also compelled to narrate for you my stories in feathers and sea-shells, divulging my secrets by repeatedly drawing out intricate patterns and formations. Because my universe of language and narrative stemmed from the moment my mother showed me how to write yue. 月.

The strokes stretched out, transforming the space while articulating the meaning. And that, is how we tell stories.

ALCHEMY IN THE PROCESS:

ON TRANSLATING

LEONARD AND HUNGRY PAUL

Andrea O'Brien

When I first encountered *Leonard and Hungry Paul* – as a reader – I was immediately impressed by the gentle humour that suffused it. Although there are no explicit markers that locate the story in Ireland, its tone, approach and the mentality of its characters were immediately familiar to me. When I lived in Ireland, I was impressed by the kindness of Irish people, something that struck me as remarkably different from Germany. Even when they banter and joke, Irish people are rarely out to hurt anybody.

Kindness is an essential element of Rónán Hession's writing. He may portray his characters' particular flaws with humour, but he never treats them with disdain or disrespect. When I set out with my translation, I was acutely aware of the need to find an appropriately gentle tone and language that avoided sarcasm, confrontation or offence. Incidentally, a fellow translator recently asked me how I would translate the word 'kindness' in a modern novel. The question arose because the German word for kindness (*Güte*) is perceived as somewhat old-fashioned and dusty, especially when used as an adjective (*gütig*).

The conversation made me wonder whether the fact that this (German) word was perceived as outdated meant that we as a society perceived the notion of kindness itself as an anachronism. While I was translating Rónán Hession's novel however, I used the words '*Güte*' and '*gütig*' without hesitation or second thought, and I find it very apt that such a gentle word that has been reduced to a niche existence in modern German vernacular lent itself so naturally to this particular novel.

NARRATIVE FLOW

One of the many strengths of Hession's prose is its easy narrative flow. Rooted in the Irish storytelling tradition that I find characterises so much of the nation's writing, Hession's novel encourages us to sit back, relax and enjoy. But to equate this unassuming simplicity with triviality would be a mistake. There is a lot at work here. While the author's sentences appear straightforward at first sight, they often convey a deeper sense of wisdom or invite us to take a refreshingly new approach to what we thought we knew about the world.

In order to reproduce this understated and skilfully crafted flow in the German translation, I called to mind the subtle and not so subtle differences between German and English syntax, how word order and structure changes the tone and emphasis of a sentence and also plays with conventions and the reader's expectations.

MAGICAL

Like all literary translators I work with a set of tools that I have collected over many years of experience, studying, reading and learning. But this technical knowledge only takes you so far. It is the creative act, the flow, the many un-reflected micro-decisions that produce art. And 'the flow' is, by its very nature, not a rational process. We can analyse the result, but it is hard to explain how we got there in logical or technical terms. Literature translation is, like writing itself, a deeply empathetic, sensual and intuitive process.

Just as prose or poetry are so much more than the sum total of their words and phrases, successful translation goes beyond the mere transfer of words or sentences from one language into another. The process can be dissected, but its workings will not be revealed. It's all a bit magical, really.

CHALLENGES

That said, of course there were passages in *Leonard and Hungry Paul* that required reflected, conscious decisions. How to translate the different phrases listed by the Chamber of Commerce and with it, the conundrum of how to sign off an e-mail? In German, we do not use phrases like 'To whom it may concern' or 'Dear Sir or Madam' – our conventions are very different and so are the 'problems' that are associated with them.

How to proceed? Use the English phrases and explain the conundrum in German? After a moment of reflection I decided that I needed to find equivalent German phrases, and realised – much to my delight – that many of these German phrases also threw up an array of very similar 'problems'. A major challenge was, of course, Paul's delightful winning phrase. In the German translation, it had to meet the criteria of 'pointing out the noteworthiness' of the preceding paragraphs and inviting the reader to consider them while 'also leaving the door open if the reader felt otherwise'. It took me a while to find my personal winner, the German phrase that covered all the bases, and it came to me – as is often the case – during a walk in the park. Obviously, I will reveal neither the original nor the German translation.

LUCKY COINCIDENCES

It is my experience that many challenges that I may initially perceive as difficult are easily solved as soon as my unconscious translation process is in full flow. And while some layers of the original may become lost in translation, others can actually be gained. One such example is the term 'fire warden', which in the original is a straightforward term that may or may not conjure up the vague image of an official. The surprise (and humour) comes from the fact that it is a girl that does the job of carrying out fire drills and she looks anything but what you would expect of a fire warden.

The German translation (and humour) also works along these lines, but the German word for fire warden (*Brandschutzbeauftragte*), in its wonderfully German officialese, conjures up a much more vivid image: that of a grey-haired, bespectacled, no-nonsense (German) official.

The discrepancy between the readers' expectations and the revelation is so much stronger and the humorous surprise much more pronounced. Lucky coincidences like these delight us translators and help us achieve a creative balance between the original and the translation.

I am very happy that *Leonard und Paul* was received by German readers with as much enthusiasm as *Leonard and Hungry Paul* was in Ireland, because it means that the translation managed to capture the essence of what makes Rónán Hession's novel so immensely enjoyable.

THE ART OF
SMALL-SCALE ILLUSIONS:
WRITING HISTORICAL FICTION

Nuala O'Connor

istorical fiction is a combination of research (which is helpful) and imagination (which is the real work, in a sense). These narratives imagine what it was like to be human in a different era, to be a person in flux, searching for answers. The writer of historical fiction gets to know her time and setting through research but, mostly, she asks herself, what are the interior dramas of these characters? What do they care for the most? What do they fear? Every story is a piece of unsettled time for the characters involved: this happened, then that happened; that happened only because this happened. The 'happening' is an unrepeatable event – a one-off – and it alters things. And, although your characters may endure life-shattering wars or natural disasters, it will often be the personal repercussions that really matter, not the mechanics of political upheaval, or other large events.

There is a speculative element to past-set fiction – the

writer cannot truly know what it felt like to live back then, but she imagines conversations and what-ifs, especially if she writes biographical fiction – narratives centring a real person's life. Historical bio-fiction is an exercise in re-animation, empathy, embodiment, and sympathy. Some feel it's a type of cannibalism, and even writers of these novels differ about how real lives should be approached and recorded in fiction. There are Faithfuls and there are Festooners. I'm a Mostly Faithful – I stick to the known facts and embroider to create an interior life for my characters; and, as an Inevitable Festooner, I employ empathic thinking, inventing scenes that probably never happened, because fictional plots have to contain an amount of drama that often doesn't exist in real lives.

For Committed Festooners nothing is off limits as regards what characters will get up to or say; some writers even shift real life characters into other eras. Personally, I'm more wedded to things being as close to how things were as I can glean from recorded facts (timelines/known incidents). But crucially, this rightness can only be as I *imagine* it, because the writer brings to fiction her own foibles, prejudices, style, history, knowledge, and so on.

Hilary Mantel said – and I'm paraphrasing – in a novel you can't separate fact from fiction, it's like trying to separate mayonnaise. So, while writers can be slavish to facts, we also know that truth is a slippery eel, and all 'truths' are presented through a particular and personal lens. The historical fiction writer examines the 'facts' from many angles and decides what to highlight. She must also filter the filters she finds and gather what seems most pertinent and – often – most interesting, fictionally.

Research helps the writer to understand what her characters know effortlessly. To (sort of) quote Eckhart Tolle, 'There is only now.' We have history and hindsight; our historic characters only have their *now*. The wondrous Mantel again: 'the novelist…lives inside the consciousness of her characters for whom the future is blank.' The writer must write her character's *now,* in ignorance, while actually knowing a lot.

POINTS TO BEAR IN MIND WHEN WRITING HISTORICAL NARRATIVES

Specifics wed the reader to the story and promote trust. Evoke setting by naming places/objects/foods; use language that is archaic or has flavours of era-specific speech patterns. Small details can anchor the reader, like how historic women really feel about being beholden to men in every aspect of life; or what sassafras tastes like in saloop. TJ Pierce called fiction 'the art of small-scale illusions.' The historical writer douses the reader in just enough detail to give the illusion of time travel to a real place. Colm Tóibín referenced illusion, too, at the Cheltenham Literary Festival, regarding his bio-fiction of Thomas Mann: 'I use the facts as more than scaffolding; I use facts to create an illusion that the reader follows in real time. The information is a starting point, then I want to follow the *illusion* that this is what happens.'

Ideally, let research sink in and become invisible. Concrete detail is useful, but too much bogs down the reader, particularly if the vocabulary is impenetrably historic. Use research to understand the era, but just because you know every hook and eye of Victorian corsetry doesn't mean you include it. Emma Darwin put it beautifully: 'Explaining in historical fiction is like backpacking: don't load the narrative with everything the reader might possibly want, just give us the things we can't possibly do without.' Choose wisely, balance detail with drama – something must happen, after all.

Historical facts are the backdrop to the drama, not the story, but large historic events change people and societies, in big and small ways, and this is good narrative fodder. Ask questions about the events you centre: Is your character an unusual witness? What are the personal repercussions for them? How can they improve their situation? What is unchangeable for them? How do they deal with that?

Each era/period has a set of attitudes that dominate. But we don't need to accept received wisdom, or the 'accuracy' of history. And fiction is normally peopled with mavericks. Know your territory (politically etc.) but let your characters push against it.

Period texts, including magazines, newspapers, novels, non-fiction texts, and advertisements, will provide accurate, authentic information regarding cultural norms like food, dress, mores, manners, flora, fauna etc.

- The British Newspaper Archive online is an excellent resource, as are the census records in Ireland and elsewhere, and various national archives (many digitised).
- Diaries and letters are usually more down to earth and honest than newspaper/historical reports. Many are digitised or viewable in libraries and archives.

- Pinterest and YouTube (often linking to specialist blogs) are useful research places. But be judicious in the use of facts you find online. Some sites trade in fantasies, misinformation, and lies – try to verify all 'facts'. Remember to filter the filter!
- Experts in any field are usually happy to answer brief emailed questions (if Google, Wiki, the library, archives etc. prove fruitless).
- On the ground research is extremely valuable, if the writer has the means to achieve it. Where possible, walk the geography of your fictional world, with all senses alight. You learn things in situ – the quality of the air, the feel of the streets – that no book can convey. As (historical) writer Andrew Miller advised at Listowel Writers' Week, 'Eyes open, heart open, feet on the ground.' Enjoy it all!

COMICS ARE FOR EVERYONE

IS IAD COIMICÍ DO GACH DUINE

Paul Carroll

I never planned on writing comics, or on becoming embedded in the Irish community in quite the way I did. My journey as a writer began in prose, and it wasn't until I worked on a web documentary about comics in Ireland as part of my postgrad thesis in 2015 that I began to really see how things worked in this country. Since the start of that journey, I've been taking stock of Irish comics as an industry and a community.

Comics as an industry isn't quite like any other area of publishing. It falls into a space between magazines and book publishing, and features all manner of formats and routes to entry. So what does 'success' mean in this area? Here, I'll be shining a light on the publishing landscape of comics in Ireland, the types of events that exist for comic creators, and the resources available for those looking to make their start in comics. A word of friendly advice before we begin: for a long time, comics will feel like an expensive hobby for a writer. Take it slow and keep proving yourself as a creator. If you fall in love with the medium, it'll be worth it in the end.

IRISH COMICS PUBLISHERS

The first thing to note for anyone writing comics in this country is that the majority of people who make a living out of it do so through international publishers. Ireland is home to only a handful of publishers (most of whom are supported by the Arts Council) who have published at least one graphic novel, and none of them follow the route of the American publishers, releasing the stories issue by issue. The O'Brien Press has published more than most, and those are focused on Irish history and folklore.

For the rest of us looking to see our work in print, the options are to pitch stories to publishers in the US or the UK, or to self-publish our work in the hope of catching the right person's eye.

Anthologies have been—and still are—one of the 'easiest' ways to make some sort of impact as a writer in comics. They come with the benefit of an editorial eye, marketing by all contributors involved, camaraderie, and sometimes enough pay at the end that the writer might also get a cut of the page rate on offer. Via Limit Break Comics—my comic collective and sometimes 'publisher'—I've been trusted to produce a few such anthologies of my own, and it is through that work that I've found something close to what I would call 'success in comics', at least insofar as producing new work is concerned.

Once you've produced some of your own work and have something to show off, and perhaps even sell, you'll need to bring it to readers. While self-published prose is still sometimes looked down upon, comics have long history of independence from larger publishers.

Aside from Limit Break Comics, other collectives that publish under labels include Stray Lines, Rogue Comics, Two Pugs Press, Back Pocket Comics, and the Cork Comic Creators.

EVENTS FOR COMIC CREATORS

While Ireland is lacking in publishers for comics with proper distribution channels, we have a wealth of events that specialise in the medium, not to mention the conventions that focus on gaming and anime.

There are four specific comics events in Ireland: the Dublin Comic Arts Festival (DCAF), which takes place four times a year; the Cork Comic Expo, which is less regular, but fronted by Will Sliney and Big Bang Comics; WICAF, the Waterford International Comic Arts Festival which launched in 2023; and the Dublin Comic Book Festival organised by Alliance Française Dublin, Illustrators Ireland and the French Embassy in Ireland.

Alongside these are conventions like Dublin Comic Con with its Artist Alley, and Octocon, which includes comics in its programming of panels and workshops and often includes comics in the Trade Hall. Outside of specific comics events, comic creators have appeared and taken part in Cúirt, the Dublin Book Festival, and the Bram Stoker Festival.

RESOURCES TO GET YOU STARTED

Until recently, there haven't been local channels for learning about how to write comics. While a few of my peers have been running workshops around the country when the opportunities present themselves, there wasn't a home for learning about comics—or Irish comic creators—for people who missed those events.

I began working with the Irish Writers Centre through the Evolution Programme, bringing comics back into the course programme and teaching the undergraduate Creative Writing students in the University of Galway about the medium. At the same time, the Tallaght Academy of Sequential Art opened its doors as the first education institution of its kind in Ireland to focus on comics as a medium.

For most others, the options are to study Animation and segue into the industry that way, teach themselves everything they might need to know, or pick a vocational module in comics when offered in art colleges.

Outside of direct learning, engagement in the Irish comic community is the easiest way to start learning the craft. IrishComics.ie is a shared publishing platform, founded in 2021 to share the work of Irish creators on a single website. Creators in—or visiting—Dublin can attend the Dublin Comic Jam, while those in Cork can visit the Cork Comic Creators.

As someone who joined from the outside with a camera, a boom mic and an interest in the medium, I can assure you that the community is open and welcoming, and incredibly friendly towards LGBTQIA+, neurodivergent, and disabled creators.

I have two final notes to leave you with.

The first: comics are a medium, not a genre.

The second: comics are for everyone. Or, as has been immortalised in an enamel pin: *Is iad coimicí do gach duine.*

A VISION OF THE WORLD

Eoghan Smith

O n a trip back to Ireland from France in 1946, Samuel Beckett had a revelation that would have profound artistic consequences. By that stage, he had authored several poems and short pieces of fiction, the novels *Dream of Fair to Middling Women* (unpublished at the time) and *Murphy* (published 1938), as well as some works of non-fiction and translations. Up until that point, Beckett said, he thought that to be intellectually equipped as a writer he had to rely on knowledge. But in an interview in 1961, Beckett admitted that his first great novels came the day he 'became aware of [his] own folly'. Only then, Beckett said, 'did I begin to write the things I feel'. It was after this epiphany that Beckett wrote the major works that are usually associated with his distinct vision of humanity in ruins: the trilogy of *Molloy*, *Malone Dies,* and *The Unnamable*, and plays such as *Waiting for Godot, Endgame* and *Happy Days.*

With the distance of time, the idea of art feels complete in the work of a writer such as Beckett; his vision of the world is clear and unmistakeably delineated in the language of his novels and plays. His deracinated landscapes and depictions of bodily and mental disintegration are uncompromising and recognisable. To maintain the integrity of his work, he was protective of how his own fiction was translated and his plays staged. But to get to this point, Beckett's aesthetic involved a transition from knowing to feeling; from comprehension to ignorance; from exteriority to interiority; from the objective to the subjective, and eventually, an effort to eliminate the subject altogether; and from wordiness towards wordlessness.

Poems, stories and dramatic works are statements of any given author's vision of the world as they see it. John Banville is fond of quoting Kafka's line that the artist is a person 'with nothing to say', but even that too is a clear statement of what a writer and their stance should be. Stories are a writer's approximation of the truth, their perspective on a state of affairs at a particular moment in time. Every writer's story says: this is my comment on how the world is as I see it. But when writers and artists talk of being true to that vision, they can only be referring to how they see things as they have come to understand them in the here and now. Writing by its very nature is the transformation of something we have experienced – an idea, a memory, a sensation, a feeling, an event – into words. Beckett's example shows that an artistic vision can also transform: it is not static but is instead open to change. The object of writing is always moving, coming in and out of focus. The writer is also moving too, evolving their art, deepening their own understanding of it, merging in new and provocative ways the imaginary and the real. In fact, jettisoning an existing impression of what writing should be doing, experimenting with different types of language, genres and styles, testing ideas and making mistakes, can help locate the essential vision that any writer is trying to project.

These processes can, importantly, help a writer to understand the kind of writer they are, what they want to write about, how they want to write, to find their approximation of the truth. Such a process of refinement enables a writer to become more perceptive, not only of the world around them, but of how they are perceiving it. Each piece of writing offers a new way of looking at the same object, each one searches for a more precise language, the right images, the most effective set of metaphors and symbols. Artistic creation requires elements such as time, patience, introspection, self-criticism and self-understanding. It requires asking the unavoidable question of why you are writing in the first instance. It requires asking what is truthful about what you are writing, and how that truth can be expressed. Perhaps the greatest challenge for the writer is not only to stay true to their work, but, as Beckett realised, to discover what it is they are being true to in the first instance.

The economics, trends and vagaries of publishing neither validates or invalidates a writer's vision, but the pressure to publish or to gain some measure of recognition can nonetheless influence an author to write in a way to which they are not committed nor in which they believe. This is the surest way to fail as an artist. It must be accepted that not all readers will be receptive to every piece of writing. This should not be a cause for concern. The deepest acts of creation require commitment to a vision of the world that will be contained within and expressed through that artwork. The writer's job is then to sharpen their perception, to continually refine that vision, to make it communicable in language, and present it such way that the truth of it can be seen. There will always be other people to say what they want and expect, but the artist can only offer in good faith what they have.

Craft

Non-Fiction

Notes on
Newspaper Book Reviewing

Kevin Power

I became a newspaper book reviewer, aged 27, for the same reason that I started smoking cigarettes, aged 22: because I thought it looked cool. Nowadays it is clear to me that neither smoking cigarettes nor newspaper book reviewing is cool, but it's tricky to discern these things when you're in your twenties.

Aged 42, I no longer smoke cigarettes, though I continue to admire them from afar. On the other hand, I can't seem to stop reviewing books for newspapers. My total number of published newspaper book reviews now approaches, or possibly exceeds, 400 – a horrifying figure, certainly, and one that should perhaps best be understood as the basis for a cautionary tale, but proof also of at least one thing: I love reviewing books for newspapers. I regard it as honourable work – which is, I suppose, what you say when you worry that your work isn't taken very seriously by the wider world. Then again, love is the best reason to do anything, especially when the money isn't great.

In all that time, reading all those books, writing all those pieces, I must at least have learned something (let's hope). Herewith, and offered with all due humility: some notes for the aspiring practitioner of the newspaper book review.

- Editors of newspaper books sections are, like all newspaper editors, tyrannised by deadlines. They have a morbid fear of empty space appearing on their pages. So, rule 1: Submit your piece on or before the deadline. If you're late, you will cause your editor to panic, and they will not commission you again.

- What do newspaper literary editors want? In descending order of importance: words; the precise number of words they asked for; words that require little to no editing; words that make sense; words that attract clicks and conversation.

- The average newspaper book review is 800 words long. Like the composer of a sonnet, the newspaper book reviewer operates within rigid formal constraints. A snappy opening (jokes are good). Thereafter, George Orwell's five-paragraph model is your basic structural material. Introduction; plot summary; pros; cons; conclusion. Within this framework, as within the framework of the sonnet, infinite variety is possible.

- A capsule plot summary must appear – if not in paragraph two, then *somewhere*. Your readers want to know, after all, what the book you're reviewing is actually about. Fancier venues – *The New Yorker,*

The London Review of Books, The New York Review of Books – tend to regard capsule plot summaries as a bit twee and old-hat. But the capsule plot summary is of the very essence of the 800-word newspaper book review, so don't get fancy until a fancy editor tells you you're free to do so.

- A value judgement must visibly be made: is the book under review good, or is it rubbish? Adjectives are your best pals, here. But the newspaper book review is as susceptible to the virus of adjectival cliché as are more noble forms, like the love letter. Currently popular book reviewing cliches include 'whip-smart' (only applicable to female writers) and 'a moving exploration of trauma and memory' (applicable to any novel). Classic book reviewing cliches include 'a page-turner,' 'compulsive,' 'taut,' 'explosive,' 'deft,' etc. Forge new adjectival permutations! The future of prose depends upon it!

- A book review is an argument. Quotation is your proof. A bad book can often be eviscerated using only quotation; a good book elevated by the same method. Either way, you must quote. If you don't, your argument lacks weight: why should your readers trust you?

- Don't review your friends. That's what blurbs are for.

- The traditional way to make a name for yourself as a critic is to trash a high-profile book with maximum wit. (Cite your own favourite recent example here.) Editors love hatchet jobs, because hatchet jobs get clicks. But that doesn't mean that you should become merely a practitioner of hatchet jobs. Such a reputation can destroy a career. Critics are judged primarily by what they praise; taste is finally a question of love, not of hatred or of scorn.

- I got into newspaper book reviewing when, in October 2008, the literary editor of the *Irish Times*, the late and much-missed Caroline Walsh, called me up and asked me if I would be interested in writing reviews. She knew who I was because I had just published my first novel. A novel, or a book of short stories, is a useful credential in the field. But having a traditionally-published book on your CV is not essential. A reasonably well-known blog or Substack; a portfolio of student journalism; journalistic experience in another field; academic publications or expertise; all of these will serve.

- Don't email a books editor to say, vaguely, 'I'm available to write reviews.' Like the rest of us, books editors want solutions, not problems. Say: 'I see [WRITER] has a new book out in October; I've previously blogged/written about them, or about a similar writer, and I'd love the chance to write about this new book.' Include links to your blog or previous reviews. Great, the editor will think; that's one slot filled. It follows that you should familiarise yourself with forthcoming books (many publications do long preview pieces in January; online bookshops are also helpful in this regard – just search 'forthcoming books' in your genre of choice).

- Say what you think. A critic who doesn't is no use to anyone.
- A rule of thumb: the more conservative a newspaper's political stance, the better they will pay. This is either because conservative people tend to be unscrupulous enough to get rich or because rich people tend to be naturally conservative – I leave it to you to decide.
- Expressing your opinions in public calls for a thick skin. Don't be combative for the sake of it. But be combative when being combative is called for.
- Critics are critics because they love art and want to talk about it. This, in the end, is the best reason to write newspaper book reviews: not for attention or prestige or money (N.B. you will not get much attention or prestige and you will not make much money), but because, for a certain kind of person – and who could I possibly be talking about? – newspaper book reviewing comes dangerously close to not feeling like work at all.

ACADEMIC PUBLISHING:

FROM PHD TO BOOK PROPOSAL

Christabel Scaife

In academic publishing, an author's first book is often based on their doctoral research, but a PhD thesis will require intensive revision before it's ready for publication. The process of converting a thesis into a book can be daunting, so here are some tips for first-time academic authors.

Always bear in mind that a thesis and a book are aimed at different audiences. With your thesis, you're writing for a very small group of people (your supervisor and your examiners) and there are certain boxes you need to tick. You want to show how closely you've studied your subject, so the thesis may contain a large number of citations to demonstrate your knowledge of the field. With your book, you're writing for a broader audience who may not care so much about this. Of course it's vital that your book should still be carefully referenced, and that you acknowledge the work of other scholars in the field whenever appropriate, but make sure you put your own arguments to the fore.

While you're thinking about this new audience, ask yourself whether it's possible to broaden the scope of the original thesis. If your PhD involved working in a very specialised area, consider whether the book might attract more readers by looking at the bigger picture. Don't be afraid to drop sections of the thesis and replace them with new research. Your book will probably be all the stronger for it.

Think carefully about the structure of the book. Does your Table of Contents have a classic PhD thesis format – for example, an introduction, four long chapters with multiple subsections, followed by a conclusion? If so, look at reorganizing the material into, say, six or seven chapters of readable length.

Write a new introduction, with your new audience in mind. In a thesis, the introduction is sometimes just a kind of preview of the text, e.g. 'in Chapter 1 I will do this', 'in Chapter 2 I will do that'. In the book, use your introduction to set the scene in a meaningful way and to set up key themes and questions that will resonate throughout the text. Make sure it gets the reader's attention and contributes something important right from the start, rather than just providing a rehearsal of the book's contents.

You also need to think about length. Books are usually somewhere between 70,000 and 90,000 words. Your thesis might be significantly longer than that, in which case try to be ruthless; be prepared to lose material that you've spent a lot of time on, in the interests of producing a coherent, streamlined book with a clear argument. If you have to drop something that you really like, perhaps you could turn it into a journal article.

Be wary of excessive 'signposting'. Signposting is where you tell the reader what you've just done and what's coming up next. It can be helpful in the thesis, but if there's too much of it in the book it will feel repetitive. Keep an eye on the flow of the writing, and don't feel the need to constantly explain or justify what you're doing.

Be careful about third-party material, such as illustrations, maps, graphs, or quotations from other people's work. You probably didn't need to seek permission to include this material in your thesis, but in a published book it might be a different matter. Check the Society of Authors website for useful advice about this.

Consider your book title. Don't use the same title as your thesis! Try to ensure that the new title is eye-catching, but also clear and descriptive. You should assume that readers are going to come across your book online, rather than browsing the shelves of a bookshop or even a library, so it's important to get the relevant keywords in there so that your work is easily discoverable.

Ask your university library to put your thesis under embargo so that the availability of the thesis doesn't cut into the potential readership for your book. This is quite a common request; libraries should be able to accommodate it in the knowledge that they'll be able to remove the embargo further down the line, once the book has been out for a few years.

You probably spent years researching and writing your thesis, and now you might easily spend another year (or more) converting it into a book. When you submit your book to an academic publisher, it will undergo a process of peer review. This may sound intimidating, but it's often incredibly helpful to get a fresh perspective on your work, so make the most of it!

With these tips in mind, you should be all set to transform your PhD thesis into an eloquent, engaging book and, in doing so, make your research accessible to a much wider audience. Good luck!

SPORT:

WRITING INTO THE DIGITAL BLIZZARD

Paul Rouse

'The mighty spirit of Tolstoi was not more refreshed by his first sight of the mountains after his journey over the vast plains of Russia, than is the soul of a true-born hurler at the sight of a good hurling match. It is like a city on fire, where the crackling of burning timber and the hissing of the flames swell into the roar of conflagration. We never heard sweeter music than that of the hurling field.'

Michael Cusack, 1887.

I n the years immediately after founding the Gaelic Athletic Association in 1884, Michael Cusack wrote brilliantly about the games which his new organisation controlled, especially hurling. Tens of thousands of words flowed through his columns in the national press, in the newspaper he founded, and in his diary. It stands as the finest body of writing about sport yet published in Ireland.

More than anything else, Cusack—who was a schoolteacher by profession—was a brilliant reporter. When he wrote about a meeting, the smell of the plume of tobacco smoke smothering the delegates lifted from the page; when he took a train to Clare to visit his homeplace, you sat in the carriage beside him as the fields sped past. And when he wrote about hurling, you stood shoulder to shoulder with him for an hour, with timber breaking all around you, alive inside the thrill of the game .

It was not all sweet music; Cusack could write propaganda but he preferred truth. He was unafraid. When he went to Kilkenny in April 1887, he described the state of hurling in the county as 'a positive disgrace.' The first problem was the city. Walking through its streets, he found 'pale, emaciated figures' discussing only the fancy dress of those who passed. 'On the steps of the Bank of Ireland another crowd of persons, who probably call themselves men, was slothfully reclining with their faces towards the sun,' while 'the huge pillars of the town hall supported the dead weight of a lot of fellows.' His mood darkened still further when he eventually found the hurling field: 'The hurling of both teams was the worst and most spiritless ever witnessed on an Irish hillside.' During the play a half-dozen of the hurlers lay down in the centre of the field for a rest in what was 'a contemptible perversion of the grand old dashing game of hurling.' In fact, far from being interested in hurling, 'the local people sneak about the corners, with humps on them, to play flying visits to the local shebeen.'

How had Cusack learned to write like this?

Firstly, the context must be considered. Sports-writing was a new phenomenon at the end of the nineteenth century and sportswriters had yet to fall into their dreary rehearsal of the formulaic previews and match reports which soon became their stock-in-trade. Even in match reports, the original sportswriters spoke with a candour which is wonderful to read. For example, when—in 1886—Ireland lost a rugby international to England for the 12th consecutive year, an Irish rugby journalist writing for a weekly paper had no doubt that it was the fault of the backs: 'We were playing two backs against six,' he wrote, 'Greene was worse than a failure because he interfered with others. Dan Ross did not come off. Joe Ross struggled gamely but without effect. M. Johnston disgraced himself.'

Secondly, though, even allowing for context, Michael Cusack had other things going for him: he read and read. Indeed, it was reading that led him to actually found the GAA. He changed from a man who played cricket and rugby to one dedicated to organising hurling as a modern game after he read Standish O'Grady's *Cuculain: An Epic* (1882). In O'Grady's hands, Cú Chulainn's deeds as a hurler were recreated for a new generation: he played a match in which 'the clash of the metal hurles [sic] resounded in the evening air' and those who watched were awed into silence. Only the very best hurlers attempted to compete with him as he rushed backwards and forwards 'urging the ball in any direction that he pleased, as if in mockery.' As well as drawing on what he read in his writing, Cusack ran his personality through his words, for ill and for good. For example, he was devoid of perspective when he perceived himself as being slighted, as was the case with *The Irish Times*, which he described as a paper 'of that most despicable of all creatures—the Orange Catholic—the slave that refuses to be emancipated—the lazy, place-hunting, unprincipled knave that would 'sell his soul for a penny roll, for soup and hairy bacon." But he was also able to laugh at himself. He responded to taunts that he was hot-headed, even crazy, by saying he was, *au contraire*, actually 'as cool as a New England lawyer eating a cucumber at the back of a tombstone during a blizzard.'

Now, 150 years on, modern sport is ubiquitous. It is a vast global industry and for hundreds of millions of people it is the most significant feature of their cultural lives. The scale of modern sport ensures that it cannot be understood only in terms of its cultural importance, of course; its political, economic and social aspects are everywhere evident. It is inextricably linked with industrialisation and urbanisation, the power of empires and, ultimately, the hyper-commercialisation that is a fundamental part of the accelerating transformations of our new millennium. This is apparent everywhere in the words that are written every day and layered across every form of media.

How would Michael Cusack write into that digital blizzard? He would surely write what he sees, write what he feels, write what he wishes, write without fear, write with humour. And write again.

ON WRITING HISTORY

Donal Fallon

T here is perhaps no society as conscious of the past, or as engaged with it, as here in Ireland. In writing any historical study, it is important to have some sense of where the research fits. Is it a work of social history, or cultural history? What has been written in the field on the subject before? In the broadest sense, history encompasses all that has happened in the recorded past. There is little point asking me a question about Ancient Rome, or in asking a historian of Ancient Rome about Dublin's Victorian tenements. And so, focus, and a sense of what school of history you are working within, is key. As a social historian of Dublin, my journey began with reading the defining oral histories of Kevin C. Kearns, like *Dublin's Tenement Life* and *Dublin Street Life and Lore.* Dublin's story, Kearns rightly felt, could only be told by including the voices of Dubliners themselves. That ethos has driven much of my work.

Even in the short time since my own journey as a historian began, the landscape of available materials has changed dramatically. Decade of Centenaries funding, the impact of the Covid 19 pandemic (when many institutions closed their doors), improving technology – and more besides – have all played some role in bringing more and more materials online. It is testament to Ireland's commitment to history that many of these resources are freely available. These are primary sources, original materials that form the building blocks of historic research.

Where to begin? Firstly, both historians and genealogists have availed much of the 1901 and 1911 Census returns, digitised by the National Archives of Ireland at www.census. nationalarchives.ie. These returns are searchable by a number of information categories. Beyond looking at addresses, you can also search by: religion; occupation; relationship to head of family; literacy status; county or country of origin; Irish language proficiency; specified illnesses; and child survival information. In the case of Dublin, the stark realities of inner-city poverty are clear from the returns. Dublin's high infant mortality means that families in the 1901 census, when examined a decade later, have often lost children to sickness. They paint a different picture of the Dublin that existed in the townships, beyond the canals in new suburbia.

My favourite online resource of recent times has been the Bureau of Military History, hosted by Military Archives at www.militaryarchives.ie. This collection of 1,773 first-hand testimonies gives us new insights into the revolutionary period. Specifically, the brief of the Bureau was 'to assemble and co-ordinate material to form the basis for the compilation of the history of the movement for Independence from the formation of the Irish Volunteers on 25th November 1913, to the 11th July 1921.' Even those not researching or writing about the Irish revolution itself should consider searching these archives, for the broader insights they can give us into the time period. A search for 'football' returns

230 results, while 'music' returns 109. Military Archives also host the vast Military Service Pensions Collection, which includes the pension and medal application forms of participants in the Irish revolution. These tend to be much more focused, requiring references and documentation in support of claims.

Beyond sources, what is most important in the writing of history is structure. I find it helpful at the outset of any written task to produce some kind of structure plan. What will paragraphs or chapters cover? Is the approach going to be chronological, or thematic? Having an idea of structure at the outset can prevent the subject drifting too much.

A lesson learned with time has been to avoid excessive use of large block quotations of secondary sources that are the work of other historians. Instead, try and work quotations into your own writing. The observation of a proof reader on a publication – that the reader wants to read your analysis, and not that of someone else – stayed with me. Your work and your voice should be front and centre, supported by such sources but not overly relying upon them.

There are some challenges which only certain historians will encounter. For example, if employing oral history in your work, there are questions of ethics and methodology which are vitally important: there is little point in undertaking oral history interviews which cannot be used later. The Oral History Network Ireland (online at www.oralhistorynetworkireland.ie) offers workshops and training that familiarise researchers with best practice in the field. The ability to include first-hand testimony from interviews you have conducted yourself is exciting, and brings something new to your study.

Writing for an academic journal and writing a historical piece for a newspaper are very different tasks. Yet the lessons around using sources, and seeking to develop a structure early on apply in both cases. History gives us a better understanding not only of the society that came before us, but the world we live in today. Rather than viewing history merely as 'a series of facts about the past', we should see writing history as an opportunity to help interpret that past, and to make assertions about it: the past, like the present, is often debated.

UNTIL THE WORDS SING:

A QUINTET ON HYBRID TEXTS

Cristín Leach

There are a few reminders I keep with me when I set out to compose a piece of writing that occupies a space between fact, memoir, fiction, opinion, and maybe something else. Auto/critico/archive-based fiction or reality/documentary-based creative nonfiction must find a shape all its own, every time, if it is really going to work. I like the hyphenated word *fact-ion*, or perhaps it should be fact'ion, for fact-fiction, because it is a reminder that this practice is related to literary journalism and to the non-fiction novel, an apparent contradiction in terms. I like it too because a faction, by dictionary definition, is a small, organised, dissenting group within a larger one. My professional background is as a writer of journalistic art criticism. This marginal, precarious practice must keep reinventing itself. It's a genre of writing that begins as a fusion of journalism, specialist reportage, cultural criticism, essay and art writing and becomes over time a source of art history. When I moved beyond newspaper work to publish two strangely-shaped books, each with an internal logic of their own, I took five creative principles with me, two borrowed from two American writers, and three from three Irish visual artists. They form a handy quintet.

~ CELLO ~

In her essay, *The Getaway Car, A Practical Memoir about Writing and Life*, the author Ann Patchett compares writing with learning to play the cello: 'If you want to write, practice writing. Practice it for hours a day… the pleasure *is* the practice.' It's a reminder that what looks like effortless skill in performance is always first honed in hours of doing, by yourself, without necessarily seeking a public endpoint. If you value writing as practice and experiment in the moment, somewhere between those reach-for-the-sky bum notes and losing yourself in the joy of playing with words, you might just figure out how to make art.

~ CHIMES ~

The painter Bernadette Doolan regards waiting as an essential part of her work. She once told me it's a good thing there's no cc-tv in her studio to watch her apparently 'doing nothing' some days, for most of the day. She's not doing nothing. What she is doing is waiting for the spark of spontaneity that comes when you deliberately, thoughtfully stop.

She's waiting for each painting to tell her it's time to begin, time to carry on, or that the canvas is actually finished. She is 'listening' to her work. Sometimes making art is about making space for the kind of gesture that can only come after a contemplative pause: sit with your work, make space and trust that if you listen, the writing will tell you what it needs next.

~ GONG ~

In December 2016, the writer Maria Dahvana Headley spooled out a Twitter thread which I have never forgotten. It read, in part: 'Do your life now… Write your book now… Help someone rise now. Teach someone your skills now. Be brave now… Do the biggest, hardest art now. You do not have forever. You have now… Share now… Open your mouth now… Come shine now. Come trust now. Come be the storm now.' Those words rumbled in the back of my mind for five years until they became a big deafening boom telling me to sit down and write my memoir. Do your art now. Be brave. Write your book.

~ CLARINET ~

I can only finish a piece of writing when I know I have found the right shape. *Negative Space* is a memoir in eight essays, but I imagined it as an album of eight heartbreak songs. The album metaphor gave me permission for certain motifs to repeat, like a beat, or a riff, including the arrival of a text message which punctuates the story in different ways more than once. With my RHA book, *From Ten till Dusk*, I originally imagined a portrait gallery, but came to the idea of the collection as a box of chocolates: each chapter in a different style, all part of one selection. I wrote a list of 'story types', which included a story that is a poem, a story in a hundred questions, a story in diary entries... These structure ideas are not obvious to readers but they were essential tools for writing the books. The journalist in me is always looking for the pull quote, a key phrase that might contain the whole world of a story. My stories often begin with phrases that strike me as having more than one meaning: 'in the evenings, by gaslight', from the archives in *From Ten till Dusk*; a remembered phrase, 'the piece is a car crash Cristín', in *Negative Space*, which serves as a forewarning of what's about to hit my marriage and my mental health. Story-shaping phrases repeat in my mind while I'm doing something else: watching TV, minding children, going for a walk. This is something the artist and RHA President Abigail O'Brien once described to me as 'mental mooching', allowing ideas to just bubble to the surface. Sometimes the resolution for a work in progress arrives while you are scrubbing the bathroom floor. I was cooking when I fully understood that not all of the research needs to stay in the text. Details removed in an edit can still flavour a piece of writing by their lingering absence, like a cardamom pod in some cooked rice.

~ CYMBALS ~

On a studio visit to the artist Gabhann Dunne in 2021, I noticed he had thrown a number of small paintings onto the floor, making a pile of discarded, beautiful, half-finished art. He told me there is a moment when the painting 'breathes', and that didn't happen with those works. When I asked him what went wrong, he said, 'They all fail in the story.' This is the last lesson of the hybrid quintet. If you follow the first four notes, you will know when the work is complete. Never be afraid to delete. Nothing is wasted when you are writing. Get lost in the flow, notice when the cadence feels right, blur the boundaries. Practise, wait, begin, trust, restart. Keep going until the words sing.

AN APPETITE FOR TRUTH:

WRITING AS AN ACT OF MEMORY

Hilary Fannin

In 2015, my memoir *Hopscotch* was published by Doubleday Ireland. I'd been approached by the publishers less than a year beforehand. They'd kindly bought me my lunch and, between a last glass of wine and a roll-up on the restaurant steps, I'd agreed to submit a completed manuscript of some kind before Christmas.

I got the train home, fed the cat, and tried not to think about the commitment I'd just made, given that I'd never actually written a book before. With the clock ticking, my confidence about as ragged as the ancient moggie, and even my dreams being invaded by snarling keyboards, I began.

I realised by the end of the first day that what I was writing was memoir.

The thing was, the publishers hadn't exactly asked for a memoir. At the time, I had a newspaper column in *The Irish Times*, loosely commenting on life as a fiftysomething-year-old, so I assumed the publishers expected me to produce more of the same: vague ramblings on surviving middle age, offbeat musings on how to refresh a marriage and the cat litter.

Like many people, I believed that memoir was the domain of ramshackle rock stars, querulous politicians, and celebrity chefs. I was, in those first weeks of writing, plagued with self-doubt. What right had I – a woman in late middle age who'd never done anything interesting with a kumquat, or smashed up a guitar or thrown a chair through a hotel window – to produce a memoir?

But what is memoir, I tried to reassure myself, but story? Your own story. An unfurling of memory, a careful unfolding of the past which ultimately illuminates the present.

I knew that, like any story, the memoir needed a destination, needed somehow to focus on a point of change. I knew I needed parameters, a beginning and an end.

Hopscotch begins with my first day in convent school, in 'Low Babies', where we tiny four-year-olds in enormous grey uniforms gathered in front of the blackboard to begin our education. It ends with my untimely expulsion from that same school as an eleven-year-old.

Covering that seven-year period, the book also examines my parents' disintegrating marriage, the revelation of my father's long-standing love affair with another woman, my older siblings' precarious and premature independence, a brutish visit from the bailiffs and the bank's repossession of my childhood home.

Despite this material, I was absolutely determined not to write a misery memoir. The book was to be a comedy, and to some extent it succeeds as that, although not entirely. What I hadn't understood until it was reviewed and reprinted was something key to memoir's growing appeal: that my story was also a story of a time, of an era of societal strictures and stringent social mores when many families were living with dark and pernicious secrets.

The tale of my parents' quixotic relationship to each other, to money, to their creativity, immaturity, and despair at being tethered to values that weren't their own, was, in its small way, more reflective of the much bigger collective story of Irish society than I realised until the 70,000 or so words were written.

Memoir continues to be a mainstay of the publishing industry, and one doesn't have to be a recalcitrant red-headed prince to write one. The most cursory investigation of publishers' lists will yield a whole crop of memoir, from the medical to the meditative. Maybe, in an age of misinformation when truth, we are told, is no longer truth, readers have an appetite for first-hand accounts, for the teasing out of the difficult, uncomfortable, profound and sometimes cathartic stories that reside in each of us.

For me, memoir writing became a tool for making sense of the past while also being more alive to the present.

I don't know, maybe all writing is an act of memory. What are we really doing when we write, if not using words to beat out, indent and begin to arrange a lifetime of images left on the senses?

Memoir is a kind medium, a genre that welcomes both reader and writer. As an occasional teacher of the form, I have never ceased to be moved and surprised by the extraordinary stories that so-called ordinary people carry inside them, the memories they are turning over and over in their minds and hearts through the decades.

I was lucky that, in telling our story, I came from a family that were spirited and generous and game enough to accept my version of events.

And speaking of luck…

We had a budgerigar in our family home before that home ceased to exist; his name was Lucky, which, to be fair to the cantankerous old bird, he certainly wasn't. About a year after *Hopscotch* was published, I was sitting in a bar with my three siblings, all of whom are nearly a decade older than me. (I was the 'mistake', the result of my glamorous and impatient mother's brush with the rhythm method, a mind-wrecking form of natural contraception that, unfortunately for her, involved counting.) The conversation turned to Lucky, the bleakly despondent family pet.

'You know, you missed a trick when you wrote about Lucky,' one of my siblings said, going on to explain that the colourful little bird hadn't, as I believed, been found dead in his cage one morning, his empty swing solemnly rocking.

Apparently, my eldest sister, possibly under the influence of a mind-altering substance, had let the misnamed bird out of his cage late one night so that he could experience some personal freedom. And when, the following morning, my mother came down to the kitchen, her false eyelashes resting on her cheeks like sleeping spiders, Lucky was hanging by his neck from the curtain cord.

'To Lucky,' we said, raising our glasses to our existentially tangled-up budgie, a not-so-sadly missed member of the family.

Proposals
& Pitches

Your First Steps towards Non-Fiction Publication

Patrick O'Donoghue

As commissioning editor for Gill Books, my primary role is to ensure excellence in the books we publish. As well as approaching potential authors, some of my favourite titles have arrived in my inbox completely out of the blue. I'll never tire of seeing these new proposals – even if sometimes there just aren't enough hours in the day to read them all. So what helps your submission stand out? Here, I offer some tips for the debut non-fiction author – and perhaps some pointers for those who are already in the saddle – which might offer some light surrounding the road to publication.

THE FIRST STEP

Familiarise yourself with the Irish publishing scene. Thankfully, the book you're holding in your hands (or reading electronically) is the ideal place to start. Visit publishers' websites, look through the range of titles on offer, and see whose output you find yourself gravitating towards. Add any publishers who appeal to the list of those you are planning to contact.

SUBMISSION GUIDELINES

Along with the necessary contact details, in most cases you'll also find the publisher's submission guidelines on their website. Take the time to review this page, as there will undoubtedly be something there that you can use in your proposal to improve your chances of success. Also, while some publishers will receive submissions all year round, others have submission windows, and will only be seeking new material during that time period.

WHAT SHOULD I INCLUDE IN MY SUBMISSION?

Submission guidelines will vary but here is a list that will tally with most non-fiction requirements: a cover letter; a brief synopsis of the text; a chapter outline; two or three sample chapters; and an author bio.

I recommend you keep the cover letter relatively short and to the point. Use it to make a connection and pique interest – but let the other documents do the heavy lifting. Address the submission to an actual person, if at all possible. Again, check the publisher's website or their social channels, and if all else fails there is nothing wrong with giving the publisher a quick call to find out this information.

The synopsis is a concise overview of the book. There are no set rules on how long it should be, but I find that 300–500 words tends to work quite well – not too short, and not too long. The synopsis is your best – and possibly only

– opportunity to grab the publisher's attention, so make it as enticing as possible. Don't ramble, and don't hold back any information: this is not the place for *you'll never guess what happened next …*

A strong chapter outline can make a real difference. This is basically a more detailed Table of Contents, with one or two lines giving a flavour of each chapter. Here, you're trying to deepen the interest you've already kindled through your synopsis.

As far as the sample chapters go, choose the best, not necessarily the first: if the strongest material is in the middle or towards the end, then include these. If the publisher is interested, they'll come back for more.

The author bio is self-explanatory, but do feel free to add in any other information that might add weight to your proposal, such as your social media following, or significant events surrounding the subject of your book.

A final tip, and it's a minor point really; I recommend you use a traditional font when submitting – you know the ones: Times New Roman; Cambria; Calibri; Palatino; Arial and so on. They're classics for a reason.

DO I NEED TO INCLUDE IMAGES OR ILLUSTRATIONS?

No, there is no need to include illustrations with your proposal. If you've written a political biography, for example, then the publisher will work with you to compile a list of images suitable for a picture section.

WHAT IS THE IDEAL WORD COUNT?

There are no right or wrong answers as to how long a book should be. (Okay, that's not true, 500,000 words is a wrong answer.) However, there are some conventions around the expected word count for general non-fiction titles. For example, a 320pp Trade (234x153mm) paperback will more than likely have a word count in and around 80-90,000 words; a 256pp pictorial/text history of the Burren might only need 30-40,000 words; whereas a political biography could easily go north of the 100,000-word mark. In any case, if the publisher likes what they are reading, they will work with you to find a word count which fits. A word of caution though – if your manuscript is over 100,000 words, then expect some cutting.

There will, of course, be exceptions to this. Fintan O'Toole's bestseller *We Don't Know Ourselves: A Personal History of Ireland Since 1958* clocks in at a sizeable 624 pages, and at a rough guess I'd say it's around the 200,000-word mark. However, unless you are also a former literary editor of one of the country's biggest newspapers, with more than four decades of experience commentating on Irish society, do not expect a warm response from the publisher if you land 200,000 words on their desk!

IS THE MANUSCRIPT FINISHED?

If you're asked this question, it's a good sign – indicating the publisher is at the very least curious to read more. If you haven't finished writing the manuscript, then manage expectations about timeframes. It's best to set a realistic deadline, so you can have the manuscript in good shape without putting yourself under pressure: don't over-promise and under-deliver.

REJECTIONS

Rejections are an unfortunate inevitability. Publishers reject titles every day for many reasons, including: the subject matter isn't a good fit for their list; the book is not commercially viable, i.e. the publisher doesn't think they can sell enough copies to be profitable; the market might be saturated with similar titles; or the publisher might simply have a full list of titles with no capacity to take on your book. Whatever the reason, try not to be too discouraged.

'Please bear in mind that this is just the opinion of one publisher,' is a phrase which the late Sean O'Boyle, the first publisher I worked for, would write to authors whose work he was declining. The line is reflective of the kindness and empathy of a man who understood the sacrifices writers make to get to the point of submitting their work.

I still believe that this is excellent advice – and I offer it here to any writer embarking on those first steps towards

publication.

IT'S ALL ABOUT THE BOOK

Madeleine Keane

The postman always rings twice in my house, such is the volume of books (at least twenty or so) that land here every week. Like many people when they hear about my work, he's interested to know if and how I get to read them. I am patient as I explain that no, much as I'd love to, I simply cannot read all the titles I receive.

As literary editor since 2001 of the country's most widely read national broadsheet, along with building shelves to accommodate my burgeoning library, my mission has always been to cover, in some way, shape or form, as many books as possible every Sunday. Around 4 million titles are released globally each year. My weekly books section comprises four pages. As they say, do the math.

MY FOCUS

My focus is firmly, firstly Irish with a commitment to including international writing too. We have a distinguished literary heritage and it's often observed that we are living in a golden age of Irish literature; yet it is also crucial to look outwards. Our bone-deep patriotism is endearing, and we are right to be proud of our great little island – particularly when it comes to our myriad, marvellous authors – but we are betimes parochial, and it is vital to remember that there's a big world of books out there.

In terms of range, my chief loves are literary fiction, memoir, and poetry. However, our readers come first, so I make space for political biography, environmental manifestos, and high society scandals, as well as psychology, travel, nature, and sport. I want to hear from and about whistle-blowers and feminists, detectives and scientists, playwrights and philosophers.

And, arguably, most important of all, the imperative to inspire, nurture and encourage the next generation of readers – our children – has always been high on my agenda.

MY PAGES

So, with these parameters in mind, what am I looking for from prospective contributors?

In terms of general features and articles, even after four decades in the business, I'm still mesmerised by the mechanics of writing – where writers get their ideas, and how they do their research; do they know the end when they start their beginning? I love that John Irving writes the last sentence of each novel first and then works his way towards that. I've never lost my complete fascination with people who go daily into empty rooms and conjure fantastical worlds.

Consequently, I'm also very interested in the world of publishing and keen to see where it's going, to discover emerging trends. Remember when Domestic Noir was the new Big Idea. So, what's next? Where did auto-fiction come from? Is there a new genre that we haven't yet invented? We must also look at literature in the ever-evolving lens of society's values and interests. Whither publishing in this digital age? What effect will Artificial Intelligence have on our industry? Can you earn a living as a writer in Ireland?

Then there are the sub-genres within genres which offer endless scope for features. Crime is a great example. If you regard the fertile landscape offered by murder, fraud, and deception, you'll see how many strands there are in this corpse-strewn category. From Emerald and Scandi noir to police procedurals, psychological thrillers and campus killers, the bloodied list includes spy stories, LGBTQ+ dramas, locked-room mysteries, cold-case whodunnits, history, romance, dystopia, and now, thanks to Richard Osman, the hot new kid on the block – cosy crime.

I'm not in love with the listicle but appreciate its value. What are the best books about betrayal? Tell me the top 10 European espionage novels, enumerate the poetry collections, the travel memoirs, the plays we must read before we die. I also love hearing as much about nascent writers as I do about those forgotten in the mists of time.

REVIEWING

The heart of our newspaper's books section is the reviews. I'm always on the hunt for new voices, new critics. If you're cold calling – wanting to write for my pages – the key to my heart is telling me what you're currently reading, why and if and how it moves you.

If you receive a commission, don't blow it. I shouldn't need to point this out, but experience means I must: meeting deadlines in a weekly newspaper is mandatory. As is accuracy – not just in details: the spelling of the author's name; the correct imprint; the shade of the heroine's hair; our house style – but in the appraisal itself, particularly, say, in a labyrinthine novel with tangled plot twists and a multiplicity of characters.

If you're judging another's writing, your own must pass muster too. As Sam Anderson noted a few years ago in the *New York Times*: 'A badly written review is self-canceling, like a barber with a terrible haircut. The best way to establish critical authority is to demonstrate in your own prose a vitality at least equivalent to that of the book you're writing about.'

Spoilers are verboten on my pages; so too is hedging your bets. Pin your colours to the mast and tell us what you love, loathe, and could leave behind. But please avoid gratuitous cruelty: remember how demanding and difficult this art is and play nicely. Don't show off. A distinctive voice matters but there's no need to make yourself the principal player of the piece. It's all about the book.

I'll conclude with advice from John Updike who was as celebrated a reviewer as he was a novelist. In 1962, he wrote: 'Review the book, not the reputation. Submit to whatever spell, weak or strong, is being cast. Better to praise and share than blame and ban. The communion between reviewer and his public is based upon the presumption of certain possible joys of reading, and all our discriminations should curve toward that end.'

LIFESTYLE PUBLISHING:

A DECENT PROPOSAL

Sarah Liddy

I dream of receiving that magical submission – exciting, unique, relevant, and so carefully considered that I pick up the phone straight away to make an offer. It's not completely unheard of: many non-fiction titles are acquired based on short proposals for books that aren't even written yet.

A lifestyle book can be anything from self-development to cookery, from gardening to health, and in recent years we have seen many Irish success stories in this space. Lifestyle publishing is not just about chart toppers though; it's an area that can back-list well, so books that might not have been high achievers on publication can continue to sell in modest numbers for many years, becoming core stock in stores.

As publishers, we don't expect writers to know or understand the market as well as we do – but we hope prospective authors will follow our submission guidelines and give themselves the best chance of success. Whatever your topic, here are a few key things to consider before submitting a proposal to an agent or publisher.

WHO ARE YOU?

This will be one of the first things the person reading your submission wants to know: what are your qualifications for writing this book – do you have a popular podcast on the topic, are you an academic who wants their work to reach a non-academic audience, do we know you from TV or radio? You don't necessarily need to have a high-profile but there does need to be something in your background or qualifications that makes you the right author for the book. It's important when it comes to promoting a book too: a publisher will want to know how you can help with the publicity process.

WHO IS YOUR AUDIENCE?

What other books might your audience buy? Publishers like comparisons, so don't be afraid to tell us what other titles are out there on the same subject. Sometimes we are looking for an Irish take on a popular topic: just because Davina has a book out about the menopause, it doesn't mean there isn't room for an Irish expert on the same subject. Let us know what will make your book both similar and different!

WHY ARE YOU WRITING THIS BOOK, AND WHY NOW?

Do you have clients who have begged you to put your expertise down on paper? Or have you built a social media following who'd like to see your content in one place? Maybe you have been planning it for ages and finally have the time – let us know.

WHY THIS PARTICULAR TOPIC?

Is it underserved by the current offering on the bookshelves (sometimes there's a good reason for this)? Has new research changed what we need to know? Perhaps your own star is rising and it's the right time to bring out a book. An important question to ask yourself is whether your topic is really a book, or whether it might be better as a blog or extended piece of journalism.

HOW WILL YOU ENGAGE YOUR READERS?

Think about how you will bring your audience with you through the book, and whether it needs photos, artwork, exercises, recaps, case studies. Non-fiction involves telling stories to create a connection with the reader, whether that is through the introduction to a recipe, or an anecdote from your own life in a self-help book. Publishers want books that resonate with readers, whatever the genre.

WHAT MIGHT YOUR BOOK BE LIKE?

It's useful to research what's already out there: think about where your book will sit in a bookshop; look at comparable books and see what length they are, whether they are in colour or black and white, what kind of illustrations or photographs are included, and how much they cost. A publisher will make many of these decisions but it's helpful to have a realistic concept when you are writing a proposal. Don't become wedded to a particular vision though, your publisher might have other ideas and decide that gold foil and sprayed edges aren't right for your book!

With your research done, it's time to put your best foot forward and write your proposal. Submissions requirements vary, but as a rule it's useful to include:

- A cover letter which answers the questions above.
- A proposed table of contents – remember with non-fiction it can be better to approach a publisher with a proposal rather than a completed manuscript. A good editor will want to partner with you, and can offer valuable input on structure, content, tone, and building engagement. The table of contents gives a publisher an overview of your vision.
- Some sample text that gives a sense of style and tone.
- Information on what, if any, photos, graphs, diagrams and other artwork you think the manuscript needs. Again, this is an area your publisher will want to work on with you, so you don't need to have all of this ready when you submit a proposal. It may well be that your publisher commissions and pays for these elements of the book if they take it on.

Finally, don't agonise! Good editors have an instinct for spotting the gold in the submissions pile. I have taken on books that were pitched to me in a couple of lines – and while we much prefer to receive a well thought out and considered proposal, it certainly doesn't have to be perfect to find a receptive editor. Good luck!

HOW TO WRITE LITERARY
FICTION THAT SELLS

Deirdre Nolan

When I sat down to write this piece I felt like a fraud. Despite over twenty years in publishing I don't know much more than anyone else what will sell and what won't.

I can read a piece of writing and feel its magic, understand that I've experienced the almost transcendental joy of being able to live another person's life, if only for those few moments.

I can know that so many other people would experience the same joy were they to read the same book as me. I understand how the book should be produced, in what format and with a compelling cover. I understand the mechanics of marketing the book, finding its most appealing aspect and highlighting that for potential readers, ensuring influential reviewers have access to the book, getting a great sales team fired up to enthusiastically sell it to booksellers.

But what makes a book take that leap from being published to being a bestseller? As a publisher I'd love to pat myself on the back and say it's because of my unique skill, a God-given talent, but the truth is it's often down to luck.

Literary fiction can be notoriously difficult to sell, and I've seen many utterly brilliant books sell no more than a few thousand copies while other less dazzling titles sell in the hundreds of thousands. This can be the result of a strong, impactful marketing campaign or the publisher's dream phenomenon – word of mouth. A book can find its way into an influential person's hands and take off from there, climbing up the charts until the cycle of exposure and endorsements causes it to become a bestseller, or it can languish on too many TBR (to be read) piles, its magic undiscovered like a gemstone stuck in a rock.

VOICE

So if you want your gem to be polished by an editor and shine for all the world (or at least part of it) to see, what do you need to watch out for in your own work? There are a number of answers to that question.

When I'm reading submissions the main thing I look for is voice. I want to read something original, something that makes me think about life in a way I never have before. It's my belief that, while there may or may not be an afterlife and/or reincarnation, we can live many lives simply by reading widely. Books make it possible to immerse ourselves in another person's world, culture, mindset, helping us to develop empathy and compassion.

A unique, engaging voice can ensure the reader learns by osmosis to think differently in some way about the world, and it's that sense that I'm always seeking. It's an elusive magic, very difficult to falsify but instantly recognisable once you discover it. In order to find that voice I think that writers need to lose their own – and their own egos. They need to get out of their characters' way, step aside and let their characters speak to them clearly, even if it's with words and actions the writer doesn't like. Trust the story, and trust your storytellers.

PACING AND STRUCTURE

As well as compelling characters, I also look for intriguing pacing and a strong narrative arc. While literary fiction doesn't need the mile-a-minute pacing of commercial fiction such as crime or contemporary romance, it still needs to move the story along in a timely manner so that the reader doesn't lose interest. You need to create drama by inflicting conflict on your characters, and often this works best by introducing a sense of danger from the off. Grab the reader early and keep them intrigued.

I read countless submissions as part of my job, and there's one issue I see occurring over and over and over – lack of structure. The most incredible story will fall flat if it isn't produced within a strong narrative arc. When you've completed your first draft, please go back and check each sentence, paragraph and chapter for structure. Each should hold the other up like a series of rainbows, small ones for the sentences, with larger overarching ones for the paragraphs and chapters, and finally a giant sky celebration for the entire book. Don't just focus on the sky, remember to check in on each smaller arc too and ensure it's well-constructed.

TESTAMENT TO YOUR COMMITMENT

Finally, good luck with the publishing process. I realise that it sounds counterintuitive coming from someone who makes her living from publishing books, but please don't see the value of your book as resting in whether or not it's published. If you've finished writing a book you're in a tiny minority of people, and your book is wonderful because it's uniquely yours. It's a written testament to your perseverance, your discipline, your willingness to work long hours and your commitment to your chosen craft.

If it's accepted by a commissioning editor that's great, it's a nice endorsement of all of your hard work – but if your book isn't taken on by a publishing house remember that commissioning editors are as humanly flawed as anyone else; they don't always make the right decisions, and whatever their opinion you have still written a book.

You are an author, and that is magnificent.

Getting published is the icing – but not the cake.

PITCHING TO A FESTIVAL:

TIPS AND INSIGHTS

Julianne Mooney Siron

I reland is renowned for the art of storytelling, so it's no surprise that almost every county in Ireland has some form of literary or book festival going on. Festivals are a great opportunity for writers to come together with their peers, to share ideas and challenges, to experience the more social aspect of writing, and get to meet their readers. In more recent years libraries have started to run their own festivals, rural villages bringing in writers and readers from around Ireland and further afield.

If you have been published by a traditional publisher, the marketing and PR department will most likely have developed relationships with festivals around the country, and will pitch their authors. Talk with your publisher; if you have specific festivals you are interested in attending then highlight these and ask if they could approach them on your behalf. If this is not an option for you, it is possible to approach festivals directly. Below are some tips to keep in mind.

RESEARCH

- This is essential to get right. If this is your first book, focus more on local festivals in a nearby town, city, or county.
- Try your local library. Libraries are a great source of support for writers and often run festivals or book club events – and it's a great way to get on the scene and gain experience.
- If your book is specific to a particular area, then contact a festival or library in that region.
- Research the festivals you plan to contact. Festivals will often specialise in genres: crime; history; travel; non-fiction; literary. Make sure the festival suits your work: there is no point applying to a children's festival when you write for adults.
- Once you have identified relevant festivals and events, make sure your timing is right. Most festivals will start programming 6 - 12 months in advance of their festival, so there is no point contacting them two months before the festival in the hopes of being programmed that year.
- Follow the festivals on social media and sign up to their newsletters. Some festivals do an open call, and you will be able to submit directly to them, according to their guidelines.

TIPS FOR QUERYING

- Address your submission to either the Festival Director or Festival Programmer. Make sure to include the following information:
- Book title: provide details about the book in an Advance Information sheet, or if it has been released with a link to the information.
- Provide your publisher details.
- Give details of any events or festivals where you have performed, and what events you have lined up for the coming year.
- If you have a particular format or idea include this in your pitch. Festivals receive a lot of submissions, so if you have a specific idea for an event, something unique, it is well worth including: festivals are always looking for new, innovative, and interactive events.
- Offer to post a copy of your book for review.
- State if you are happy to be on a panel. If it is your first book, most festivals will have emerging writers' panel discussions or readings.
- Try to visit the festivals you are interested in; for financial reasons it's not feasible to go to everything – but if there is a particular event you really want to be involved in, it's well worth going to see what it's all about. Use the opportunity to meet other authors, get a feel for the different events – and you could even introduce yourself briefly, so the organisers and curators can put a face to a name. Festivals are a great networking opportunity.

Even if a festival has to say no, remember, they receive hundreds of submissions every year and as much as they would like to programme everything there is just not enough funds or space in the programme. Don't get disheartened, respond to the email and say you'd love to be kept in mind for future years. Then get back in touch the following year. Festivals will do their best to programme as many new writers as possible – it might just take time.

TOLKA:

A LITERARY JOURNAL'S INSIGHTS

Catherine Hearn

T*olka* is a biannual literary journal of non-fiction, based in Dublin. Founded by three friends in the Autumn of 2020, we publish all kinds of non-fiction, from essays and memoir to reportage and auto-fiction, and we have a particular interest in promoting stylistically innovative and formally promiscuous writing. We open our submissions window twice a year for a month at a time. The first is usually between December and January, the second between June and July. Submissions do not require a fee, and we publicise these open calls in our newsletter and on social media.

Our commissioning policy is based on an even split between the open submissions process and a commissioning practice which allows us to publish work from both established authors and emerging writers from various backgrounds. This dual-approach allows for an inclusive practice, and also allows us to commission writers that we love, such as Roisin Kiberd, who wrote us a piece about Jeff Bezos encountering God during his forays in space.

Tolka's three founding editors – Catherine, Liam and Seán – draw on their own expertise and experience to solicit and commission exceptional pieces of non-fiction. Four contributing editors - Martin, Chloé, Madeline, and Caoimhe - are also employed to connect *Tolka* with burgeoning talent and help to shape the overall arc of each issue. Additionally, we have a translator-in-residence, Brian Robert Moore, who is tasked with sourcing and editing stylistically innovative work-in-translation.

We don't include an editorial in our issues, or explicitly state what we're looking for in our submissions policy, as we don't want to be overly prescriptive, and often, we don't know what we're looking for until we read it. Instead, each issue is shaped through careful curation; Issue One opens with Liadan Ní Chuinn's first lines, 'When I was at University I had to cut up a body (I'm sorry, I'm sorry)', from their powerful piece 'twenty twenty'. The issue concludes (spoiler) with a beautiful fragment from Ana Kinsella's 'Wayfinding': 'The best bit of any ballet is the break in the music, during a dancer's solo, when all you can hear is the furious scuffling of pointe shoes along the wood of the stage and the collective hush of a whole auditorium holding its breath.'

While we have published some of the most innovative contemporary Irish writers, such as Eimear McBride, Brian Dillon, Niamh Campbell and Nidhi Zak/Aria Eipe, we also strongly promote new writing, and we publish writers from around the globe. We highly advise reading previous issues of *Tolka* before submitting your work. Many writers, who have had submissions published in *Tolka*, have told us they were inspired by previous issues.

Below are tips if you are considering submitting to us – but most will apply wherever you are sending your work.

- Ask someone you trust to read your writing before submitting: this can give another perspective on how finished a piece of writing is. Similarly, ask yourself: is this as polished and meticulously edited as it can be? Am I ready to let this out into the world? At the same time, trust yourself to know when a piece of work is ready!

- Avoid making your work experimental or 'formally promiscuous' for the sake of it: this conceit is intended to encourage writers to push the boundaries of non-fiction, and to make it clear that your writing does not need to be limited by genre. However, there's little point in turning half your essay into a prose poem, unless that formal choice chimes perfectly with the content of the piece. Someone who does this really well is Brenda Romero. Brenda's first *Tolka* piece, 'Conception', details the writer's experience of IVF and her struggle to conceive a child, and it takes the form of a 'choose your own adventure' dice game. The form perfectly encapsulates and reflects the very random and non-linear process of IVF and the long, winding road that many women face in their efforts to conceive.

- Do not try to write to the submission window deadline: it's unlikely that you'll conceive of, write, edit and submit a great piece of work within a month.

Instead, the submissions window should be an opportunity to polish and possibly rework a piece that you've already written.

- Avoid overly academic language: because we're a non-fiction journal, we attract a lot of submissions in the form of academic essays. Usually, unless they're considerably reworked, these are not what we're looking for. While we welcome pieces that are well researched and grounded in a variety of disciplines (science, history, politics, etc.) we're usually seeking a more personal or narrativised approach, rather than scholarly research papers.

- Submit widely and repeatedly: Ireland has a very rich and expansive journal culture, each with their own style and preferences, and just because your work may not be a fit for *Tolka*, it doesn't mean it's not a great piece of writing. Before deciding where to submit your piece, investigate a number of journals to find out where it would best fit. A piece rejected by a different journal might be exactly the one we're looking for!

All successful submissions to *Tolka* will undergo a minimum of two rounds of edits (although editorial feedback can vary and may not always be necessary), including a round of copy-editing. Through this process, we aim to improve the quality of the piece itself and also the abilities and practical knowledge of the writer. We assign all of our contributors one lead editor who is dedicated to that piece and will liaise with the writer directly.

We pay all contributors fairly and transparently for their work. With feedback and guidance from the Arts Council, we now pay a rate of €500 per submission. Aside from publishing their work, we also promote and advocate for the writers we publish, including them in as many events, readings, festivals and media opportunities as possible, as well as recommending their work to other editors and to agents.

Our ultimate hope is that *Tolka* acts as a home for expansive forms of new writing, writing that extends the creative and critical possibilities of non-fiction, writing that may not belong anywhere else.

The
Publishing
Experience

COCONUT SHY:

THE ECONOMICS OF PUBLISHING

Ronan Colgan

O n 14 April, 1993, in the feverish atmosphere of half-time in a packed Chicago Bulls' stadium, a 23-year-old local man called Don Calhoun was pulled from the crowd. The challenge he was set was to attempt a shot at the basket from over 75 feet. It was a three-quarter court shot and felt to be almost impossible, particularly for an amateur, randomly chosen from the audience. The prize for making it was a cheque for one million dollars.

Contests like this were common at the time and were insured by promotions companies. According to a senior executive in the industry, 'the perfect contest was like the most tempting carnival game: just feasible enough to make people think they can do it but actually extremely difficult'.

Anyone who has investigated the economics of publishing, as either a prospective author or publisher, will be familiar with this sentiment. It can be a challenging industry to make money from. It can feel like standing in front of a fairground shack, throwing everything you have at a coconut.

It doesn't help that these economics are highly complex and endlessly variable. Each different genre, from literary fiction and illustrated children's books to academic publishing and poetry, have their own models; within that, each publisher will have their own approach, areas on which they spend more or spend less. And, within that, each book will be different. No attempt can be made to speak *ex cathedra* on this subject. Somebody will always do things differently.

Whole books could be written on this subject, and these books would be important, valuable and could change aspects of the industry. But would they sell in large numbers? That is really the heart of it.

However, notwithstanding the caveats above, there are some relatively universal constants. In the spirit of attempting to demystify this particularly opaque side of the industry, let's explore two of the most frequently asked questions: firstly, why do books cost what they cost?; and, secondly, how much money will an author make?

To try and answer both those questions at once, we might take a sample book and dissect it as best we can. The largest category of the Irish publishing market is non-fiction and, within that, it is history and biography, so this is where we will turn.

So, our notional book is an Irish non-fiction title, 300 pages in length. There is no colour plate section but there is an index. The publisher and author have debated going down the traditional route of releasing in hardback first and then moving to paperback, but it's been decided that, having requested print quotes for various quantities, hardback would push the retail price higher than either the publisher or the bookshops believe would work for the intended readership. The author has a track record of previously published books; she avoids social media but initial media interest is likely and there is a good marketing plan in place. The decision is to print in paperback and the print run is 3,000 copies. The retail price is set at €20.

In order to get a sense of why this retail price is set, we can work backwards and look at where that €20 goes.

Firstly, 50% of this will go to the bookshops. If this seems high, it's worth remembering that the bookshops need to have a high-street presence and everything that goes with that, like bricks-and-mortar rent, staff, utilities and commercial rates. Bookshops have never been accused of making too much money and this is not an oversight. It's also worth bearing in mind that Amazon have the buying power to demand higher discounts than bookshops, without the talented staff, proximity or tax obligations. Support your local bookshop.

So, from the €10 per book remaining, €2.50 of this is spent on sales and distribution, the process of informing, championing and physically delivering every book to potentially every bookshop around the country. That leaves €7.50 per book.

From the €7.50, the print cost per book is €2, leaving €5.50. The copyediting, proofreading and indexing costs come to €1.50 per book, leaving €4. The cover design and internal layout come to €1 per book, leaving €3.

Of the remaining revenue, €1 is allocated to the roles of the commissioning editor, the editorial assistant, the marketing and publicity people – and of course the finance person who helped calculate all of these costs, paid all of these invoices and, critically, processed the author royalty payments. That leaves €2.

The author royalty was agreed at 10% of net receipts, which means the amount the publisher receives after book-shop discounts but before any other costs. In this case, the publisher receives €10 so the author royalty is €1 per book. And the remaining €1 is the profit to the publisher.

And so to our second question: how much did the author make? In the end, this book sells 2,500 copies and the author's print royalties are €2,500.

However, she is invited to speak on various panels and festivals, which these days regularly come with a fee. She is shortlisted for a number of small awards and one prestigious award in Canada, which surprises everyone – except those who have read the book, because she writes beautifully.

And while the market for our notional book is simply the size that it is, as the sales showed, its relative success means she is approached by another publisher to write a book with an international focus. During the meeting they reflect on the fact that the Irish book market, while vibrant, is roughly the same size as the Manchester book market. This strikes a chord with the author as her grandparents were from Manchester. This book is published and sells closer to 25,000 copies and Spanish and Italian translation rights are sold. The author receives 60% of the international rights fee. The French publishers debate it but ultimately decline. *C'est la vie.*

This author may not exist but her story does. Some authors make money from their writing and some don't. Some create careers out of their books, some create books out of their careers. Authors are often necessarily supported in their work by the Arts Council of Ireland, the Heritage Council, Culture Ireland, as well as through their royalties. And there are countless examples of Irish authors achieving great success, both critical and commercial, with their Irish publishers.

It is perhaps worth bearing in mind two last points.

Firstly, two of the lowest selling genres are poetry and academic publishing. And it is these genres that are most likely to produce a book that changes the world.

While publishing sits at the conjuncture of art and commerce, and books that sell are the things that make the author and publisher money, there are nuances and there are surprises and there are wildly different definitions of what success is. It might feel like a carnival game, and it is certainly not simple, but the difference is that both you and your publisher are on the same side of the shack, standing side-by-side, throwing everything both of you have at those coconuts.

And lastly, to Don Calhoun, our basketball fan pulled from the crowd. Obviously he made the shot. Anything is possible.

BEING BRAVE CAN PAY OFF:

DEFAMATION LAW AND

PUBLISHING NON-FICTION

Mark Tighe

Getting sued and having your home or savings put at risk is not something authors should be fretting about before publication. However, that is the stark peril that authors of Irish non-fiction books have to face up to.

Ireland is known to have one of the most financially punitive and restrictive defamation regimes across the EU. Although we do not have criminal defamation laws like some EU countries, our costly civil defamation system means that one defamation complaint could financially destroy an author or their publisher. I know of one historian who is struggling to find a publisher of his almost-completed work of the rise of the far-right movement in Ireland because it is seen as a work that is legally problematic.

At a 2021 Oireachtas Justice Committee hearing, Didier Reynders, the EU Commissioner for Justice, noted how the Commission's report on the Irish justice system had said that 'frequent defamation legal cases, the high cost of defence and the high damages awarded by the Irish courts are seen as an inducement to self-censorship and a constraint on media freedom.'

Late in 2019, Paul Rowan and I decided we would develop our reporting on John Delaney and the Football Association of Ireland (FAI) from the Sunday Times and go into greater depth on the scandal in a book. The risk of a defamation case against us was our prime consideration when choosing a publisher.

Our stories on the emerging scandal of Delaney's staggering mismanagement of the FAI, that included paying tens of thousands of euros to his former girlfriend, were generating a record-breaking number of fresh subscriptions for our newspaper. So, we believed there would be a big demand for a book that could go deeper into Delaney's rise and fall.

Public appetite for the story meant that three different publishers made us offers to bring what would become *Champagne Football* to print. The size of the advances on offer was not our biggest consideration when deciding which we would choose. Instead, we asked each publisher what was the scope of the defamation cover they could offer us as authors.

Previously, when I was considering working on a book about a wealthy and litigious Irish businessman, I was advised to transfer my stake in our family home into my wife's name, to protect our family financially. Our question to the three publishers generated three different answers. One, the Irish branch of one of the biggest book publishers in the world, withdrew its offer.

A large Irish publisher, which had made us the best financial offer, said it could not offer us a guarantee of any protection if Delaney or anyone else decided to sue us personally.

The third publisher, Penguin Ireland, said that as long as our material contained no deliberate mistruths it would take charge of any defamation cases arising from the book. Our choice was clear.

The reason theoretical defamation complaints were so prominent in our thoughts was because of the track-record of the man we were writing about. One of the reasons Delaney's time at the FAI lasted for almost 15 years was because many journalists were afraid to write critically about him.

Between 2011 and 2019, Delaney was involved in 78 legal actions, many of which were defamation cases. In 2016 and 2017, in the aftermath of coverage of the arrest in Brazil of Pat Hickey, the Olympic Council of Ireland (OCI) President, much media coverage was given to the fact that Brazilian police said they wanted to talk to Delaney, who was an OCI vice-president, about the ticketing scandal that prompted Hickey's arrest.

Delaney issued a slew of writs on the back of this coverage, complaining it unfairly tarnished his reputation. FAI documents would later reveal he received five legal settlements totalling €267,500 from media organisations.

Newspaper journalists knew how sensitive Delaney was. In one case in 2007, my now employer, the Sunday Independent, published a light-hearted diary piece in the sports section that said there were nine pictures of Delaney in an eight-page FAI newsletter. The piece joked that there was a cult of leadership around Delaney in the FAI akin to leaders such as Stalin and Ceausescu. The following week the newspaper was forced into issuing an unreserved apology for the 'grossly unfair' item. The apology, at 63 words, was nine words longer than the offending piece.

As cases around the world have shown, it is possible to defame someone just by using an emoji, as has happened with the use of an innocent face emoji in the UK and a mouth-zipped closed emoji in Australia.

In Ireland, the largest ever defamation award was €10m awarded to Donal Kinsella, a business executive, who was defamed by a press release relating to him sleepwalking while naked. This award was reduced to €250,000 on appeal.

The damages regime for High Court defamation cases was effectively set in a 2022 case involving Paidraig Higgins, a pilot, who sued the Irish Aviation Authority. The Supreme Court set out five levels of defamation awards in its judgment. It said 'very moderate' cases could lead to damages of up to €50,000, medium cases could achieve up to €125,000 and serious defamatory cases with mitigating factors could get up to €199,000. Very serious cases could achieve damages of up to €300,000 while 'exceptional' cases could receive in excess of €300,000.

While the government has promised a new defamation act to reform the 2009 Defamation Act, it is unlikely to be passed by this Dáil. While it has proposed some welcome reforms such as the removal of juries from High Court cases which should make trials less costly, the government is planning only a limited introduction of a 'serious harm' test. This would require plaintiffs to prove that a publication damaged them.

Almost uniquely in civil law, in defamation cases the complainants do not have to prove they were harmed by complained about publication. The government proposal to introduce a harm test would only be applied to defamation cases taken by corporations (like Ryanair, a regular litigant), or in cases of 'transient' defamation, which would cover defamation in cases where people are accused of theft from a retailer. Quite how a harm test can be introduced for some cases but excluded for the majority of cases over concerns about its constitutionality has not been properly explained by the government.

Being brave can pay off. In our case, *Champagne Football* generated zero legal complaints. It was the best-selling Irish published book in 2020 and has sold in excess of 82,000 copies, including ebooks and audiobooks. With a general election on the horizon, writers and publishers can put pressure on politicians to commit to making the Irish defamation landscape less foreboding for those wishing to publish non-fiction books that tackle serious issues.

BRINGING IT TO THE STUDIO:

FROM TEXT TO AUDIOBOOK

Kevin Curran

In the six years I was writing my novel, *Youth*, I never considered an audiobook version. Yet it turns out I wrote a perfect novel for the audiobook experience.

1. It was relatively short, 70k words, which made it only a 7 hour listen (something I was later told by an expert is the perfect length).
2. It was in first person.
3. It was in first person vernaculars.
4. The four first person teenage vernaculars overlapped, which made the tone of voice and energy diverse, and the experience episodic.
5. There was also a narrator, but this fifth voice only appeared at the beginning of the novel for ten pages, and then at the end of the novel for 2 pages.

So, when the publisher got in touch to say they wanted to do an audiobook, I was delighted…but tempered my expectations. I mean, how many audiobooks have you heard that have five different actors? And how would we get the young actors into the studio in such a short space of time?

I didn't need to worry because the publisher, namely Bridget Farrell, knew how to get things done.

Over the space of six weeks in March and April I went to Sonic Recording studio in Stoneybatter and spent a day each with five different actors. Kate Gilmore read the narrator, Jordanne Jones read Tanya, Gabriel Adewusi read Angel, Florence Adebambo read Princess, and Conal Keating read Dean.

Each actor had about fifteen thousand words to read over the course of a day. The engineer sat at the desk, and I sat out of sight, on the couch behind him. I wanted to let the actors read their lines and immerse themselves in their character without having me adding any pressure or expectations.

Of course, the odd time I'd jump up and press the mic to give some feedback for a line, or to make a suggestion – or in some funny instances, correct pronunciation! How do you say *Guildea* (the Balbriggan way)? How does *Kurwa mac* sound in Polish? What about when Angel's mother spoke Lingala? (In this case I had a fluent Lingala speaker record themselves saying the lines and I forwarded them on to the actor!) How do you say SZA? What about Megan Thee Stallion's *WAP*?

On one occasion, Bridget from Lilliput, who of course had done other audiobooks before, sat in for a session. Like me, she followed the manuscript as the actor recorded their lines. Her head would lift when she noticed a missed word, expecting me to stop them. But once it wasn't an obvious mistake, I felt the flow was more important. If the actor brought an intensity and realism to the character's voice, I was willing to let a word here or there differ from the printed manuscript. Yes, of course the text is important, but for me the audiobook should be about the energy and the drama an actor can imbue into a moment, into a scene, into a performance, through the mic and into your headphones!

For a 1st person audiobook, especially one relying so heavily on local vernacular, and the 'voice' of the character, it is all about the energy, intensity and credibility of the voice.

Prior to recording, I sent each actor a 'Character Sheet' and a few pages of 'Character Direction'. I also spoke with the actors before they went into the studio. In some cases I spoke for an hour on the phone with the actors, going through their character, how I imagined they would tell their story, what exactly I felt was their story, where they were from, i.e., North Dublin or Central Dublin, Congo or Nigeria, or where their parents where from. All of this fed into the accents and the voice they would bring to the studio.

In one case, I provided an actor with about ten YouTube clips of lads from Balbriggan and the Drill music scene talking either in interviews or in 'Live' Instagram posts. This enabled the actor to really bring an authentic voice to the recording. The same actor also asked to hear the voice of his love interest in the book – she was one of the other narrators and an actor had recorded her part a few weeks earlier. He wanted to hear how she spoke so he could try and replicate her voice (to some small extent) in the scenes he read.

Making an audiobook like *Youth* was so positive and thrilling, it's hard not to feel the pull to write something similar, just to experience the process again. But for me, this is the wrong way to write. I wrote without even thinking about an audiobook, and luckily just happened upon a story that lent itself easily to an exciting audiobook experience. This was in no small part thanks to the actors involved.

Each actor brought subtlety, nuance and emotion to scenes I had never considered before. I read all of my drafts out loud when I revise. Yet, in the studio with the young actors, I was delighted to be surprised by how they interpreted scenes and dialogue. Some shouted lines, others whispered in close to the mic, others laughed, or kissed their teeth. It was an absolute joy to see them at work, interpreting my words the way they did.

And that's why now, I can step back from the audiobook and tell people, with pride, about how good it is. Yes, the words are mine, but the emotion, the drama, the energy and the comedy is all about the actors, and their ability.

If the writing of the book was a collaboration between myself, early readers and my editor, I'm glad to say the audiobook was a collaboration between myself, an experienced studio engineer and five talented actors.

COUNTING DOWN TO YOUR
BOOK LAUNCH

Ruth Hallinan

TEN: SIGN A CONTRACT

You've done it: after years of hard work, your manuscript is now the best it can be – congratulations!

If you want to see your book in a bookshop, you will most likely need to follow the path of traditional publishing. First, you need to submit your work to a publishing house – but which one? Go into your local bookshop or library and take a look at titles that are similar to yours in terms of genre and writing style. Flick to the copyright page and take a note of the publisher – this is a good place to start. You can also find a list of Irish publishers on the Publishing Ireland website.

Check websites for details on how each publisher receives submissions. Some only want to receive work from literary agents and won't read work from authors directly. However, there are many Irish publishers who want to hear from authors, so having an agent isn't essential.

Once you have submitted your manuscript, it could take weeks or months to receive a response. Rejections are disheartening, especially since you have worked so hard on your book – but it is important to remember that commissioning is a matter of taste as much as being a business, and what one editor rejects could be exactly what another is looking for. Consider any feedback you receive, and try again somewhere else.

The moment of receiving a contract is exciting for both author and publisher. Your contract grants the publisher a license to publish your book in certain ways called 'rights'. You always own the copyright to your own book, but you allow the publisher the exclusive right to print your work when you sign a contract. Read it carefully; if you have an agent, they will check you are being offered a fair deal. Make sure you understand each clause and ask questions if you are not sure.

This is a good time to ask what marketing, publicity, and distribution plans are in place for your book. Be realistic about the strengths of the publishing house you are working with: only big, multinational publishers can afford to offer six-figure advances, but small, independent publishers will likely give you much more one-on-one attention. The standard deals for publishing houses vary widely depending on size, how they are funded, and what their specialty is – which is another reason to be clear about your ambitions right from the start. Now that your contract is signed, sealed, and delivered, it's on to the next stage!

NINE: PROMOTE YOUR BOOK

How does your book end up in a bookshop? Bookshops decide what to stock long before the physical book is ready. They can place pre-orders anytime from two weeks to nine months before publication. Sales reps present information about your book to key buyers who then decide how many copies to stock. The publisher needs to provide bookshops with 'reasons to sell', i.e. publicity material, in-person talks, book signings, prize nominations, anniversaries, etc. Without these selling points, it's difficult to secure large stock orders from bookshops.

The publicity plan will vary depending on the genre of your work and the remit of the publisher. Marketing and publicity professionals will talk with you about their plans early in the process and will ask you for feedback. Tell them about any ideas or aims you have for your book and any helpful contacts you have such as journalists or other authors. Media outlets have different deadlines, so it's best to line everything up as early as possible.

EIGHT: CHOOSE A COVER

Cover design is the most important part of marketing and publicity: a good cover will be eye-catching and communicate the genre or tone of your book straight away. You may have some ideas, but publishers, sales reps, and publicity professionals work with books every day and will have a strong sense of what design will compete in the market.

If you genuinely dislike the proposed cover design, talk to your publisher to understand their reasoning. It's ideal for you both to agree, so respectful communication is essential. A design you have made is unlikely to get the green light unless you are a professional in this field. Ask permission before sharing cover drafts online: the designer may have used images for mock-up that have not yet been licensed, so you could accidentally incur a copyright infringement fine if you post images without approval.

SEVEN: POLISH YOUR MANUSCRIPT

After signing your contract, there will be an editorial schedule in place to get your book ready for printing. You might encounter different kinds of editors. A structural editor focuses on the overall shape of the story: they might suggest cutting or adding a character, combining chapters, researching a whole new area to include, or changing the ending.

A copy-editor or line editor will go through each paragraph carefully and check the continuity of the story. They could still suggest significant changes, such as cutting paragraphs, but these won't be as wide-ranging as a structural edit.

Finally, a proofreader will check the text to ensure correct spelling, grammar, and punctuation along with anything else that might have been overlooked.

This part of the process can be lengthy. If you are asked to rewrite parts of your book, keep in touch with your editor to let them know that you are sticking to deadlines. Everyone wants the best result possible, so don't be disheartened if you receive a lot of edits – this just means the publisher is invested in your book.

SIX: CLEAR COPYRIGHT

During the editorial process, you may also need to clear copyright permissions. When you sign your contract, make sure you know who is responsible for seeking copyright clearance and who might be liable for any copyright infringement fines if text is published without approval.

Authors are often responsible for seeking copyright permissions since they have chosen to include the quote, lyric or extract in their text. Copyright can be a complex area, but, essentially, if you are publishing a book for commercial purposes (that is, not an educational book), then you need permission to reproduce anything you use. Some venues, especially multinationals such as Universal, Sony or large publishers, can take months to respond to a request. Send your copyright queries as early as possible in the process.

FIVE: KEEP PRODUCTION ON TRACK

Running alongside publicity and editorial is the production schedule. This determines how long each stage should take in order to go to print on time. You might never meet the production manager, depending on the size of the publishing house, but they will determine the look and feel of your book. Production includes physical printing as well as creating ebooks and audiobooks, depending on the plan.

FOUR: SELL RIGHTS

Your contract outlines what rights the publisher has. If they have 'world rights', they can sell different versions of your book to other publishers, for example, a French edition or a US edition. The publisher may enlist the help of a rights agent who will pitch your book to other agents or publishers. Rights sales are never guaranteed, but publishers are always hopeful that other publishers will see the value of your book, just as they did.

THREE: SEND TO PRINT

If your book is scheduled to publish in September, that doesn't mean you have until August to make changes! Your book could be sent to print weeks or months ahead of publication, especially if it's being printed abroad. At this stage, you will not be involved in production anymore, but you should keep in touch with marketing and publicity to help promote pre-orders as much as possible.

TWO: DISTRIBUTE WIDELY

When your book has been printed, it will be stored in distribution warehouses. Your publisher may use distributors in Ireland, Britain, the US or other European countries – you can ask where your publisher distributes when you sign your contract. Distributors supply books to shops, but the promotion of your book may have to come from your own efforts as well as the work of marketing and publicity.

ONE: LAUNCH

The day has finally come – your book launch! Some publishers, particularly in Ireland, organise book launches for authors in bookshops or other significant venues. These are a great opportunity for the author to meet their readers, sign books and sell copies! The launch day is exciting for both the author and the publisher, who have each been working hard for months to make the book a success.

The word 'launch' can be misleading – although it's often taken to mean the first of something, you can have as many launches as you like, in different towns, cities, and countries. It can also give the impression of being the start of the publishing process, when in fact it's closer to the end. Yes, it's the beginning of your book being out in the world – but it's also the culmination of the all the production and promotion your publisher has done. Enjoy the moment!

POST-PUBLICATION:

WHAT TO EXPECT

Ivan O'Brien

S o your book has been published: what now?

While it might be tempting to think that the quality of a book means that it will find its audience and sell itself – that is simply not the case. There is an enormous degree of work involved to get a book noticed, talked about, read and purchased.

With over 100,000 books published in the UK every year, and over 1,300 published in Ireland, there is intense competition for column inches, broadcast time and table space in bookshops.

As readers, we expect to hear authors talking about their book and in Ireland we are fortunate to have many avenues where books are discussed.

Publishers usually have detailed sales, publicity, and marketing plans for every book they publish. The planning for this will begin a few months before publication, and often covers broadcast (TV and radio, national and local), print (magazines and newspapers, national and local), online (blogs, online publications and social media) and events (launches and festivals, as well as bookshop, library and school events). The media love the content that books bring, and most talk shows feature authors for this reason.

Your publisher will build a mix of suitable opportunities, and will have a coordinated campaign usually beginning about two weeks before publication, until weeks or months afterwards. Many publishers will expect an author to be available to contribute to this work for at least a few weeks around publication: not doing so at this vital time can damage the sales prospects of a book – as this is when booksellers will see the impact of this publicity (even if it doesn't generate sales immediately), which is important for gaining and retaining good placement in shops.

Publicity work is, in many ways, the exact opposite of what most authors consider their comfort zone: writing usually involves privacy, quiet and long periods of focus, while publicity is essentially a selling or pitching job; it can be quite high-energy and often extremely public. It's a good idea to discuss in the early stages of the process just what your publisher expects of you, and what you are comfortable doing.

It's okay to find a public role difficult and your publisher should coach and help you here. In some cases the publicity might focus on you, the author, rather than the book: this might feel strange – but it's often the way book marketing works.

You might want to consider if and how you will employ social media. Some publishers may feel strongly that it's a necessary part of publicity; others may accept that not everyone is comfortable or engages with these platforms. For authors who are active on social media, some prefer to keep their personal and professional profiles separate. If you are active on social platforms, be careful about what and how you are posting and engaging: does this align with your role and expectations as an author?

If you don't currently use social media, it's generally not a good idea to start an account specifically for your book – you're unlikely to understand the tone and landscape of the platform, and therefore won't use it to your best advantage.

If you are promoting your book online, ask your publisher what the preferred call-to-actions are: should you direct readers to the publisher's website, your own website or a preferred retailer? They will be happy to advise.

Booksellers love to see authors who come into their shop, locate their books, and offer to sign copies. If you can't find your book, it's entirely possible that it's in the shop but just not where you expected to find it – so do politely ask a bookseller. If it's not there, it might be that they have sold out and have more on the way, or that the supply chain has been a bit slow. Don't be tempted to give a retailer a hard time but do tell your publisher about any gaps and they will work to close them. Booksellers are your very best allies so make sure you establish good relationships.

The sales, publicity and marketing side of books can be difficult to get to grips with – but it's an absolutely essential part of the process.

PROMOTING YOUR
SELF-PUBLISHED BOOK

Liz McSkeane

Whave I set up Turas Press eight years ago to publish my own work, I soon realised that the production of a book, whether in print or digital
format, was only the beginning. It was thrilling to hold
a title I had published in my hands—but I began to appreciate the scale of the challenge that lay ahead: reaching
readers.

How can we self-published writers attract readers to our
books, when we share such a competitive space with large
publishing companies and their enormous PR budgets and
marketing departments?

PREPARING THE GROUND

One of the earliest lessons I learned, which applies to both
fiction and poetry, whether print or digital, was that promotion begins long before the boxes are delivered from the
printer or the file is uploaded.

The production values of a self-published book must be as
good as those of any traditionally published title. Depending

on your skill set, this may mean enlisting the services of professionals in cover design, typesetting, editing or proofing.

Engaging with other writers and the wider literary community is the single most important, and fruitful, aspect of preparing the ground for a self-publishing venture. This includes taking part in workshops, courses, attending readings, launches and festivals, either in person or online, and engaging with other writers and industry professionals on social media.

It is also important to connect with places such as the Irish Writers Centre—but also literary organisations at a regional and local level. Get to know your independent booksellers too; they often have readings, do their own book promotions, and are more likely to stock self-published books than the big chains—and don't forget to connect with special interest groups relevant to your book.

CHOOSING THE STRATEGY

Depending on your resources, and your willingness to spend time on non-writing activities, you may choose to:

- Hire a publicist and/or a digital marketing professional to draw up and implement marketing plans.
- Handle some or all aspects of the publicity yourself.

WORKING WITH A PUBLICIST

By hiring a publicist or digital marketing expert, you benefit from their industry knowledge of where and when to place your work, and from their long-established relationships with feature editors, bloggers, picture editors, radio and TV producers. They will draft proposals and promotional materials with or without your input. In my experience, this strategy means that you're more likely to have coverage in general features and magazine-style content and programmes, rather than in reviews.

The financial outlay of hiring a publicist is a key consideration. Although this approach greatly increases your chances of appearing in high-profile outlets, there are no guarantees: the final decision rests with the editor.

While I've found the expertise of a professional publicist beneficial when promoting fiction in print book format, I've reached the audience for poetry more easily through the various DIY strategies outlined below.

Ebooks are publicised through online advertising on various digital platforms, and also by reader reviews—strategies which are also available to print books. However, anecdotal evidence indicates that digital advertising of books is most effective when there are already positive reader reviews. Therefore, the time to spend money on digital adverts is after your book has positive comments from readers, rather than before.

DOING IT YOURSELF

You can carry out the following actions over time, well in advance of your publication date:

- Create a website or a landing page where your book is featured.
- Establish a social media presence and engage with

key people in the literary community.

- Request endorsements from established writers and reader reviews from your peers.
- Email editors of literary journals, books pages, radio and podcast producers to request reviews of your book. Include local, community and regional outlets and mention any literary achievements.
- Identify and enter any competitions for which your self-published book is eligible.
- Identify current events, anniversaries, commemorations which connect to your book and contact the relevant interest groups.
- Explore all outlets and platforms where readers can access your book: bookstores, libraries, special interest shops or organisations, online platforms, and arrange to place it in as many of these as possible after publication.
- Set up an online shop to sell your book.
- If your book is in print format, create an ebook and upload it to the various platforms.
- Organise a book launch and invite everyone who has helped, and who you hope will help in the future.

DIY TOOLKIT

In order to carry out these activities, you will need:

- Photos of your book cover at the highest resolution possible, as these can be resized downwards for emailing.

- A headshot of yourself at different resolutions: well-taken photos using a smartphone are acceptable, but not selfies.
- A press release and/or a Title Information Sheet.
- A list of addresses and social media handles for your target contacts.
- Book blurbs and summaries of different lengths created for different purposes.
- A set of 'pitch' letters asking editors, bloggers etc. to feature your book.
- A short video/audio clip (optional but increasingly important) of you discussing your book.
- Advance Review Copies: pdfs of your manuscript but also print copies for novels and creative non-fiction.

If you don't already have the skills to create these materials, you can learn. High-quality, low-cost skills training in website design, content creation, digital and social media marketing and more is available throughout Ireland from the countrywide network of Local Enterprise Offices.

Many agents and publishers give guidelines on their websites on how to write a pitch letter, synopsis, blurb and more.

If all of this sounds daunting, remember how much more daunting it was to have faith, take the plunge and publish your own book.

You did that. You can do this.

DESPERATION

TO VALIDATION:

THE LEARNING CURVE OF

SELF-PUBLISHING

Pamela G. Hobbs

I t was desperation that drove me to self-publish my first two books. Or perhaps a more apt word would be frustration; both, in fact, are appropriate. Being one of the twelve winners at the Irish Writers Centre Novel Fair was a huge boost to my confidence, and validation for my writing – but it was also, for me, an unhealthy mix of unrealistic expectations and hope.

Despite kind words and gentle rejections from agents and publishers in the weeks following the event, the old imposter syndrome set in fairly rapidly. But that weird part inside, the little voice that said *someone will love your story*, would not stay quiet. So, I listened. And out of the aforementioned desperation and frustration, I jumped.

NAÏVE ERRORS

Self-publishing was already a minor success story in 2015 when I made my first foray into its murky depths. I was a greenhorn, and completely devoid of the necessary skill set – hence my poor first attempts. I made several egregious errors, some out of ignorance, some from financial constraints.

I used one of my own paintings – an abstract landscape – as the cover art. Bad first move. It in no way gave any indication of the content – zero representation of romantic suspense, my genre; I hadn't taken the time to research covers of similar books, those by authors I read regularly. I had tunnel vision: *get it out there.*

My second mistake derived from this tunnel vision: haste. I became obsessed with having my book available for people to read. In hindsight, there was no hurry, no deadline, no panic, except the self-inflicted kind.

My third (and a close tie with the mistake of the awful cover), was the lack of editing. At this stage I was barely on social media; all I had was a Facebook page. I wasn't connected with writers' groups or online forums for advice and help. I barely knew what a first draft meant, never mind the necessity for several drafts. I wrote it, checked it for obvious errors, printed it out, re-read it, found some more errors and changed them.

Voilà! Ready to publish.

I cringe now at how naïve I was, how unprepared. And this isn't even taking into account the rather steep learning curve of actually following KDP's (Kindle Direct Publishing) steps to publication. There are a lot of tricky menus and verbiage to get to grips with in terms of understanding and user friendliness. I floundered, but nevertheless persisted.

PRINT ON DEMAND

In 2017 I went one step further and decided to go for print on demand. The second book in my series of five was written. It still hadn't been professionally edited – even though I knew how important it was – since I was unable to pay for the service. I gave it to one other person to read, and with their helpful feedback I made some structural changes.

However, this time I looked up stock images from the internet, which didn't entirely reflect my genre, but was still a major improvement. What I didn't realise was the ante was now seriously upped with regard to the skills at my fingertips: book size; format; front cover; back cover; blurb; the bleed from the cover image; the varying margin widths; the pixels of the image. It was overwhelming, and I knew no one who could help.

Trial and error ensued. I got proofs back; they were unacceptable. I had chosen large size format, 15cms by 23cms, and there was a strip of plain colour down the side: so unprofessional. I re-did them. By this second book, I had more confidence; it was, at the time, enough. I was writing book three and was glad my books were out there. And the really cool thing about it? You can track your sales and, if in Kindle Unlimited, follow how many pages are being read in real time.

VALIDATION

During these days of self-publishing I continued to apply to *Date with an Agent* (as part of the International Literary Festival in Dublin) and various festivals offering advice and critiques. This paid off. Before my third book was really under way I got the call – an Irish publisher wanted to give me a five book deal, the whole series. They were happy to re-publish the first two on completion of professional editing and cover changes, both services included in the contract.

I know of romance writers who only self-publish and they put out perhaps four books a year; it is their business, their livelihood – and some of them are *New York Times* best sellers. Would I self-publish again? Yes – but with way more ammunition in my arsenal: I would revise, rewrite, and edit multiple times; I would listen to the manuscript on the 'read aloud' function in Word (brilliant for picking up simple proof reading and grammar errors); I would offer the manuscript to beta readers (trusted people who can critique your work); after all of this I would hire a professional editor. As far as design goes, I would investigate Canva, which many authors use for all kinds of things, including the cover, book trailers, and social media posts.

Writing is the easy part. The rest? Damn hard no matter which way you go – but worth it when a reader says how much your book meant to them. Now *that* is validation.

WRITING CRIME FOR
A DIGITAL PUBLISHER

Patricia Gibney

W hen I was writing what turned out to be my debut novel *The Missing Ones*, I didn't have a clear
plan of what type of book I wanted to write, I
just wanted to write a book – but as my work progressed it
evolved into a crime novel. I love to read all genres but my
main go-to is crime, especially a crime series. I love to have
a mystery to solve, a main character to follow from book to
book, and an interesting cast of characters to shout for – or
shout at!

I wrote that first book for myself without a notion of
who might, if ever, publish it. It took me five years of
blood, sweat, and many tears, to finish writing *The Missing Ones.* I got there in the end. The end? No way. It
was just the beginning. And I think this is important to
realise when you are starting out. Writing the first draft,
fine-tuning and polishing it for submission, is just the
first phase of many.

I knew I wouldn't be able to do all the ancillary work associated with getting a book published, so I set out to secure an agent – and I was lucky with my initial attempt. Ger Nichol of The Book Bureau was the first agent I submitted to and I was thrilled when she took me on.

After Ger sent *The Missing Ones* out on submission, and following some of the dreaded rejections, she was presented with a proposal for four books in the Lottie Parker series from Bookouture, a London-based digital publisher. I was ecstatic, to say the least. My contract was for four books over two years, with two books being published annually. A point to remember here is that there is usually no advance with digital publishing – income is dependent on the success of the book or series.

This was my first foray into having a book published and I quickly discovered I had a lot to learn. With digital publishing, the closer the books in a series are released to each other, the more beneficial it is. This is because the reader can download the next book instantly. From a writer's point of view you need to realise what this entails in terms of the time involved for your work, and how to handle it.

The advice I would give is to develop a good relationship with your editor; make it a two-way relationship. You have to be able to tease out things together and discuss many aspects of the book and your schedule.

Writing your book is just one phase of the process, because then you have the job of editing, proofing, and promoting. A good idea is to request a detailed work schedule which you can agree with your editor. This schedule should give you deadlines for each phase and the weeks and days allotted: time lines and submission dates for draft, line and copy edits, and proofing dates. If the book is available in paperback format as well as an ebook you have two versions to be proofread: this is a time consuming job, and occurs near the end of the process – usually with a short timescale, so it needs to be factored into your schedule.

The further you get into a series, the more a good working relationship with your editor is crucial. I find having brainstorming sessions via Zoom or over the phone with my editor about character development or plot lines helps negate unnecessary edits down the line. Get your cards on the table early and tease them out.

Promotion and marketing are a huge part of the digital publishing world. Your book needs to get noticed on a virtual bookshelf of millions. The title and cover cause a lot of stress for authors, but the marketing team know what works. You reach a stage where you let your baby out in the world and let the professionals take over. That said, it is advisable to have a presence on social media and create author pages. Announce when your book is on pre-order and when it is published. Publicise the blog tours and thank the bloggers for their time and reviews. Tweet and post, and don't be afraid to shout your own name and that of your book from the rooftops.

When I finished writing *The Missing Ones*, I never dreamed that I would be writing book thirteen within seven years. It is hard work but I love coming up with new and intricate plots to challenge myself and my readers. Writing crime books is a constant game of unravelling threads, reeling in red herrings, and solving mysteries. It is an amazing journey.

Facts &
Figures

Everything you Need to Know about the ISBN System

Nielsen

The Nielsen BookData ISBN Agency for UK & Ireland receives a large number of enquiries about the ISBN system. The most frequently asked questions are answered here; for more information visit www.nielsenisbnstore.com.

WHAT IS AN ISBN?

An ISBN is an International Standard Book Number and is 13 digits long.

WHAT IS THE PURPOSE OF AN ISBN?

An ISBN is a product number, used by publishers, booksellers and libraries for ordering, listing and stock control purposes. It enables them to identify a particular publisher and allows the publisher to identify a specific edition of a specific title in a specific format within their output.

DOES AN ISBN PROTECT COPYRIGHT?

A widely held belief is that an ISBN protects copyright. It doesn't, it is an identifier, a product code. The copyright belongs to the author. In general, publishers don't tend to buy copyrights for books. They license the copyrights, which the author retains.

WHAT IS A PUBLISHER?

The publisher is generally the person or organisation taking the financial and other risks in making a product available. For example, if a product goes on sale and sells no copies at all, the publisher loses money. If you get paid anyway, you are likely to be a designer, printer, author or consultant of some kind.

WHAT IS THE FORMAT OF AN ISBN?

The ISBN is 13 digits long and is divided into five parts separated by spaces or hyphens.

Prefix element: for the foreseeable future this will be 978 or 979.

Registration group element: identifies a geographic or national grouping. It shows where the publisher is based.

Registrant element: identifies a specific publisher or imprint.

Publication element: identifies a specific edition of a specific title in a specific format.

Check digit: the final digit which mathematically validates the rest of the number.

The four parts following the prefix element can be of varying length.

Prior to 1 January 2007 ISBNs were ten digits long; any existing ten-digit ISBNs must be converted by prefixing them with '978' and the check digit must be recalculated using a Modulus 10 system with alternate weights of 1 and 3. The ISBN Agency can help you with this.

DO I HAVE TO HAVE AN ISBN?

There is no legal requirement in Ireland or the UK for an ISBN and it conveys no form of legal or copyright protection. It is simply a product identification number.

WHY SHOULD I USE AN ISBN?

If you wish to sell your publication through major bookselling chains, independent bookshops or internet retailers, they will require you to have an ISBN to assist their internal processing and ordering systems.

The ISBN also provides access to bibliographic databases, such as the Nielsen BookData Database, which use ISBNs as references. These databases help booksellers and libraries to provide information for customers.

Nielsen BookData has a range of bibliographic metadata and retail sales monitoring services which use ISBNs and are vital for the dissemination, trading and monitoring of books in the supply chain. The ISBN therefore provides access to additional marketing opportunities which could help sales of your product.

WHERE CAN I GET AN ISBN?

ISBNs are assigned to publishers in the country where the publisher's main office is based. This is irrespective of the language of the publication or the intended market for the book.

The ISBN Agency is the national agency for the Republic of Ireland, the UK and British Overseas Territories. A publisher based elsewhere will not be able to get numbers from the ISBN Agency (even if you are an Irish or British citizen) but can contact the Nielsen BookData ISBN Agency for details of the relevant national agency.

If you are based in Ireland you can purchase ISBNs online from the Nielsen BookData ISBN Store: www.nielsenisbnstore.com.

HOW LONG DOES IT TAKE TO GET AN ISBN?

If you purchase your ISBNs online from the Nielsen Book-Data ISBN Store you will receive your ISBN allocation within minutes. If you are purchasing ISBNs direct from the ISBN Agency via an offline application, it can take up to five days. The processing period begins when a correctly completed application is received in the ISBN Agency and payment is received.

HOW MUCH DOES IT COST TO GET AN ISBN?

Refer to Nielsen BookData's website or email the ISBN Agency: isbn.agency@nielseniq.com.

WHAT IF I ONLY WANT ONE ISBN?

ISBNs can be bought individually or in blocks of ten or more; visit the ISBN Store to find out more.

WHO IS ELIGIBLE FOR ISBNS?

Any individual or organisation who is publishing a qualifying product for general sale or distribution to the market. By publishing we mean making a work available to the public.

WHAT IS AN ISSN?

An International Standard Serial Number. This is the numbering system for journals, magazines, periodicals, newspapers and newsletters. It is administered by the National Library of Ireland.

WHERE DO I PUT THE ISBN?

The ISBN should appear on the reverse of the title page, sometimes called the copyright page or the imprint page, and on the outside back cover of the book. If the book has a dust jacket, the ISBN should also appear on the back of this. If the publication is not a book, the ISBN should appear on the product, and on the packaging or inlay card. If the publication is a map, the ISBN should be visible when the map is folded and should also appear near the publisher statement if this is elsewhere.

I AM REPRINTING A BOOK WITH NO CHANGES – DO I NEED A NEW ISBN?

No.

I AM REPRINTING A BOOK BUT ADDING A NEW CHAPTER – DO I NEED A NEW ISBN?

Yes. You are adding a significant amount of additional material, altering the content of the book.

I AM REPRINTING A BOOK WITH A NEW COVER DESIGN – SHOULD I CHANGE THE ISBN?

No. A change of cover design with no changes to the content of the book should not have a new ISBN.

I AM CHANGING THE BINDING ON THE BOOK TO PAPERBACK RATHER THAN HARDBACK. DO I NEED A NEW ISBN?

Yes. Changes in binding always require new ISBNs even if there are no changes to the content of the book.

I AM CHANGING THE PRICE – DO I NEED A NEW ISBN?

No. Price changes with no other changes do not require new ISBNs and in fact must not change the ISBN.

THE IRISH CONSUMER MARKET OVERVIEW

Belle Edelman

T
he Nielsen BookScan service is the largest contin-
uous book sales tracking service in the world, with
16 years of year-on-year comparison of sales information of the Irish Consumer Market (ICM). It tracks individual titles, genres and authors sold to consumers within
Ireland by collecting point-of-sale data from retail channels
including bookshops, supermarkets, and online retailers,
giving us approximately 70+% coverage of all books sold
in the Republic of Ireland. The present article provides an
overview of the ICM in 2023, including the bestselling titles, and will delve into trends and changes in market share
of various genres and of individual publishing houses.

Print book value sales in the Republic of Ireland increased
by just under 1% in 2023 from 2022 to €170m. Roughly
13m books were bought, amounting to around 300k (-2%)
less than the previous year, ending an 8-year streak in year-
on-year growth of volume sales for the country. The average price paid for a print book meanwhile increased from
€12.71 to €13.08 (+3%), broadly following the pattern of
the UK and other territories of rising prices and falling vol-

ume sales, although less than the average national rate of inflation for the year at 6.3%, as reported by the Consumer Price Index[1].

Within the three broad categories – Adult Fiction (henceforth referred to as Fiction) accounted for 31% of volume sales, Non-Fiction (which combines the broad categories of Non-Fiction Trade and Non-Fiction Specialist) accounted for 35% of volume sales, and Children, Young Adult & Educational (henceforth referred to as Children's) accounted for 34% of volume sales. Volume sales increased across Fiction by 3% to 4m books sold, which amounted to approximately 130k more books sold than in 2022, and value sales were up an impressive 9% to €50.5m, boosted by a 5% increase in Average Selling Price (ASP) to €12.63. Meanwhile, Non-Fiction volume sales were down -2%, to 4.5m books sold, but value sales remained steady at €74m and ASP remained steady at roughly €18.57. Children's was the only category that fell in value sales, down a rather significant -7% to €44.7m, and volume sales were down -8% to 4.4m, meaning 143k less books within this category were bought than in 2022. The ASP for this broad category rose 1% to €12.63.

The bestseller chart for the year 2023 reflects this prevailing appetite for Fiction, with the top 4 titles all falling within this broad category. Indeed, 11 out of the top 20 bestselling titles were Fiction, whilst seven were Non-Fiction, and only two were Children's, with none of the top 10 titles falling

---

1   Consumer Price Index December 2023 – CSO – Central Statistics Office. (2024, January 16). www.cso.ie.

into this broad category. 15 out of the top 20 bestselling books were published in the UK, 4 were published in Ireland, and 1 from the United States. Notably, the top 3 were all frontlist titles from Irish authors, published that same year, and 13 out of the top 20 books, and over half of the top 50 titles, had some Irish connection, whether through authorship, publisher or subject matter.

From 2022 to 2023, the proportion of volume sales that were published in the United Kingdom was 9.9m, increasing from 74% to 75%. Total volume purchases that were published in Ireland amounted to 2m, falling from 16% to 15% of total purchases from 2022. The proportion of titles that were published in the United States amounted to 1.2m, falling from 9% to 8%, and around 2% were published elsewhere. Out of the prominent publishers, roughly descending in order of size, more than a fifth (+22%) of volume purchases were published within Penguin Random House, which grew its sales by 4% on 2022. 12% of volume purchases came from Hachette, who were down -4% on the previous year. 9% of volume sales were from HarperCollins, down -6% from the previous year, 5% of sales were from Pan Macmillan who were steady on the previous year. The largest publisher group from Ireland was Gill Group, accounting for 4% of volume purchases, down -1% in volume sales. Simon & Schuster fell -8% in volume sales in 2023 after a staggering 2022. Bonnier Books increased its volume sales by +8%, Scholastic increased its volume sales by 3%, Bloomsbury's volume sales fell -3%, Faber were up 15%, Usborne increased its volume sales by 4%, O'Brien Press was up 9%, Edco -13%, Viz Media up 13%, OUP up 6%, Walker -15%, Wordsworth up 3%,

Atlantic Books -3%, Irish Academic Press down -6% and Profile Books up 7%.

GENRE

General and Literary Fiction remained the largest individual category for the year overall, steady in volume on 2022 and increasing 5% in value and ASP. Other categories within Fiction also grew: Crime, Thriller and Adventure was the second largest category (and incidentally, the largest category in the UK) and grew 4% in volume sales and 10% in value sales. Romance and Sagas, after more than doubling in volume and value sales from 2021 to 2022, fell -1% in volume sales in 2023, but rose 2% in value sales. Sci Fi and Fantasy is proving to have broader appeal than ever, nearly doubling in volume and value sales since 2019, and ballooning 22% in volume sales and 20% in value sales in 2023, equating to 60k more books sold. Historical and Mythological Fiction grew 12% in volume and 27% in value on the previous year and Horror and Ghost Stories experienced a massive surge in sales, up 48% in volume and 72% in value. War Fiction meanwhile dropped -28% in volume sales and -20% in value, Erotic Fiction fell -6% in volume and -11% value, and Westerns fell -2% in volume but grew +6% value. Finally, Graphic Novels, which had been growing in popularity for a few years, fell -5% in volume and -3% in value.

The largest category within Non-Fiction, Biographies and Autobiographies, was up 3% in volume sales and 8% in value sales (and within this category, Autobiography: Royalty was up 2358% in volume and 3295% in value, which can reasonably be attributed to the publication of *Spare*). History and Military was up 10% in volume and 11% in value sales, Food and Drink was up 14% in volume and 8% in value sales. Atlas, Maps and Travel has been on the up following the pandemic, more than doubling in volume and value sales from the year 2020, and up 22% in volume and 36% in value in the year 2023. Regional History was up 12% in both volume and value, and Humour, Trivia and Puzzles was up 2% volume and 6% value, whereas Literature, Poetry and Criticism was down -1% in volume but up 1% in value. Meanwhile, Personal Development was down -14% in volume and -10% in value, Leisure and Lifestyle was down -7% volume and -5% value. The Arts (including Fine Arts, Architecture and Film, TV & Criticism) was down -11% in volume and -12% in value. Mind Body and Spirit was down -14% vol and -9% value, Religion was down -16% vol and -15% value, Dictionary and Reference was down a notable -18% volume and -24% value, whilst Politics and Government was down -12% in volume and -9% in value.

While Children's saw the biggest drop among the broad categories, there were some pockets of growth. Young Adult Non-Fiction was up 8% in volume and 6% in value, Novelty and Activity Books were up 12% in volume and 6% in value, Children's Comic Strip Fiction & Graphic Novels were up 3% volume and value and Children's General Interest and Leisure was up an impressive 26% in volume and 30% in value. However, Children's Fiction was down -9% in volume and -7% in value; Young Adult Fiction was down -6% in volume and -1% in value, although notably still 36% up on 2019. Picture Books was down -3% in volume and -2% in value. Children's General Non-Fiction was steady volume-wise but down -5% in value, Pre-school and Early Learning was down -6% in volume but steady in value. School Textbooks and Study Guides were down -38% in volume and -29% in value. Ultimately, 287k less textbooks bought than in 2022, which can be attributed to the Department of Education's recent initiative[2] to provide all Primary School Students with free textbooks, a scheme which bypasses the retailer and therefore entailing that these purchases are not counted through BookScan. When School Textbooks and Study Guides are removed from the dataset for analysis, the drop in volume sales overall of Children's overall is a more moderate -4% and -3% in value sales.

So far in 2024 up to 27 July, volume sales have amounted to 5.9m, which is -5% on the same period in 2023. With sales amounting to €74m this equates to -6% in value. The ASP meanwhile has gone up 1%. Further comparing these two time periods, Non-Fiction sales have seen a decline of -10% in volume sales and -12% in value sales, but also a decrease in ASP of -4%. Sales within the broad category of Children's have fallen a further -5% in both volume and value, and a fall in ASP by -2%. Adult Fiction has remained steady volume-wise and increased 3% in value and ASP on the same period last year. Some smaller pockets of double-digit percentage growth this year so far include Short Fiction & Anthologies (+51% volume, +71% value), Science Fiction and Fantasy (+35% volume and value), Travel Writing (+17% volume, +22% value), Children's Comic

2   Minister Foley announces year 2 of free schoolbooks in primary and special schools. (2024, May 8). www.gov.ie.

Strips and Graphic Novels (+20% volume and +21% value), and Children's Annuals (+59% volume and +42% value).

Overall, what we are seeing here is the Irish print book market settling after a very encouraging few years of growth, which culminated in a record-breaking year in 2022. The impact of the cost-of-living crisis alongside rising prices overall, both in Ireland and the rest of the world, has undoubtedly had an effect. Indeed, this mirrors similar trends we have seen in the other countries that we measure. However, with inflation rates beginning to fall, and some smaller genre categories experiencing growth in popularity, there are reasons to be optimistic. This, coupled with the fact that Ireland has a thriving literary scene that is making waves around the world speaks to an exciting future for the Irish print book market.

IRELAND TOP 20 TITLES 2023

Position	Title	Author	Publisher	Volume	Value	ASP	Binding	Product Class	Country of Publication
1	Strange Sally Diamond	Liz Nugent	Penguin	41k	€624k	€15.15	P	Crime, Thriller & Adventure	Ireland
2	Prophet Song	Paul Lynch	Oneworld	39k	€687k	€17.07	P	General & Literary Fiction	United Kingdom
3	Bee Sting	Paul Murray	Penguin	39k	€668k	€16.98	P	General & Literary Fiction	United Kingdom
4	It Ends With Us	Colleen Hoover	Simon & Schuster	39k	€397k	€10.29	P	Romance & Sagas	United Kingdom
5	Spare	Prince Harry	Transworld	38k	€934k	€24.33	H	Autobiography: Royalty	United Kingdom
6	Bored of Lunch: The Healthy Slow Cooker Book	Nathan Anthony	Random House	38k	€556k	€14.62	H	Health, Dieting & Wholefood Cookery	United Kingdom
7	Bored of Lunch: The Healthy Air Fryer Book	Nathan Anthony	Random House	37k	€557k	€14.95	H	Food & Drink: General	United Kingdom
8	Aisling Ever After	Emer McLysaght, & Sarah Breen	Gill	35k	€532k	€15.08	P	General & Literary Fiction	Ireland
9	The Hike Life: My 50 Favourite Hikes in Ireland	Rozanna Purcell	Bonnier Books	30k	€624k	€20.60	H	General Folded Maps & Walking Guides	United Kingdom
10	My Father's House	Joseph O'Connor	Random House	30k	€495k	€16.56	P	Historical & Mythological Fiction	United Kingdom

11	Guinness World Records 2024		Guinness Publisher	29k	€390k	€13.25	H	Encyclo-pedias & General Refer-ence	United Kingdom
12	Small Things Like These	Claire Keegan	Faber	28k	€290k	€10.25	P	Gen-eral & Literary Fiction	United Kingdom
13	Diary of a Wimpy Kid: No Brainer (Book 18)	Jeff Kinney	Penguin	28k	€384k	€13.66	H	Chil-dren's Fiction	United Kingdom
14	Poor: Grit, courage, and the life-chang-ing value of self-belief	Katriona O'Sullivan	Penguin	28k	€455k	€16.48	P	Auto-biog-raphy: General	Ireland
15	No One Saw a Thing	Andrea Mara	Tran-sworld	27k	€418k	€15.33	P	Crime, Thriller & Adven-ture	United Kingdom
16	Lessons in Chemistry	Bonnie Garmus	Tran-sworld	26k	€267k	€10.38	P	Gen-eral & Literary Fiction	United Kingdom
17	So Late in the Day	Claire Keegan	Faber	25k	€254	€10	P	Gen-eral & Literary Fiction	United Kingdom
18	Dog Man 11: Twenty Thousand Fleas Under the Sea	Dav Pilkey	Scholastic	25k	€318k	€12.76	H	Chil-dren's Comic Strip Fiction & Graphic Novels	United States
19	Seven Husbands of Evelyn Hugo	Taylor Jen-kins-Reid	Simon & Schuster	25k	€242m	€9.72	P	Gen-eral & Literary Fiction	United Kingdom
20	Body of Truth	Marie Cassidy	Hachette Books Ireland	24k	€395k	€16.52	P	Crime, Thriller & Adven-ture	Ireland

CLARIFYING COPYRIGHT

Samantha Holman

F irst the good news, copyright is an automatic right under Irish, EU and International law: this means that as soon as you create an original work, your rights are protected. Copyright, essentially, is a form of intellectual property that protects original literary, dramatic, musical, and artistic work – regardless of artistic merit – and gives the creator the exclusive right to reproduce, distribute, perform, display and create derivative work.

Copyright protection begins as soon as you have created a new work in a tangible form. It also extends only to the expression of an idea and not to the idea itself. This accounts for a run of novels or stories on a similar theme but with different expressions, characters, locations. Your actual work is protected but not the concept itself.

The term of protection for a copyright work is the lifetime of the author (or longest living author in the case of a joint authorship) plus 70 years. A work comes out of copyright protection on the 1st of January of the 71st year after the author's death. This also means that you need to consider the post-mortem life of your body of work. Think about how your work might be used in the future and give clear instructions about your wishes for your estate to follow.

Keep a copy of your work in a safe place or send it to yourself by registered post and keep the receipt and envelope sealed. This will help you prove that you were the original author of a work if any dispute should arise.

The © symbol is not required on your work to gain copyright protection; however it is a very useful indicator to others that you are aware of your rights, and helps other creators to contact the rightsholder if they wish to reproduce, adapt or translate any of your work.

Writers also need to think about the issue of quoting, translating or satirising other original work. There is no magic formula for how much of someone else's work you can quote in your own, other than it must not be a substantial part, and must fall under one of the permitted uses (fair dealing defences or exceptions) in the Copyright & Related Rights Act 2000 as amended.

There is a 'fair dealing' exception for the purpose of criticism or review. You may use extracts from a work under this exception, as long as it is accompanied by a sufficient acknowledgement. The law does not give specific guidelines as to what constitutes a fair dealing but you should take into consideration:

- the length and importance of quotations;
- the amount quoted in relation to your commentary;
- the extent to which your work competes with or rivals the work quoted;
- the extent to which the material quoted is saving you work.

Some years ago, the Society of Authors and the Publishers Association in the UK agreed that they would usually regard as a fair dealing an extract of up to 400 words of a prose piece, or a series of extracts, none exceeding 300 words, to total 800 words; extracts to a total of 40 lines from a poem, provided this did not exceed a quarter of the poem. These guidelines do not have any standing in law but provide some useful guidance.

For example, if you wish to quote poetry, prose or song lyrics at the start of each chapter of a book, you need to seek permission in advance. Permission for song lyrics is particularly slow and needs to be given sufficient time to be granted. Titles are not protected by copyright, however, so you can leave your reader to work out your particular reference by referring to the title of the song.

Translation of a poem, piece of prose or song lyrics is an adaptation of a work which requires permission in advance of the translation being made.

There is a recent exception in Irish law which permits parody without asking for permission. For a parody to be successful as a defence, it is necessary to align closely with the source work. However, if the source work forms a substantial part of the new work then you need to seek permission in advance. The parodist must conjure up the source work but cannot take a substantial part.

There is no special exception that allows you to use a work without permission just because it is used for a not-for-profit or charitable purpose.

It is important to err on the side of caution if you wish to use an image in a work, especially if you are publishing under an open access route. Make sure you have sourced your image from a legitimate source and that you have permission to use it in the way you wish. Just because something is readily available online doesn't mean that you can reproduce it without permission. Also look out for works that have been made available under a Creative Commons licence. If you are considering using Creative Commons to license your own work, choose carefully and with an eye to future uses.

For more in-depth information please visit ICLA's website (www.icla.ie) which has an FAQ for authors, including granting and requesting permissions and what to do if your work is infringed.

Opportunities & Resources

Gaining Perspective:

Arts Council applications

Claire Hennessy

T he first thing you need to understand is that no one
is out to get you.

I know you may want to believe that someone is,
or might be. That there is a conspiracy against you. That
there is something more dramatic and, well, narratively-in-
teresting afoot than 'not enough money'. You are a storyteller; you demand more than these tiresome … accounts.

The mundane truth about funding applications in the arts
is that it is so often about 'not enough money'. It is the same
in publishing-land; supply outweighs demand by an awful
lot. There may be space for ten books on a publisher's list;
there could well be another ten, twenty, or fifty that would
easily fit.

Now multiply that by ten, twenty, a hundred – or sometimes a thousand – to get a sense of what bursaries are like.
There may be money to fund twenty artists, but there are
two hundred applications. (It is worth looking at the 'Who
we've funded' section of the Arts Council website, which
includes figures on the number of applications versus awards

offered in previous years.) A small percentage of those applications will be chancers, as with any endeavour, but most will be sincere, creative, committed humans.

It is competitive, in other words. Unlike, say, the SUSI grants for those in higher education, eligibility does not guarantee funding. It's also worth remembering, if you're a younger or newer writer (the terms are not interchangeable), that you're not just competing with writers at your level, but at all levels. The term 'starving artist' exists for a reason: writers (like other artists) are not paid well, except for rare exceptions, and it is possible to be an award-winning writer and still be in a financially precarious situation. (A handful of these writers will end up in Aosdána with annual support and be ineligible for these awards, but not all.)

All of this is to say: have a bit of perspective. This is not to talk you out of applying – on the contrary! Apply for whatever's on offer – but be smart about it, and understand what you're doing.

There are sometimes specific schemes that will emerge that have extra/special criteria. For example, during the Covid lockdowns there was a particular scheme that included an element of public performance/access, some way of showcasing the work, and making it available to others at a bleak time. But in general, awards like the Literature Bursary or the Agility Award are designed to 'buy time' for artists – to allow them to work on their craft, usually with reference to a specific project. You don't need to demonstrate the market value of your work, or that your book will make a great TV series. This system exists because we live in a world where the market does not always value artistic work.

With this in mind, then, think about what you as a writer bring to the table. What do you write about; what do you care about? What is distinctive about your work? (This is the point at which self-deprecation may creep in, because in Ireland we are not trained to have self-esteem of any sort. Notions!) Look. As a human, an individual, you are unique: how does this show up in your work? You will have to include a sample of said work: does it reflect what you're saying about it?

This doesn't need to be overly fancy or academic. But you do need to be able to answer some variation of the question 'what are you hoping to do, and why do you want to do it?' You're looking for money: what will it let you do? What does focusing on your writing for a certain period of time look like? (Probably not the same as a lot of other work – that's okay. You don't need to think in terms of quitting the day job, though scaling back may be an option for you. It might mean paying yourself fairly for the evenings or weekends you commit to your creative work, or being able to spend a week or two at an artists' retreat.) Are there some specific things you want to do (e.g. buy a new laptop, take a workshop) that are legitimate things to ask for under the award guidelines? (Read the guidelines. Always read the guidelines. The more you read them, the less scary they become.)

It's important to remember that these awards are merit-based rather than means-tested. You may well 'deserve' funding and not get it, because the thresholds for 'deserving of funding' and 'a priority funding-wise' are very different. In an ideal world, everyone deserving of funding would get it. In the world we actually live in, this isn't the case.

The more you can accept these things, the more – oh how I loathe this word – resilience you will have. It's an overused buzzword, but we do need it in the arts. We need to be able to send work out into the world understanding that the default response is a no – and to understand that 'no' does not mean that we, or the work, are lacking in talent.

Keep the word 'award' in mind. If you can do this, it will help you to remain sane when or if a no comes. It will help you apply the next time, and the next. The word 'award' will remind you of other prizes out there, and the times you haven't agreed with the chosen winners of the Booker Prize, the Oscars, Eurovision. 'Grant', I think, will send you down a dark track; it is so tempting – particularly the first time you've applied – to get into a rage over how unfair it is to not receive funding when you have done all the right things.

If you must rage, then do it away from your smartphone. Set a time limit on wallowing. Try again next time. Keep writing. Keep writing. Keep writing.

LIBRARIES AND PURSUING
A CREATIVE LIFE

Jackie Lynam

L ike many, I was a reader before I was a writer. My parents read stories to myself and my sister from the time we were babies, and fortunately for us, they were staunch supporters of the public library. My mam grew up in the North Strand near Dublin's city centre, and left school at 14 to work full-time so she could financially assist her parents, who were raising 10 children on my grandad's unreliable docker's wage. She was a devoted member of Dublin Corporation's Charleville Mall library; on her 14th birthday she ran into that beloved red brick building beside the Royal Canal, to claim her adult membership card – in her words her *best birthday present ever*.

The world had expanded for her just as her formal education ended. She discovered authors such as Somerset Maugham and Daphne de Maurier, whose stories led her into worlds far away from her poor inner-city childhood. She adored autobiographies of actors and singers, and later used the library to read up on health, psychology, and other areas of interest. The library provided her with a life-long education.

This love of books, reading, and libraries was passed on to us, and we were frequent users of the library throughout our childhood. When I was 21 I got a full-time job in Dublin City Libraries and I became immersed in the world of words from the other side of the desk.

Through my work in the Dublin UNESCO City of Literature office, I got to meet many writers, and I organised and attended numerous library talks, and some of that love of creating stories must have seeped into my brain because in 2013 I started writing myself.

I turned to writing in my early 40s, as a way of putting shape and order on the thoughts that were swirling around my head: I was trying to process grief for my dad, who had died from Alzheimer's Disease, the challenges of motherhood, and the different ways in which my body was failing me. I had no plans to show anyone my writing.

However, one evening in early 2017 I was scrolling through my phone and came across notes I had written about my post-hysterectomy check-up, two years previously. Out of nowhere these lines formed in my mind: *Notes tapped hastily into my phone, endometriosis, ovary gone, did he say left or right?* I didn't know what was happening but thankfully I had the sense to type them, and the words that followed, quickly into my notes folder before they disappeared. I had written my first prose poem.

I took some of the musings I had typed into my laptop and began shaping them into poems. I was incredibly lucky that I found support and encouragement in those early days when I really had no idea what I was doing, and a year later I started submitting poems to online journals. Over the last seven years my poems have been shortlisted for competitions and published in journals and anthologies. I have also written newspaper articles and radio essays. Tapping into a creative side of me, which for decades I didn't even realise existed, has brought me huge joy.

It was a remark by writer Elizabeth Reapy that changed everything for me as a writer. She was conducting a writer's workshop for beginners in Pearse St. Library, as part of her Writer-in-Residence programme. I was there to check everyone in, but Elizabeth invited me to stay and take part in the workshop. 'Nine out of ten people won't get your writing but one person will,' she said. That was it. That was the encouragement I needed to keep going. Elizabeth talking about her experience as an editor of an online journal, of rejecting pieces that later appeared in different publications, was exactly what I needed to hear at that time, and I've never forgotten her advice.

Over the years, hearing writers speak about their process, the challenges they face, the highs and many lows, has been a revelation. It has demystified any notions I had about writers leading glamorous lives. But more importantly it showed me that it's possible be a writer. At any age.

I believe to be a *good* writer you need to be a reader. And that's where libraries excel. In your local library you have access to thousands of books – physical, ebooks and audiobooks. It's possible to research and write your book in the local library. You can join a book club to discuss and critique what works and what doesn't in books you'd never choose if you were just reading for yourself. Libraries also facilitate writing groups who meet regularly and provide support and encouragement to each other. And it's all free.

As well as guides to writing, you can borrow books in different genres that teach you about plotting, pacing and dialogue. You can read newly-published books as well as classics and other books that may not have had the marketing budget to reach mass audiences. You can discover voices from around the world, from people who speak different languages to you, who have different religious and cultural beliefs, and all will attempt to show you what it means to be human.

As I approached my 50th birthday I gathered together a collection of some of my poems, newspaper articles and radio essays and published them myself in a book. I dedicated this collection, *Traces*, to my mother Nora who so generously instilled a love of reading in me, and whose motto has always been that you are never alone when you have a book. I hope people might even find *Traces* on a library shelf one day and that it could even inspire other readers to pursue a life of creativity.

WRITING GROUPS:

FINDING YOUR TRIBE

Peter Clarke

In 2008 I took a writing workshop with the poet, Catherine Phil McCarthy. At the last session, a woman approached me and suggested I join her writing group, and since then I have been part of the Bealtaine Writers Group, feeling well and truly at home.

According to Donegal poet Matthew Sweeney, a writing group is simply a bunch of writers who meet regularly to read and discuss each other's work, in a critical yet supportive environment—keywords for a group to work well. Giving and receiving constructive feedback is important to a group's success, just as support and encouragement are crucial.

BENEFITS OF BEING IN A GROUP

I took a straw poll in a group who had been together for many years, to see what they had gained from the experience. They listed the following:

- Feedback—honest, positive
- Discipline—encouragement to keep writing
- Inspiration to try different forms
- Encouraged to read other poets
- Hearing one's work read by someone else
- Began poetry writing in my eighties
- Performing for colleagues
- A contrary master

WHERE TO MEET

Where to meet may be the first question. Local libraries, which have space, help host writing groups, as do education institutions. Community organisations with premises are also a good idea. It's better not to meet in each other's homes if possible, to avoid a feeling of needing to entertain and cater for people, which could become stressful or competitive. Keep the focus on the business at hand: the quality and development of the writing.

AGREEMENTS

Important to any writing group is agreeing how to work, particularly around encouragement, listening, creating fair 'airspace' for each member, leadership, moderatorship, and running costs. A critical element is understanding the purpose of the group. Are you setting out to help improve your own and each other's writing? Is it a social group that happens to share writing? Is publishing the main aim? Are you a general writers' group welcoming all genres or do you specialise? These are separate drivers and if not articulated can create divisions which can become difficult to resolve.

PRACTICE

The Bealtaine Group have been meeting for around twenty-five years. The group was founded by a group of newly retired people who wanted to continue writing after a workshop with the poet Eithne Strong. Since then, many have published collections and individual pieces, have gone on to do a Masters in Creative Writing, and together have produced three anthologies. This all points to how the group practises—in their reading, writing and feedback, and in the development of the group through commissioned classes from established poets, and the continued growth and learning of each member.

All or none of this activity in a group is perfectly fine so long as it fits with everyone's vision. There is a trope of the writer in the attic alone dying for their art—but often writers benefit from and enjoy some level of collaboration and connection with their peers.

Another thing to consider is how work is presented. What has worked well for the groups I have been part of is for each person to bring enough copies of the piece they want feedback on, so everybody can read along and make notes. I find it very useful to collect those copies of my work so I can mull over the written comments as well as what has been discussed.

JOINING

If you are considering joining a group, it is helpful to have a good idea of what level of participation suits you best, what you want, and, in turn, what you are willing to contribute. So check that the activities of the group meet your current needs. Conversations with members and sitting in on one or two meetings will give you a feel for the group.

How the group treats potential new members, making them welcome, sharing work, listening, and making the climate of the group open to discussion with new members are some of the factors which determine how a newbie will feel about staying.

Groups who are together for a while seem to have the bonus of good personal relationships which help with feedback and the social needs of writers. Caution, here though: there is a risk of a clique forming which prohibits new people from joining. Over the years there will be a natural attrition and therefore a need for new people to keep the group going.

SIZE OF A GROUP

Numbers in the group are a consideration. The general practice of writing groups seems to be meeting once a month more or less, for two hours. Members need reasonable time to read and have the group comment. I have worked in groups that vary between 6 and 18 and found that the upper end puts pressure on the time for reasonable comment.

10 to 14 seems to work for me, and even fewer for a detailed discussion on the work.

ENDING

Finally, sometimes a group comes to a natural ending. It can be useful to recognise this and rather than limp along, figure out how to end things well.

TEACHING WRITING:

A MARRIAGE MADE IN HEAVEN?

Gerard Beirne

The one thing I knew is that I never wanted to teach. Not just writing. Anything. And yet, here I am, having taught and facilitated writing classes for over thirty years. For over half of those years, I have taught at universities in the US, Canada and Ireland. However, it feels as if I have taught just about everywhere else too: schools, prisons, seniors' homes, writing centres, arts centres, government departments and business organisations. I have worked with all age groups and have taught courses and workshops in a variety of genres: poetry, short story, novel, memoir, creative non-fiction, academic writing and business writing. I have been a Writer-in-Residence at second and third level institutions and in a variety of arts facilities. I have mentored writers one-to-one and on group mentorship schemes.

So what went wrong? How did I end up spending so much of my life doing what I swore I wouldn't do? Well, initially I had to. I accepted a Teaching Assistantship in order to fund my fees at Eastern Washington University while taking my MFA in Creative Writing. While there, I also completed a one-year teaching internship. To my surprise, I liked it. And to my greater surprise, I seemed suited to it too.

WHY DO I TEACH WRITING?

Firstly, I don't really teach writing. Instead I facilitate an environment where a student's writing can develop and grow. If I instruct in anything, it is in the mindsets, attitudes, and approaches that writers use and benefit from. I explore with my students our writing practices and how they interrelate with both the process of writing and the structures that different genres employ. As I tell my students, 'You will never know what I have taught you, and I will never know what you have learned.' But the evidence is visible in their writing which clearly develops throughout the time we spend together.

But *why* do I do it? It sustains me. On a practical level, it puts food on the table. But my teaching sustains me in a far more meaningful way: it feeds my writing too. When I enter the 'classroom', I bring my writing self in there too. For sure, I have more experience and knowledge about writing and literature than the students I engage with, and, of course, they are coming to me to learn and develop; but it's not content based. Our discussions and reflections on practice, process, structure and craft educate me also.

HOW DO YOU GET STARTED?

Well, you could follow my route and complete an MA or MFA in Creative Writing and look for Teaching Assistant-ships along the way. You can even go on and do a PhD. In the US, where MFAs are the norm, the degree often leads to teaching English Composition at community colleges or universities where compulsory academic writing courses are also the norm. Things are different here in Ireland although that is slowly changing. Many universities now have Creative Writing Programmes and advertise for full or part time staff. Having a Masters level qualification or a PhD, alongside a strong history of book publication, could open up those opportunities. Some universities offer Writer in Residencies too, as do some local county councils.

However, while a Creative Writing degree of some level is helpful, it is not essential. A strong publication history can go a long way, and there are a host of other options available.

IF YOU WANT TO BE A TEACHER, DO YOUR HOMEWORK

These options include courses run through adult education centres, libraries, arts centres and organisations like the Irish Writers Centre (they even have a convenient page on their website called 'Become a Facilitator' with all the necessary details). So, research what is happening in your locality. Ask at the library, talk to coordinators, contact your local arts officer.

HONE YOUR PITCH

That's right. Pitches aren't just for agents and publishers; they are for writing course and workshop proposals too. Like any pitch, you need to demonstrate your professionalism, your knowledge and experience. The pitch should be succinct and to the point but be prepared to back it up with a more complete course outline.

SET UP YOUR OWN WRITING COURSES

You can also run your own courses (in-person or online). If in-person, do your market research. If you are satisfied that there is a need in your locality for a particular course, you may have an opportunity there. If online, the world's your oyster (within reason). Of course, competition is rife. You need an angle, something that distinguishes your course from someone else's. If you are a successful writer, the angle may be your name. If not, you need to decide what it is that you have to offer that someone else does not. *Be authentic.* No bluffing, no grandstanding. You owe it to the writers you will be working with. Don't oversell yourself.

Beyond this, keep in mind that you will be running a business. This requires a range of business skills such as event organisation, advertising, promotion, finances etc. Do not underestimate the amount of organisation involved. Take it from one who knows.

A FEW WORDS OF CAUTION

Not every good writer is necessarily a good teacher. So, while the teaching of writing may seem like a tempting option, it's not for everyone. I would advise against the 'See One, Do One, Teach One' methodology. Teaching is a skill. If you embark on this route, I encourage you to reflect on your teaching practice constantly and to regularly upgrade your skillsets. Additionally, teaching, especially full-time teaching, can be stressful and exhausting. Make your decision wisely.

A FEW WORDS OF ENCOURAGEMENT

With that in mind, if you do decide to embark on a teaching career alongside your writing, and if you are suited to the task, you will be rewarded many times over. It can fuel your own writing, and there is no greater joy than witnessing the pleasure that writing brings to others.

CREATIVE COLLABORATION:

THE AUTHOR–EDITOR RELATIONSHIP

Averill Buchanan

Probably the most important relationship you'll have on the way to publication—whether you're taking the traditional route or self-publishing—is with your editor.

Twentieth-century publishing history is strewn with tales of fascinating partnerships between famous writers and their editors. Some were controversial—those between Raymond Carver and Gordon Lish, for example, or Thomas Wolfe and Maxwell Perkins, spring most readily to mind—because the level of editorial intervention was considered tantamount to co-authorship. Others were more harmonious and nourishing, like Harper Lee's with her editor, Tay Hohoff, who for almost two and a half years helped Lee transform the manuscript of *Go Set a Watchman* into *To Kill a Mockingbird*. If you're interested in reading more about the good old days of 'gentlemanly publishing', try Robert Gottlieb's memoir *Avid Reader* (2016) or Diana Athill's *Stet* (2000), which recount those editors' professional and personal encounters with some of the best-known writers of their time.

However, twenty-first-century publishing is driven more by profit margins and tight deadlines than hand-holding and the cultivation of literary talent. In-house editors still exist, of course, but the relationship you're likely to have with them nowadays will be more businesslike and less obliging of 'artistic temperament', more disciplined and less disposed to wait for the muse to strike.

If you have a publishing deal, the in-house editor you work with will most likely be the one who loved your manuscript from the start and has already been championing your work. Their involvement can range from working directly on the text itself to liaising between you and the other departments within the publishing ecosystem. First contact with them might seem more like an interview, but it's really to get to know you better, explain the processes involved and put you at your ease. You could be working together for quite some time, so you'll want to establish clear boundaries (working hours, for example), preferred channels of communication (email, phone, WhatsApp), and expectations—of each other and for the book.

Having said that, it's still important that the two of you get along on a personal level. A healthy author–editor relationship is built on trust and mutual respect, where the author is open to editorial advice and suggestions and the editor is mindful of authorial intention and autonomy. It's not a battle of wills; it's a creative collaboration. Editorial skills aside, the other qualities you'd hope to find in a good editor include sensitivity, empathy and honesty. Ideally, your experience of being edited will be a constructive one. You'll feel supported but challenged, understood but pushed to explore your full capabilities.

You'll be looking for the same qualities if you choose to work with a freelance (self-employed) editor. Many freelancers offer a range of services that can be tailored to authors' specific needs and they're often able to accommodate shifting goals and deadlines. However, finding the editor best suited to you can be a daunting task, especially if you've never worked with one before. There's more to it than looking for someone with a meticulous eye for detail and a track record in your genre. In addition to vetting potential editors for the professional skills and personal traits you're looking for, you'll also need to discuss the business side of things— timelines, fees, what's included for those fees—to ensure you're both on the same page.

So how do you find a freelance editor who gets you and your writing? The editing process is a dialogue between author and editor, so you'll want to be sure the editor is giving you the kind of feedback you need, using language you understand. Referrals are a good place to start: a friend or writing colleague may be able to recommend someone they think will suit you. Some freelance editors are willing to do a sample edit so you can see how they work. However, if you're hiring an editor for a manuscript critique or developmental edit—big picture stuff—sample edits aren't that useful, so you might want to ask for a phone or Zoom call to test your rapport.

Here in Northern Ireland, it can be difficult for local authors to find a freelance editor they feel comfortable with. In 2014, the Editors' and Proofreaders' Alliance of Northern Ireland (EPANI | www.epani.org.uk) was founded primarily to make it easier for local publishers, businesses and authors to find the right editor for their project, someone who speaks their lingo and who they can meet in person. But of course geography is no barrier to great author–editor collaborations. Most of the editors listed in the EPANI directory are members of both the UK-based Chartered Institute for Editing and Proofreading (CIEP) and AFEPI Ireland. So while our members are perfectly placed to work with local authors, businesses and publishers, many of us also have clients further afield.

Being local but global has also opened us up to publishers and authors worldwide who seek specific knowledge of Northern Irish culture and vernacular. For example, US-based authors who have set their novels in Northern Ireland occasionally approach our members for help with the nuances of historical and cultural details. We may be small but we have a mighty reach. With access to a wide network of editorial colleagues around the world, we're happy to recommend other editors if we feel they might be better suited to the work or more immediately available.

The publishing landscape is constantly evolving, but what remains the same is the need for a collaborative relationship between author and editor that brings out the best in both. Taking the time to find the right editor for YOU, whether they're in-house or freelance, via referrals or personal vetting, national networks or local resources like EPANI, will go a long way to ensuring that the path to publication is a creatively exciting, enriching and positive experience.

TO STUDY, OR NOT TO STUDY?

A MASTERS IN CREATIVE WRITING

Liz Quirke

O nce upon a time, writers found their way to their craft through solitary endeavour and graft. We picture the romance of it; the low lit lamp, the weight of the pen in the hand, the feel of the keys under fingertips. There is a charge to this image, a frisson between muse and maker, a sacred attention to creation, the promise that by putting in the requisite effort alongside sparks of genius, that before or after death the novel/poem/memoir will reveal itself and the writer will be rewarded with monetary compensation and/or immortality. Lofty ambition, yes. Erroneous supposition, not quite.

At the heart of writing is an uncomfortable collision, where the writerly ambition and ego mixes with endeavour and the hope that the work will connect with an audience. In contemporary culture, with the advent of six figure advances and prize pots, there is also the understanding that, for some, writing is a valid career choice. It is this latter aspect that encourages people in their droves to try to professionalise their practice by entering into that most controversial of pathways: the Creative Writing Masters programme.

[Full disclosure, this writer teaches creative writing at undergraduate and postgraduate level, and possesses a PhD in the discipline. It is probably also necessary at this point to disclose that I was not student of Creative Writing at MA/MFA level, training in other tangential writing arts and apprenticeships.]

There seems to be an argument by those who have come into their craft by more journeyman routes and efforts, a view which is regularly the fodder for long Facebook posts about how unnecessary a qualification in Creative Writing is to 'become' a writer, that writing cannot be taught, that a practitioner is somehow cheating the system by following a route that at its core is academic.

But does this matter? And what should people consider about these pathways ahead of an application. Well, to be frank, the decision to undertake a Creative Writing degree at undergraduate or postgraduate level begins and ends with the writer and their intentions. But, what should a person consider before they decide to commit a year or three to attending a classroom with peers all facing forward with similar endgames of publication in mind? How do we know which level to pitch for? And what are the alternatives?

Taking the undergraduate route first: Like any other course, students of this discipline will come to the classroom through second level examination or mature student applications. For many courses, the entry is based, like many creative arts disciplines, on a portfolio that demonstrates a talent. For others, it is based on a points system, or a personal essay, or the ability to pay fees. Postgraduate study comes with the same framework; the application, the assessment, the fee structure. The larger question is what happens in a university level workshop, and is that sort of tuition necessary? And at postgraduate level, what is the draw?

As with my earlier caveat, I am writing this from inside the wire. I spend weeks and months every year working with students in the pursuit of professional writing standards and recognition by publication, and each year the same benefits to students are borne out around peer interaction and protected time.

For my money, the workshop environment and peer interaction is the thing that students find most beneficial. The protected time to work on a singular dissertation project can be the most challenging and the most rewarding result. It has to be said that at least one of those aspects can be achieved outside of a third level institution—Ireland has a very strong infrastructure of writing supports away from academia, with organisations such as the Irish Writers Centre providing supports in the form of mentorships, short courses and writing space for their members. Personally I cut my teeth in the attic of the Galway Arts Centre for years before I moved into the world of academia, and aspiring writers can find their tribe at a grassroots level as a test space for their work, before committing to a route that once started moves like a juggernaut.

Creative Writing programme leaders read hundreds of applications every year and have a limited number of spaces to offer, which has the effect of giving a rarefied tenor to the idea of the qualification. To maximise the chances of getting a space, there must be a movement at the grassroots, to develop a sense of a writing self before entering into the classroom. Once you arrive through the doors, be prepared for one of the most challenging and rewarding times of your life.

AS GOOD AS IT GETS:

FREELANCE EDITORS AND AFEPI IRELAND

Brian Langan

Is my manuscript finished? It's one of the eternal questions writers ask themselves. While some writers are happy to consider their work done after one or two drafts, others can spend months or even years tinkering with it, unsure of when they should push it out of the nest, confident it will have the strength in its wings to take flight. There are numerous stories of regretful writers who sent their work to agents or publishers too soon, or self-published prematurely, realising too late that first impressions last.

While a manuscript that's been accepted by a traditional publisher will usually undergo a rigorous editorial process in-house, it first has to cross that barrier of being accepted by a publisher or an agent. What can you, as a writer, do to get past the guardians at the gate? And if you're choosing the self-publishing route, how can you ensure that your work is ready for publication? That's where the work of a freelance editor comes in.

For a fee, a freelance editor can help you make your manuscript as good as it can be. The type of edit involved can be tailored to your requirements, ranging from the broad sweep of a short beta report; the robust and detailed critique involved in a manuscript assessment; the deep delve of a developmental or structural edit, tackling issues with character, plot, narration, structure and pacing; the detailed sentence-by-sentence work of a copy-edit to ensure that the text is accurate, clear, concise and appropriate to your audience; or the error-catching final tidying-up of a proofread.

Most of all, a freelance editor acts as a fresh eye on your work, and can help you to answer: *Yes, your manuscript is as good as it can be.* Many experienced editors can, at that stage, also give feedback on how publishable it is, and may perhaps even offer advice on how you can best present your work to agents and publishers.

In Ireland, freelance editors can apply to join the Association of Freelance Editors, Proofreaders & Indexers of Ireland (AFEPI Ireland), a professional organisation which fosters high standards in editing, proofreading and indexing, protects the interests of its members, and helps to match authors, indie writers, publishers, businesses, public bodies and charitable organisations with suitable editorial freelancers.

AFEPI Ireland is a professional organisation run on a voluntary basis by an executive committee and a five-person membership committee. Its main aims are to advocate on behalf of, and protect the interests of, its members; to provide professional up-to-date advice and training; and to foster high standards in editing, proofreading and indexing.

All our members go through a rigorous vetting process when they first apply to join. The membership committee assesses each application carefully, looking for evidence of high-quality training and/or editorial experience of some kind, backed up by two references from satisfied clients or previous employers.

There are two levels of membership: Associate and Full Member. Associate membership is suitable for those who are relatively new to editing, proofreading and/or indexing, or who have limited training and recent experience. Members who join at this level are encouraged to upgrade to full membership once they have gained further training and experience. Full membership is offered to trained, experienced editors, proofreaders and indexers. Many full members have worked in-house for Irish, UK and US publishers, while others come from academic backgrounds or have worked in an editorial capacity outside the publishing industry.

AFEPI Ireland places great importance on training, and on ongoing professional development to help its experienced members stay nimble and adaptable in this fast-changing industry, collaborating with the Publishing Training Centre (PTC), the Chartered Institute of Editing and Proofreading (CIEP) in the UK, the Society of Indexers, Publishing Ireland and the Irish Writers Centre to maximise opportunities for high-quality industry-recognised training for our members.

For publishers, independent authors, businesses, organisations, state bodies, designers, students (with permission from their college/university) – anyone who uses our services – AFEPI Ireland's directory of Full Members is a particularly useful tool for sourcing the right freelancer for each project. This online directory can be browsed by the editors' names and is also searchable by the type of work required, skills, genre, specialism, etc. Aside from editing, proofreading and indexing, most of our members boast other related skills, such as advice and consultancy services, design, ebook formatting, project management, translation, typesetting and writing. They also cover a diverse range of specialisms and subject knowledge, and work on different kinds of text: for example, academic, autobiography and memoir, business, young adult and children's, educational, ESL, fiction, Irish language, law, public administration, sciences and STEM, training manuals and websites.

AFEPI Ireland freelancers are bound by our Code of Practice, which enshrines its duty of care to clients, whoever they may be. Under its terms, members are required to provide a competent, confidential service, to behave with integrity, and to act in a professional manner at all times. We promote best practice not only in editorial skills, but also in the conduct of our businesses.

Whether your work needs a heavy edit, some 'tidying up', or even just the reassurance that, *yes, your manuscript is as good as it can be*, browse the AFEPI Ireland members' directory online at www.afepi-ireland.com. You're sure to find a perfect match!

Open Access:

WHAT DOES IT MEAN FOR YOUR WORK?

Ruth Hegarty

The Royal Irish Academy was set up over 230 years ago for 'the advancement of knowledge' as it was described in our founding charter. At that time, it was an outlet for gentleman scholars. Access to knowledge has become a whole lot more democratic since then.

To stay true to those original values we've decided to move our six research journals to be open access (OA), and to achieve this we're working hard to change the way they are funded.

WHAT IS OPEN ACCESS?

OA publishing is the practice of providing online access to scholarly information that is free of charge to the reader and is reusable. It was born with the invention of the internet, and grew as the prices for journal subscriptions skyrocketed, and governments, librarians and academics moved to use their budgets to make research more publicly available.

The first major statement on it was the Budapest Open Access Initiative in 2002. The movement has been strongest in Europe, with a prevalence in disciplines such as physics and other sciences rather than in the humanities.

For the Irish government, OA is the gold standard for publicly funded research. Their ambition is outlined in the National Open Access Plan for Open Research 2022-2030:

> By 2030 Ireland will have implemented a sustainable and inclusive course for achieving 100% open access to research publications. Provisions put in place to support a diverse open access publishing ecosystem and the retention of authors' rights will ensure Irish researchers have the freedom to choose from a range of quality options for making their research open access.

HOW IS IT FUNDED?

A funder, an author, government or libraries pay a publishing fee before the work is published, as opposed to the traditional models which has the reader pay at the point of access.

Up until now, our journals have been sold by subscription to individuals and to libraries. Now we're also signing what are called 'transformative deals' with the university libraries where the subscription fee has two elements: a 'read' fee and a 'publish' fee. The publish fee allows any author who works for the university the option to publish open access.

An author can pay to have their article published immediately – 'gold' open access – using an 'APC', an article publication charge. They can also use the 'green OA' model and archive their work in a repository, in line with their publisher's policy at no cost to them.

These arrangements have meant that over the last two years over half our journals are now open to everyone to read. Our hope for the future is that journals will 'flip' to be entirely open access, as libraries agree to pay us to 'subscribe to open': in return we will make journals open access to all.

WHAT DOES IT MEAN FOR YOUR WORK?

For an author, if you choose well, it should mean that your work will be more widely read, that you can share it freely, and that your work could end up in places that your publisher could never reach through traditional models. You retain the copyright and choose the rules on how it can be shared, using one of the standard Creative Commons licences.

Employers and funders, including universities, may now assert rights over your scholarly work, so you need to check before signing any agreements with publishers that would limit your rights to publish OA.

Open access shouldn't make any difference to your right to choose a publisher and to continue publishing with your preferred publisher. In fact, governments say they are keen to protect and fund independent publishing houses and to discourage consolidation in a small number of large publishing houses.

WILL CREATIVE WORKS BE INCLUDED?

Creative works funded by government are not included because the focus of the open access movement is on scholarly works. Authors can still decide to publish their work open access if they wish, but it isn't a requirement.

WHERE CAN I FIND MORE INFORMATION?

I am leading a NORF funded project called PublishOA.ie. We have published guidelines for authors and for publishers on what they need to know and think about when they want to publish their work open access. There are a number of standard requirements which are changing as open access publishing develops. These guidelines will help you ensure that your work is not only free to read online but that it meets these requirements: for example, that it has the right copyright licence applied to allow others to reuse your work, and that it is archived properly for the future and is easy to find online.

FURTHER SOURCES ABOUT OPEN ACCESS PUBLISHING:

- Publish OA (www.publishoa.ie)
- Directory of Irish Publishers (www.publishoa.ie)
- Directory of Open Access Journals (www.doaj.org) and Books (www.doab.org)
- Creative Commons (creativecommons.org)
- The Irish Open Access Publishers (www.ioap.ie)
- National Action Plan for Open Research 2022-2030 (https://norf.ie)

Flash Fiction:

WHAT YOU CAN LEARN FROM MY JOURNEY

Fiona McKay

HOW IT STARTED

In 2020, I stumbled across Writers' HQ, an organisation offering free writing courses. I cynically scrolled to find the hidden catch: there wasn't one. I had a novel I was supposed to be editing, but instead took some of the courses on offer – free and paid for – including one on short fiction.

To further procrastinate editing, I signed up for a flash fiction course in January 2021.

Looking back on my spreadsheet, the eighth flash piece I sent out was longlisted in a small competition. I was hooked. There is joy, community, and a whole lot of dopamine in submitting work – especially when it gets accepted. As someone who had been writing a novel in a total vacuum, this was a revelation.

WHAT IS FLASH FICTION?

Flash is short – under 1000 words – but can go all the way down to 100 or even 50 word stories. But if flash is less than a short story in word count, it is more in other ways. What flash isn't, is a scaled down version of a short story. The maxim 'start late, leave early' is often used. Don't limber up with a long introduction or lots of exposition. Start in the middle of the action and add in touches of the backstory as you go – enough for the reader to pick up what's going on.

Flash makes use of the white space on the page; the reader can infer what happens off the page in the jumps between narrative sections. This makes for a satisfying read. It leaves an after-flash of meaning, like the bright image behind your closed eyelids if you've looked at the sun, creating a much longer narrative than the one presented. Flash needs layers of meaning which inform each other and make the narrative more resonant. And there must be something 'true' in it – what Writers' HQ calls The Nugget of Fundamental Human Truth. This is not to say that the story itself must be true, but the emotion has to be real: it has to tell 'a' truth.

The beauty of writing flash is that it informs other writing too: Kathryn Scanlan's *Kick the Latch* is a novel-in-flash, as are Meg Mason's *Sorrow and Bliss*, and Jenny Offil's *Department of Speculation*. Learning to write flash fiction will benefit all your work.

FROM FLASH TO PUBLICATION

When I started writing Flash in 2021, I found it exciting how much could be achieved in such small spaces. I started submitting work and began to accumulate acceptances and list in competitions. I took classes with flash experts and learned that workshopping pieces with other writers is the best way to improve my writing. I began to meet other writers through social media, online courses, and events.

In autumn 2021 I applied for Arts Council Ireland Agility funding. When my application was granted, I changed my social media bio to 'writer' – if they believed in me, I could too. I wrote a novella-in-flash and a flash collection, both of which saw success in competitions and which ended up being published in 2023 by small independent presses: *The Top Road* is published with AdHoc Fiction; *Drawn and Quartered* is published with Alien Buddha Press. I could not have imagined having two books out in the world two years after I started writing flash: reader, anything is possible if you keep writing.

RESOURCES

- The Irish Writers Centre runs flash courses with Marie Gethins.
- Writers' HQ, based in the UK, has great work-at-your-own-pace courses for paying members, and Flash Face Off for free members, with peer feedback and a weekly spoken word event on Zoom *(www.writershq.co.uk)*.
- *SmokeLong Quarterly*, the US flash-narrative literary journal, runs SmokeLong Fitness, a peer-workshop with weekly craft tasks and small-group peer feedback *(www.smokelong.com)*.
- Crow Collective runs free writing groups and inexpensive online classes at times to suit people all across the globe *(www.crowcollectiveworkshops.com)*.
- The Flash Cabin runs workshops and classes *(www.flashcabin.com)*.
- Kathy Fish runs asynchronous courses and generative classes – demand is high, so applicants are in a lottery for courses *(www.kathy-fish.com)*.
- Flash Fiction Festival runs online festival days and an in-person festival, with guest speakers *(www.flashfictionfestival.co.uk)*.
- Retreat West for community and courses *(www.retreatwest.co.uk)*.
- These are only some of the many classes, courses, and workshops that are available. Follow flash writers on social media to see what classes they recommend.

WHERE TO SUBMIT

There are a multitude of literary journals featuring flash: *Splonk (www.splonk.ie)* and *Banshee* (*www.bansheelit.com*) are great examples of Irish literary journals that love the form.

There are great lists out there of literary journals: Brecht de Poortere ranks journals by their Twitter following *(www.brechtdepoortere.com)*. Erika Krouse *(www.erikakrousewriter.com)* has another list.

Chill Subs (www.chillsubs.com) is an interactive literary journal tracker that helps find the right journal for your story.

Submittable *(www.submittable.com)* and Duotrope (*www.duotrope.com*) are submissions portals used by journals and competitions which also have information about submission opportunities.

The literary community on Twitter is also a great place to hear about journals and competitions. Follow the writing crowd!

The Landscape of
Irish Language Publishing

Cathal Póirtéir

If you are hoping for fame and fortune to come from your writing, then working in Irish will be even more challenging than writing in English. Glittering literary prizes are unlikely in any language, so personal and artistic satisfaction are the more likely rewards. Some people write in Irish only, while others include Irish as one of their writing languages. The bilingual writer has been a feature of Irish letters for centuries, but is often better known for their work in English. There are hundreds of writers working in Irish today – but only a few are well-known to a wide public.

The number of people who read books in Irish is small compared to the vast readership available to the most successful writers in English. However, there is a loyal market for fiction, non-fiction and poetry in Irish, with over a hundred books published every year.

Most writers who work in Irish do so for personal fulfilment and cultural solidarity with the Irish speaking community. A majority of writers in any language find it hard to live on their creativity alone. However, there are a small number of talented and determined individuals who have dedicated themselves to writing in Irish full-time. In such a niche market, fees and royalties from publishers need to be augmented by participation in literary festivals, writers in schools schemes, media appearances, bursaries, residencies and other supports.

Some Irish language poets are perhaps more widely recognised than prose writers, partly because of their performances at readings and in the media – with those whose work has been translated into English being more likely to be invited to participate in public events.

Fiction and non-fiction in Irish is less translated than poetry, and rarely included in anthologies of Irish writing, therefore less well-known to readers in general. A reason for this lack of visibility is the absence of reviews of their work in the book pages of the national press, and in arts programming on radio and television. Market forces may play a part in that invisibility – but book sales in Irish often go beyond those of well-publicised and reviewed poetry collections in English, so sales volume is not the only reason.

IRISH LANGUAGE OPPORTUNITIES

One festival that spotlights writing in Irish is *Imram*, which showcases the best poetry and prose in innovative presentations in a number of Dublin venues. *Imram* usually takes place over a week or ten days in autumn but also produces mini-festivals and short tours to arts centres around the country.

Annual literary competitions for work in Irish have been organised by *Oireachtas na Gaeilge* for a century or so, and are highly valued by both emerging and established writers. They also administer the *Gradaim Foilsitheoireachta* awards in three categories: books of the year for adults, for younger readers, and for books in translation.

The publicity garnered by *Imram* and by *Oireachtas na Gaeilge* awards and presentations augment the efforts of Irish language publishers and bookshops to make people aware of the excellent contemporary work available in bookshops and online.

Popular prose works and children's books may sell in the thousands if writer and publisher work very hard at publicity – with the few books that make their way onto school and college courses selling better again. Individual poetry and short-story collections are likely to sell in the hundreds, while individual poems may be featured in Irish or bilingual anthologies.

IRISH LANGUAGE PUBLISHERS

Irish language publishers, like writers, put in huge efforts for small rewards but with the help of grant schemes run by the Arts Councils and *Foras na Gaeilge*, several small publishing houses produce attractive and important books. The most active publishers include *Coiscéim, Cló Iar-Chonnacht, Leabhar Breac, Éabhlóid, Barzaz, Futa Fata, LeabhairComhar,* FÁS and *an Gúm*.

There are a handful of Irish language magazines who publish journalism, reviews, short stories and poetry, for example the monthly magazines *Comhar* and *Feasta*, and of course *Books Ireland*, where my monthly feature '*Leabhair idir Lámha*' has been running since 2016.

Journalism in Irish is produced daily by the online tuairisc.ie as well as in *Seachtain*, an insert in Wednesday's *Irish Independent*. Some national and regional press publish regular columns in Irish, most notably *The Irish Times* and *The Irish News*.

There are some opportunities on radio and television for Irish language writers; the most important of these is TG4 which has been commissioning a wide range of television programmes from independent producers since 1996. The station regularly needs scriptwriters to write (or translate) material for documentary programmes and television drama.

Ros na Rún is TG4's popular drama series, running now for over twenty years, employing a team of freelance writers to provide storylines and scripts. TG4 also runs schemes like Cine4 which encourages the development of feature films in Irish, and has supported short run series and stand-alone television drama which have given many writers an opportunity to learn screenwriting skills and earn at least part of their living.

Taibhdhearc na Gaillimhe is the national theatre for Irish language drama and manages a limited number of productions every year, usually including a pantomime. There are a small number of theatre companies around the country, notably Belfast-based *Aisling Ghéar* and *Fibín,* a Connemara based children's theatre company, who perform and tour when financially possible.

From time to time RTÉ Raidió na Gaeltachta invests in radio drama, most often in a comedy series but sometimes in adaptations or other drama. RTÉ Radio 1's *Drama on One* produces a play in Irish occasionally as do BBC Radio Ulster. There are also schemes available to encourage commercial and community radio stations to commission and produce radio drama.

Aontas na Scríbhneoirí Gaeilge is the association for Irish language writers. It provides information, representation, and networking opportunities for its members, including writers living overseas. Its website has a searchable online directory with detailed information on 500 living writers.

WINDOWS TO THE WORLD:

LITERATURE IRELAND

Sinéad Mac Aodha

'Without translation, we would be living in provinces bordering on silence.' – George Steiner

In Literature Ireland, we believe that George Steiner's famous quote on translation encapsulates exactly why our promotion-through-translation work is so important: if people who do not read English or Irish cannot read Irish literature in their language, they will not understand us as well as they should. Reading books in translation is a window on a society, on a time in history, and on a people. Our role is to help make that happen and to foster cultural understanding and exchange.

Literature Ireland is the national agency in Ireland for the promotion of Irish literature abroad. We work to build international awareness and appreciation of contemporary Irish literature, primarily in translation. There is no such thing as a typical week for the team: each brings its own surprises, with new translation proposals arriving in our in-boxes, and potential partners contacting us to discuss their latest literary translation projects.

Our favourite moment is when a brand new box of translations arrives in the post. This could be the latest Anne Enright in Vietnamese or Patricia Forde in Welsh – or perhaps it's Colm Tóibín's new novel in Japanese or John Banville's in Spanish. We have recently supported books by both Sally Rooney and W.B. Yeats in Ukrainian – and were moved to tears by the resilience of our Ukrainian colleagues.

There is a strong literary seasonality to what Literature Ireland does. The year is punctuated by three translation grant rounds that we hold for international publishers once a quarter; we started off with this core programme in 1994. By providing support for translation costs, we hope to encourage foreign publishers to publish writing from Ireland, to pay their translators well, and to provide them with enough time to do a good job. Our aim is to have literature from Ireland read and enjoyed right across the world. Every application is assessed by an independent expert to ensure that texts are well translated from English or Irish to the target language of the publisher. We have the greatest respect for the translators who do this very difficult and sensitive work. Since we started operating in 1994, we have supported just over 2,500 works of Irish literature in fifty-eight languages.

Literature Ireland coordinates the national stand at the major international Frankfurt and London book fairs (which share a cumulative footfall of over 210,000). Flying the flag for Irish literature is a huge privilege and something we are very proud to do. At Frankfurt, we host a networking reception for over three hundred professionals from the sector. We normally invite the Ambassador to make a welcome speech to our international guests and to tour the Irish publisher stands.

We also produce an annual catalogue, *New Writing from Ireland*, which we circulate ahead of (and at) the Frankfurt Book Fair each October, where we meet foreign publishers, literary agents, translators, and festival directors. The catalogue provides a snapshot of what's happening in contemporary Irish writing and helps inform our fifty plus meetings during the fair. Literature Ireland is not a literary agency; we don't sell rights, but we can certainly complement the work of agents by providing our own expert opinion regarding what might work in a certain territory or indeed on a certain publisher's list. Our organisation now has almost thirty years of experience in this field and a strong network of publishing and other contacts across the globe.

Keeping on top of the exceptionally vibrant contemporary literature scene is a challenge – fortunately, the whole team loves reading. We also like to attend book launches and to meet emerging writers. Meeting personally is helpful when we are asked to advise and help programme events abroad – this happens often. We have writers travelling to Bosnia Herzegovina, Estonia, Germany, Korea, Denmark, Italy, Latvia, and Mexico this year to connect with readers in those territories. We liaise with local programmers and festival directors, and in some cases fund or co-fund travel costs and writers' fees. Sometimes, our role is purely advisory. We also support writers by funding a limited number of residencies abroad each year. We believe this is important for writers as it provides them with opportunities to seek inspiration in new contexts and to network and share ideas with their international peers. In the coming years, we have plans to expand this aspect of our work significantly.

Recently, we have taken on a new project, running a week-long annual summer translation workshop online. The idea behind this is to provide intensive training for early-career and emerging translators who wish to focus on translating Irish literature: it's crucial to help develop a new generation of experts. Our tutors are extremely accomplished and popular; in the case of the French programme, several students have returned three years in a row. Ultimately, funding permitting, we plan to run such workshops in-person. So far, we've run these in Czech, Dutch, Bulgarian, French, German, Polish, Spanish and Italian. Last year's Spanish translation workshop took place across four time zones!

Literature Ireland runs a small number of residencies in Ireland for more established translators. These residencies help recharge the translators' cultural batteries and provide opportunities to explore new voices in the Irish literary scene, to meet new writers and, in some cases, to visit the place where the work is set. Our residency run in partnership with University College Cork is a particularly successful example of this kind of work. We love spending time with visiting translators and showing them all the country has to offer. We work closely with our funders Culture Ireland and the Arts Council, and also with the Department of Foreign Affairs. In the coming years, we plan to focus especially on Central and South America, Germany, and Southeast Asia – but we welcome applications from right across the world.

OFFERING LIGHT:

THE IRISH WRITERS CENTRE

Valerie Bistany

_____

WHY WRITE?

I have always empathised with Captain Boyle in Sean O'Casey's *Juno and the Paycock*, who lamented that 'th' whole worl's in a terrible *state o' chassis*'. (When was it not so?) As if in reply, Samuel Beckett remarked, 'to find a form that accommodates the mess, that is the task of the artist now.' How sagely put!

Writers are the philosophers in our midst: the act of writing creatively is to make time to reflect on one's own values and ideas, and to explore complexity in a safe setting. In honing language to articulate stories which connect, whether they are popular or not, a writer's words give shape and meaning to our global culture. Really, it is not about what happens out there in the world, but how we respond to it, through words and stories. New ways of thinking have never been so achingly needed as they are now.

WHO WRITES?

We all do, don't we – or at least we can. But the sheer gall – or guts – to call oneself a writer is a different matter altogether. It can take some writers many long years, even post-publication, to come out publicly as a writer. Donal Ryan believes that ' … writers are ordinary people. With ordinary lives. I think the idea of the narcissistic, tortured artist, ripping up pages and drowning in bourbon has finally dissipated and been replaced by a more sobering, if less romanticised version, of what it means to be a writer… I know authors who are farmers, carpenters, social workers, married, single, unemployed, young and old. The desire to write is an equal opportunities affliction.'

This is reflected in our experience in the Irish Writers Centre: we have folks from every walk of life as members, all benefiting from the different opportunities we offer – from bursaries and residencies, to courses and programmes, from being part of a writers' group, to attending literary events – or just hanging out in our lovely Georgian building on Parnell Square, writing.

Some writers are hugely experienced – professional members and facilitators who help us to deliver our activities. Others are pure beginners; maybe they received a voucher for Christmas and are trying out a creative writing course for the first time. Most writers are somewhere in between, on the journey to perfecting their craft and career.

WHAT CAN THE IRISH WRITERS CENTRE DO FOR ME?

Wherever you might be on your writer's arc, you will be welcome at the IWC, and you will be supported and encouraged in your writing endeavours. You will become part of a literary community, a *meitheal,* if you so wish. Despite the writer in the garret cliché, we know that writers work better when they connect, share information, seek feedback, learn to edit their work, and develop resilience to rejection.

In recent years, the IWC made a particular effort to reach out to underrepresented writers; there are specific programmes (such as Foundation Programme for early career writers), bursaries, and various mentoring supports. The pandemic accelerated the launch into online provision – we were able to break out of the building and create access to every corner of the island, and indeed the world.

For professional writers, or those on the way, there are specific resources: the Meridian series is designed to help writers to become more resilient, to develop their career skills and writing craft, and to address their well-being. Evolution Programme is a totally unique bespoke development intervention for published authors over a six-month period, who are supported individually and collectively in their creative needs. The National Mentoring Programme, an all-island initiative widely supported by arts offices, offers an unparalleled opportunity for emerging writers on the cusp of publication to learn from a mentor of their choice. Our residencies are many and varied. The Novel Fair, a speed-dating opportunity between debut writers and publishers and agents, has resulted in over 30 publications. (You can read more about the impact of the Novel Fair in Jennifer McMahon's illuminating essay in this handbook, *It Begins with a Bell*.) There are also opportunities to participate internationally. One recent partnership is with Varuna, the National Writers' House in Australia, with whom the IWC ran Lamplight, an online craft development programme for a group of Irish and Australian writers, featuring Kit de Waal and Marcus Zusak.

There is not enough space here to recount the breadth of the IWC's work – but the website is a mine of information, so I would encourage you to browse! And the best part is that the developmental aspects of this work are available at low or no cost, made possible through state funding, with the Arts Council of Ireland as the IWC's primary funder. Transparency and equality of opportunity is offered by public call, and subscribing to the weekly newsletter on the website is the best way to stay in touch.

WHAT IS THE IWC'S VISION FOR WRITERS?

Artistic voice is any artist's life study. In Spanish, *dar a luz* translates as *to give to light* – a poetic construct for giving birth: the image it evokes is the crowning of a baby's head as it emerges from the mother's body. As a former leader of the IWC, this is how I see the artistic voice – it emerges from the deepest core of oneself as a fragile, ungainly entity, which needs nurturing if it is to thrive.

The vision and desire of bodies like the IWC is 'to give to light' the voice of each writer who has something to say, and to live in a world where writers prosper, esteemed for the words and ideas that illuminate our lives and further our understanding.

IT STARTS WITH A BELL

Jennifer McMahon

You thought you'd be frantic, but a welcome serenity has settled in your mind. You've been here before for the prep day, so you know the territory. The other eleven writers in the room with you, each one a fabulous emerging talent in their own right, have become dear to your heart. Like you, they've earned their seat at the table. They're wishing great success for you, and you for them. Your pitch is honed, rehearsed, tried and tested. There's nothing more you can do. Now it comes, with the polite ringing of a bell.

Your first appointment finds you, smiles, shakes your hand, and sits down across from you. She's a big deal in the publishing world. You thought she'd be intimidating, but she's nice and excited to meet you, and she wants to hear all about your novel and your writing. You've got fifteen minutes to tell her. That's a big ask, but you've practised and practised, and right here, right now, you're a Novel Fair winner, and that counts for everything. The energy is buzzing, the air is shimmering with possibilities, and you're doing just great.

I was there, where you're going to be. On February 17 2023, I was in that room, giving my all. On March 16, I received an offer of representation from Brian Langan at Storyline Literary Agency, and two days later, I accepted. I wasn't the first, though. Around ten days prior to my receiving Brian's offer, fellow Novel Fair winner Barbara Leahy signed with Ger Nichol from The Book Bureau. Our careers are just beginning, and who knows what's ahead for us?

Let's talk about how to get from where you are now to hopefully securing representation or a publishing deal at the IWC Novel Fair.

YOUR NOVEL

Art demands excellence, and you're an artist, so make it great! Seriously, that's your primary focus in the run-up to September, when submissions open. Those bits that make you cringe? Fix them. That character you're not so sure about, because she's only a second cousin to the protagonist and all she has is a walk-on part? Evaluate and cut. Kill your darlings. Take out every unnecessary word, explanation, misplaced comma. Make every sentence count. You want your manuscript to yell out to the judges that you've got talent and an amazing story to tell.

YOUR SYNOPSIS

A synopsis is a wonderful tool, and I rarely start a new novel without first writing one. Three hundred words isn't a lot in which to summarise your masterpiece, so here are some tips:

Keep in mind that a synopsis is a technical and not an artistic document. Its only purpose is to communicate the entirety of your story, including the whodunit. It's not about language or clever metaphors, so keep it simple.

Start with a one-line premise which expresses what your story is really about. Expand it into three lines, one for each act. If you're not using the three-act structure, adapt this point to suit your novel. Now expand those lines to a little more detail.

Focus on the principal characters and the core story. Forget subplots.

Make it clear what your protagonist's arc is. Who are they at the start of the novel, and what have they learned by the end? If they've learned nothing, if they've regressed or haven't changed, make that clear.

Write it long, then cut.

Rewrite and rewrite. My synopsis went through over thirty revisions. Persistence pays, believe me.

USE BETA READERS & GROUPS

If you're not a member of a writers group, find one, and workshop your opening chapters. Make use of beta readers. You'll find many good ones online at reasonable prices. Take their suggestions if you think they're valid. Accept constructive criticism. Above all, be open to possibilities.

BUDDY UP

If you know another writer who plans to submit to Novel Fair, buddy up with them. I was very fortunate to have my friend and fellow scribe Cassie Smith-Christmas, also a Novel Fair winner in 2023, to share the journey with me, start to finish. We read and re-read, critiqued and evaluated each other's work, over and over. I swear, I couldn't have done it without her.

PULL THE TRIGGER

Don't let that deadline pass you by. Submit it, and then forget about it. Get on with writing your next novel, because the results are out of your hands.

KEEP YOUR PHONE ON

If you're a winner, they'll call. I can't remember the exact date that Betty Stenson from the IWC called me, but I do know I cried. You'll probably cry too, so keep a pack of tissues next to your phone.

GIVE YOUR ALL

Between Betty's call and the opening of Novel Fair, put everything you have into your preparations. The IWC prep day will be a big help, but the work is down to you. More than ever, you need your buddy. Hone your elevator pitch. Research agents and publishers. Connect with the other winners, and do online video calls to get to know each other, and to practise together. You and your fellow winners need each other right now.

GIVE YOURSELF A HUG

I mean it. For finishing a novel. Very few people do. For submitting to Novel Fair. If you win, that deserves an extra-big hug. And remember, you're a writer, an artist, and among the elite.

So, here I am a few months on, a represented author, working on the edits for what will likely be my debut. In my case, I have three completed novels, plus a short-story collection. Sure is nice to have options, right? But you only need one, and the novel you have in front of you, the one which bears your name as the author, could be the very one which launches your stellar career.

Hey, I think I hear a bell ringing.

Could it be ringing for you?

WHAT DOES A
LITERARY AGENT DO?

Vanessa Fox O'Loughlin

Maeve Binchy famously said that that your relationship with your agent is like a marriage. This is so true – but it's a business relationship too.

An agent's job is to make money for a writer, and in doing so, make a living through earning their commission (typically 15% in home markets and 20% elsewhere). This doesn't just mean making the best and as many deals as possible – it includes helping an author to produce the best work they can, guiding them if they are unsure, and often being a mentor and sounding board.

INDUSTRY KNOWLEDGE

It's in everyone's interests that you produce the best book you can. If you're caught up in the creative process, it can be difficult to have one eye on the business side. This is your agent's job. Most writers aren't business people – this is one of the reasons agents are so important.

An agent will help you make sure your book is in the best possible shape before submission; then they will approach publishers with the work. Their skill is in knowing the industry: they know exactly who will be interested in the book, and where to send it. If several offers are on the table, they will help guide you to the right decision.

This doesn't always mean the offer with the most money – there could be other factors at play, like the size of the publisher, and where they see the book on their list. Is it going to be a lead title? Are they bringing in a fabulous marketing package? What have they done with similar books in the past?

NEGOTIATOR

Once the deal is done, an agent will advise on and negotiate the contract. This is *crucial*. All publishing contracts are boiler plate; a publisher expects you to negotiate. Your agent will advise on what rights to hold back, and which rights the publisher is likely to be able to exploit. They'll ensure your royalties are fair and your advance is the best that it can be.

Your agent will also sell subsidiary rights – audio, TV and film, foreign language – either directly or through sub agents, and this is where you will begin to make money as a writer. The work is done, the primary sale has been made, so every subsequent sale is icing on the cake.

Your agent will then look after payments. Many publishers need to be invoiced for payment, and as advances are often paid in three or four instalments (on contract signing, acceptance of edited manuscript, first publication, and paperback publication), they'll keep track of that too.

One of the most important elements of the agent role is to preserve your relationship with your editor; they are the buffer, the negotiator when things need sorting out. Perhaps you hate your cover, or your editor feels strongly that your book needs a new title but you dislike their suggestions – your agent is there to smooth the waters and bring everyone to an amicable agreement. They really can end up doing a lot for their 15% commission!

If you don't have an agent, but are offered a publishing contract of any sort, it's vital that you get advice on it before you sign (and not from the family solicitor who has nothing to compare it to). The Irish Writers Union and the Society of Authors both offer free contract advice for members – their membership payment could be the best money you ever spend.

FINDING THE RIGHT AGENT

Getting an agent isn't always a magical solution to publication – agents get rejected too, and sometimes they can't place a book no matter how much they love it. But they will keep going as long as they can, and will help their author weather those rejections as much as possible. Having someone in the industry believe in your work is incredibly valuable, and they will guide you forwards. There are many reasons books don't find a publisher, which often have nothing to do with the writing – market forces and trends aren't something anyone can control – but your agent will have the experience to explain what's happening.

If possible, send your work to several agents. You only need one to say yes – but do make sure that you connect with that one agent, that their vision for your book is the same as yours, that they 'get' you. Make sure you meet them – in person ideally, or on Zoom at the very least, and that you feel you can work with them.

It feels massively counterintuitive to turn an agent down, but if one is interested, then others will be – have confidence in yourself. If you're terrified to email your agent, or don't feel you can chat to them, you're not winning. Making sure that you have a sensible termination clause in your agent contract (3 months maximum) will protect you both.

One important point to remember is that agents work on commission, so they have to quantify every book that comes to them in terms of whether they can sell it – and if they can sell it for an amount that justifies the work that they may need to put into first the book itself, and then the sales process. You may have written a beautiful book, but if it is very niche, or suited to a smaller publisher, the economics of that book may mean that an agent can't take it on. Agents don't take on individual books, they take on authors, so if they love your writing they may ask to see the next book – but you do have to have something for them to sell for a formal relationship to begin.

There are many more writers out there than agents, so finding one is a bit like finding the perfect date. Many brilliant writers do very well unagented, but in an ideal world, your agent is your advocate, business partner, and mentor, and their role can be invaluable.

GET TO KNOW TO YOUR BOOKSELLER

Aoife Roantree

One of the best things you can do as you work towards launching a book is to get to know booksellers.

Booksellers love to talk about books, so ask how business is going, what books are selling well, or what they're reading. When it's time to approach agents or publishers, the industry knowledge you will gain from these conversations will stand to you. Tell booksellers about what you're reading (our brains are primed to gather crumbs like this from all sorts of places, you might overhear us telling another reader the next day about the same book solely based on your recommendation) and what you're writing (get us invested in the book early).

A bookseller's advice could be useful in other ways: they have years of experience in evaluating book design, format, and price, and in observing and assessing readers' responses – so listen to them.

When you're getting ready to launch your book, you might remember a particular bookseller you spoke to whose reading tastes aligned with yours: maybe you or your publisher could send them an advance copy or PDF of your book, so they can read it and hopefully recommend it to their customers. Do not underestimate the power of the hand-sell. I know of busy bookshops where classic 'staff picks' are regularly among the shop's bestsellers – books published ten, twenty, or ninety years ago, still selling hundreds of copies a year in a single shop, purely based on bookseller recommendations.

It might seem blindingly obvious, but: be nice to booksellers. They are often very busy, and many bookshops manage with minimal staffing, so try not to take up too much time if they look like they're under pressure. And don't underestimate the power of a small treat: authors, illustrators, or publishers who arrive with a packet of something sweet will be remembered fondly.

Building relationships like this is even more important when it comes to your local bookshops. If you are a regular customer and you have a good relationship, your bookseller will be much more likely to take a chance on your book. You may also want to hold a launch event – this can be a great way to sell lots of books to your friends and family, and booksellers have a wealth of experience in this area.

If your book has a traditional publisher, they will probably have a sales team or use a sales agency who will tell bookshops about your book. I don't recommend doing sales pitches direct to booksellers yourself in this situation – if everyone did this, booksellers would have no time to get anything else done. In the case of your local bookshops, you could – in the course of one of your regular visits – tell them about your book. Don't be too pushy, this is unlikely to get anyone onside.

If your book is published by a smaller independent publisher or is self-published, your contact with a bookseller may be the only way they will hear about it. Again, don't be too pushy. If the book can be supplied through a wholesaler or large distributor, the bookseller will be taking less of a risk and may be more likely to take a chance on your book. Remember that all bookshops curate their stock (there is only so much shelf space), so if they decide that your book won't work for them – perhaps because of their customer base or location – don't take this personally.

Remember that the bookseller's job is to sell your book, not to market it for you (lots of bookshops engage in marketing, and your book might be included, but you shouldn't rely on this as your only avenue). You could partner with a bookshop you love to push sales: you could tell your friends, family, and social media followers about them; you could offer signed or personalised copies exclusively from that bookshop, and so on.

Studies have shown that when a bookshop closes, some customers will simply buy and read fewer books – so it's in all our interests to support them. And of course, the benefits flow both ways – hopefully your book will be a bookseller's new favourite, and they will recommend it to their customers, selling lots of copies as a result.

So thank you in advance from the booksellers to the creators – because without great books, where would any of us be?

Children's Books

Community in
Children's Literature:

What makes an excellent children's book?

Ruth Ennis

Recently, I've been wondering how I found myself tucked away in this corner of the world: the corner of children's literature, born from a love of storytelling, inspired by those who craft it, and shaped by the need to connect to what is important to us while we're young. Children's literature is often positioned as the first form of storytelling we're exposed to; it's a vital step in the building of our humanity, particularly in Ireland where storytelling is so innately within us. I can think of nothing more important than ensuring excellence in a reader's first experience with books. It's reassuring to see this ethos shared in the children's book community in Ireland.

I'm a firm believer that the right book can change any young reader's life for the better, and I've dedicated my work to that goal. It's a path carved out by those willing and generous enough to share their enthusiasm and commitment to great children's literature with me. While I'm still learning,

I'm excited to share a few things that I consider crucial for those eager to join me and many others in this part of the world.

My journey through children's books began as an undergraduate where, for my final dissertation, I studied the representation of children in theatre. I later pursued a Master's in children's literature, with a focus on the depiction of nature in children's poetry. A common thread between these fields of interest was a sense of a child's agency, and prioritising the child's voice in stories for children. To this day, these studies influence my understanding between a good children's book and a great children's book: are the events of the story happening to your characters, or are your characters driving the story through their choices, personalities, and mistakes? It's a small but important distinction; in a young person's life they are so often left with little agency regarding where they go, what they do, who they see, and more – but how wonderful must it be for them to find comfort in books, seeing characters that reflect their lives acting in ways that are fundamentally authentic to them?

I later worked in bookselling and publishing, two experiences that taught me how a book goes from page to stage. It's a tricky thing to navigate, creating a body of work for an audience that we grow further away from every day we get older. The publishing and distribution process is paved by necessary gatekeepers who write, edit, sell, promote, and recommend books to young people, all of whom are committed to getting each book into the hands of the young reader who can appreciate it. The best advice I was ever given was this: before you write a word of your children's book, read. Read five books that were published in the last five years that are as similar as can be to the story you're writing: age group, genre, voices that you want to emulate. Only when you read what is similar to your book can you make it unique. Booksellers and librarians are your best friends in this part of your journey; they have a wealth of knowledge and resources that will help you find the books you need.

Knowing your audience is foundational to writing good children's literature. That familiar audience can stem from a young person you know: a family member, a student you teach, even a passing interaction with a child. But I think the most genuine, vulnerable, and impactful stories are written for the child you know best – the child you were. This is especially necessary for writers from marginalised communities – people of colour, the LGBTQIA+ community, the Traveller community, neurodivergent people, and more – where their stories were not as well-represented in books available to them growing up. Prioritising what moments were important to you as a young person and shaping the core of your story around their associated emotional residue is a sign of great children's literature, because that emotionality is timeless. The joy of the first time you laughed until you cried, the fury in first experiencing something unfair, the nervous excitement of trying something totally new, what did it all feel like? Capturing these lightning-in-a-bottle feelings in a story, no matter how fantastical the world around it becomes, is going to be what the reader remembers when they put the book down. That said, the one emotion you probably shouldn't prioritise is nostalgia, which tends to be context specific, relates to the author writing the story rather than the emotionality, and can lead to the reader feeling alienated compared to their contemporary experiences.

Most recently I've worked in the charitable book-sector, where I've been granted the opportunity to work with schools and to understand which types of books readers prefer. There is an overwhelming demand for more accessible reads, shorter books, illustrated works, graphic novels, and I'll always make the case for verse novels. What links these disparate forms is a tendency towards equalising visual and textual literacy. A huge factor in the appeal of these kinds of books is the boost in confidence they can offer in a young person's reading ability. A child's visual literacy may be stronger than their textual literacy, and the fact that the two can be mutually supportive is something to be celebrated. The demand for these formats is growing and I look forward to publishing trends developing to reflect that.

All I have learned comes from listening to and talking with writers, illustrators, booksellers, reviewers, librarians, publishers, and more. There's such a sense of pride and joy in the Irish children's literature community, where each member has been consistently generous in sharing their experiences to serve the goal of producing excellent books. The community can be found in a number of resources, locations, and events: Children's Books Ireland and Illustrators Ireland memberships; #ProperBook information events; specialised children's bookshops like Halfway Up the Stairs; children's literature college courses in Trinity College Dublin and Dublin City University; and the online community of children's books lovers on social media. There is something new and exciting to learn in this little corner of the world every day, and I look forward to seeing the community grow.

LEAVE IT ALL IN THE CLASSROOM:

EVENTS FOR CHILDREN IN SCHOOLS AND LIBRARIES

Sarah Webb

I'm writing this on the train. I'm on the way home from an event in a school in Malahide and I'm exhausted. This is a good sign as I know I gave it my all. To tweak a sporting term, I left it all in the classroom!

Events are an important part of many professional children's authors' lives. They are one of the ways we can encourage and support children on their reading journey. They also encourage children to be creative and to play with their own creativity. When they see a living, breathing author or illustrator in front of them, they realise that they too can be a published author or illustrator one day.

Children's author Eve McDonnell agrees: 'Something truly special happens when an author visits a school. From the child's perspective, a new pathway of possibilities opens up… They too could do this job! They too could create.'

Events are also important from a publicity and marketing perspective. Children's books do not get the same media attention as books for adults: events are a way of getting your book in front of young readers.

Many children do not get taken to book events or festivals. For some an event in their school or local library is the only time in their lives they will ever meet an author or illustrator. For this reason, I take every school and library visit very seriously indeed.

The single most important thing I can tell you is this: **A children's book event is not about you. It's about your audience.**

Think about that for a second. It takes away a lot of the pressure. If you can make children feel seen and listened to, then you will have done your job well.

In an article in the Sunday Independent Shane Hegarty says that 'the key, always, is to let children speak. To let them be involved. To make any talk as much about their ideas as it is yours.'

A book event is not a selling tool, although if you do it well and connect with your audience it might well sell books down the line. Note in Ireland there are often no book sales directly attached to many school and library events. However, you will be paid for doing these events (more on that in a moment).

I believe one of the main roles of book events for young audiences is to inspire children to read. Your book or books, yes, but also other people's books. To help create readers.

Events are also beneficial to authors. It keeps you connected with what children are thinking about, reading and watching. As well as writing, I also work in a children's bookshop and it gives me a wonderful insight into what children are actually reading. And they are still reading, which I believe is something to be cherished, nurtured and encouraged. Good book events help children engage and connect with reading. As our current Laureate na nÓg, Patricia Forde says, 'Events bring children and artists together to enjoy books as a community and to learn about expressing themselves through words and images. This is the next generation of readers, of writers and of illustrators. We have to invest in their future.'

I've seen hundreds of children's book events over the years and the ones that stand out are those where the author makes the children *feel* something, or think deeply, or hoot with laughter—where there is genuine connection and respect for the audience.

In Ireland we have some incredible storytellers who deliver outstanding events such as Eoin Colfer who always has the audience in stitches, and Marita Conlon-McKenna who is such an incredible storyteller that when she's talking to children you could hear a pin drop. Deirdre Sullivan who talks with such honesty and wisdom to teens, and Chris Haughton who is so good with toddlers and young children that I call him 'the toddler whisperer'.

Alan Nolan is one of the most experienced authors in Ireland when it comes to children's book events. He has travelled the length and breadth of Ireland, talking to thousands of children about books, imagination and wonder. 'When I was in school we never saw hide-nor-hair of an author. That's why I really love going into schools, libraries and festivals, talking about books with children now. It's so important for me to interact with my audience, to find out the kinds of things that they are into now, and to encourage them to speak up, draw, read and be creative. I find that it inspires my work.'

What all these people have in common is this – they are 100% themselves when doing events. They are honest and open and respect their audience deeply.

Here are some tips for delivering school events:

BE YOURSELF

What are your strengths? Are you funny? Sincere? Can you tell great stories? Draw live? Deliver thoughtful writing workshops? Play to your strengths. There is no need to tap dance for the children, you are not a children's entertainer (unless you like tap dancing, then go for it!).

PREPARE, PREPARE, PREPARE

You cannot do too much prep work. Create an event you are proud of. Put time and energy into it. Children are highly visual and love looking at photos and images. Most schools have whiteboards now; you can use them to show a creative powerpoint presentation with carefully selected images.

You can also use the presentation as useful visual prompts for your talk.

BEFORE YOUR EVENT

I like to talk to the teacher by email or on the phone before every event, asking them about their class and what they are interested in. I send on the first chapter of my latest book so they can read it to their class and prepare questions for me.

I send on the powerpoint so it's all set up for when I arrive – far less stressful that way!

IN THE CLASSROOM

First, I ask the children how they would like me to settle them down if needs be. A finger to my lips. Three claps. They can decide. The teacher can help you with this. I don't always need it, but with lively groups it can be useful!

I tell them exactly what is going to happen and what I expect: e.g. 'I'm going to talk to you for a little while about how I became a writer and share some photos with you of me growing up. I am happy to take questions during the talk and I'll be asking you questions. Stick your hand up if you'd like to ask something. I'd love to see your own writing and art at the end after the talk and you can ask me questions then too.'

STARTING OFF

I start off my school events by asking the children what Irish and international authors they like to read. The teachers too!

I keep the talk (I generally talk to 3rd to 6th class) to around 30 to 45 minutes and take questions throughout, plus 10 to 15 minutes at the end. I'd suggest 40 to 45 minutes for an event for younger classes and 60 minutes for the older classes.

AFTER THE EVENT

I invite the children to show me their writing and/or art-work. I spend time looking at each child's work. This gives quiet children who would like to ask me something time and space to do so.

If I come out of the classroom or library knowing the children, really knowing them—how they think, feel, what books they like and dislike—I know I've done a good job. Talking to children about my writing and my love of books is a privilege and I never take it for granted.

HOW TO BOOK A SCHOOL OR A LIBRARY VISIT

The first step is to create your own event around yourself and your books. Then you can contact your local school or library and ask them what event opportunities are open to local children's authors.

Send them a short outline or 'blurb' of your event with your biography at the end. Include your book cover and your author photograph. If you are unsure about what to say in this blurb, see below for an example, or try looking at author's websites for their event blurbs, or check out the programmes of book festivals like West Cork Literature Festival, Towers and Tales, or Dublin Book Festival who hold lots of events for children. Once you have some local experience with events you can broaden this out.

Here is an example of a short workshop blurb for one of my own events at Dalkey Book Festival:

The Weather Girls – Bringing Irish History Alive

A Creative Writing Workshop for Children with Sarah Webb

Age 9+

Join Sarah for a fun writing workshop with a history theme, based around her book, The Weather Girls which is set in Ire-

land in 1944. Children will find out about Ireland during World War 2 ('The Emergency') and the coastal Éire signs, including the Dalkey one! They will then write their own story or poem inspired by history.

FEES AND WHY IT'S IMPORTANT TO CHARGE FOR YOUR EVENTS

Children's Books Ireland recommend a rate of €300 for school visits (2 hours). You can find their Say What You Pay document outlining their recommended fees on their website.

Libraries tend to pay an average fee of around €200 per event. Check with individual libraries for details.

Traditionally published children's authors can join the Writers in Schools Scheme. Their fee is €200 per visit, plus travel expenses. More about their pay structure is available on the Poetry Ireland website.

Many authors depend on events for part of their income so it's important to price your time and experience appropriately. Doing free events undermines your colleagues. Unless it is a marketing event with your publisher, or a charity event (although I always invoice them with the value of the event I have 'donated') it's best practice to charge a fee.

Children's author Ann Murtagh says 'Events are an important source of income for me, but they are also a hugely enjoyable and a valuable means of connecting with my readers. I find them energising, insightful and crucial to my writing process.'

Good luck with your events!

PLAYING WITH POEMS:

WRITING POETRY FOR CHILDREN

Lucinda Jacob

DOES IT HAVE TO RHYME?

No, of course not! But this is the question I get asked more than anything else, from aspiring children's poets as well as children themselves. And what's not to love about rhyme? It's joyful, fun and, hand in hand with rhythm it sits with our very heartbeats. Well, badly handled rhyme is not to love, but more of that later.

SERIOUS FUN

Snot and knickers? Grisly teachers? Bouncy, funny poems full of lavatorial humour will go down well with most children, but it *is* a particular phase they go through, and children are pretty quick to sense that poetry like this can be trying too hard to charm them. It's my strong feeling that once the playful fun of poems featuring all things disgusting has been experienced, children quickly feel the condescension of writing that is trying too hard to get alongside them by saying something like, 'Nudge, nudge, let's all agree your teacher is a horror.' But, that said, write your poems according to *your* voice, sensibilities and feeling for fun!

My own inspiration comes not so much from sitting at my desk but from getting out and about, observing things and talking to people. We are blessed to be a nation of talkers, and many of my poems have come from the fabulous things random strangers have said to me. 'Do they think that mermaids are going to come and read in it?' This was a comment about the building of a new library which inspired my poem, 'In the Library Beside the Sea'. 'Marine Road—it's the road of flying grannies.' This absolute gift of a comment came from a man who caught my eye having just saved an older lady from being blown over on said road, and which became my poem 'Marine Road on a Windy Day'.

KNOW YOUR CRAFT – AND KEEP LEARNING

I enjoy using all sorts of poetic forms and structures and I find that my preliminary notes will often suggest the form a poem will take. There might be rhymes in there that I can build on, or a phrase or line that is asking to be repeated through the poem, and if it needs to be free verse there may be elements such alliteration and assonance that will strengthen the writing and create pleasing repetition and pattern in the language. So, get to know your craft. If you are using rhyme, please, please make sure your poem scans and the rhythm works! Rhyme that doesn't scan is very tricky to handle and while to do so may seem fun and child-like, if you are going to break a structure you must know that structure inside out or it may fall flat. Try every form, from cinquains and haiku to ballads, sonnets, free verse and everything in between. You may never use them but think of this practice as great exercise for your poetic muscles! There are lots of 'how to' books out there to help you. Try a few, you will like some more than others. Sign up for writing groups, workshops and master classes, even if they are for 'adult' poets. You will always gain something from them to enrich your writing. Something vital to note is that a poem that will delight a child, whether funny, serious, happy, sad or angry needs to be *for* a child and not from the point of view of an adult describing childhood.

HOW TO REACH YOUR AUDIENCE AND READERS

Public libraries can be your best friend, or at least the li-brarians and arts officers can be. Do use your library; it may sound obvious but get in there and see what is going on. Browse the shelves and borrow poetry books by poets you love and those you haven't even heard of, whether their work is intended for adults or children. Read, read, read and keep expanding those poetry muscles! Do sign up for library and arts newsletters and if you would like to work with children look out for calls for practitioners on their websites and so-cial media. I appreciate that not all writers want to facilitate creative writing but doing so can be a great opportunity to read your poetry to your intended audience, to see how it is received by them, and to encourage the next generation of poets. And by encouraging actual children to read and write poetry with you, you will be creating readers! And it's fun! I certainly find giving workshops to children one of the most invigorating things I do.

Schools often look for writers to visit their classes, but you will most likely need to be Garda vetted and do make sure you are never left alone with children. Once you are published, look into joining the Writers in School Scheme which puts school visits on a formal footing and is a wonderfully supportive organisation.

Join Children's Books Ireland! This great organisation is for anyone who has an interest in children and books. I love to hear what other children's writers are doing in any genre and years ago I volunteered to review books for their magazine, again exercising the writing muscles. Plus, it was in a queue for coffee at one of their conferences that I got chatting with a publisher who suggested I send her some of my poems and that was how I first got published.

PUBLICATION?

There is no obvious path to publication for this 'niche within a niche' that is poetry written for children. For poetry written for adults, poets usually start by submitting to poetry journals, building a body of published work and, hopefully, working towards a pamphlet and first collection. But don't let this lack of obvious route put you off. The good thing about most Irish children's publishers is that they often will look at unsolicited work. But don't just send a flurry of poems to them without checking first. Look at their publications, find out if they are interested in publishing poetry, and check if and when they are likely to look at new work, and follow their guidelines for submission. Keep an eye on their social media and websites as some will indicate that they will look at new proposals within a finite timeframe and you won't want to miss that.

Be imaginative in looking for homes for your poems. Local papers are often looking for copy with a local flavour and many produce pages aimed at children, particularly coming up to school breaks, holidays and festivals. With the right timing a short article including a poem and how you came to write it, and with a fun writing activity to go with it, could be just what a busy copy editor is looking for.

And good luck! We are a nation rightly known worldwide for the richness of our poetry written for adults. I would love to see this richness (and volume!) reflected in the poetry we write and publish for children. We need more children's poets!

WRITING FOR YOUNG PEOPLE:

NAVIGATING SOCIAL MEDIA

Lori Moriarty

I have never been able to master 'the floss'. This has more to do with my lack of coordination than a lack of will but also, and it's important to state this at the top of the article, there probably won't be a direct correlation between your ability to dance and sales of your books. That important clarification out of the way let's have a look at the best way to navigate the ever-changing social media landscape as an author of books for children or young adults.

A quick google of the subject of this piece is going to send you down a rabbit hole of online articles. They will talk about trends, hashtags, and platforms while also worshiping some deity known as SEO (Search Engine Optimisation and not a pop star like I had initially thought). With the rise of online book communities and the many articles pondering the power of Booktok, social media has become a valuable tool for authors. Largely none of these articles will address authors writing for children or young people, and certainly not authors based in Ireland writing for these audiences.

This rise in emphasis on social media for authors coincides with a growing awareness that the Irish children's top ten best-seller list rarely features any books by Irish or Ireland-based authors or illustrators. Campaigns such as Sarah Webb's *Discover Irish Kids Books*, organisations such as Children's Books Ireland and offices such as the Laureate na nÓg have started harnessing the potential of social media to spread awareness of the incredible authors and illustrators living here. The popularity of events such as Patricia Forde's *Whole Wild World* tour online, especially on Instagram, show us the broad appeal of this content and also provide an online foundation upon which authors can build their presence. As Ruth Ennis notes in her piece on children's literature in this handbook, there is a whole community of book lovers online and it really is time for children's authors to take up some of the space.

PLOTTING

Whether you're a plotter or 'pantser' when it comes to your books, for social media you do need to sit down and have a scroll (helpful here to set a timer on your watch so you don't accidentally lose a day to cat videos). Find what style interests you and approach your social media plan with intention. Look at other authors, maybe find someone writing in a similar area as you and gather some ideas. A guide to the tone or format favoured by the various social media platforms is easily found elsewhere and is obvious from a quick scroll. The first question to ask yourself is what do you hope to get out of this? Are you going to use social media for marketing, growing a community, networking or charting your writing process? You can want it to be all these things but do be clear about your aims because the key to social media as an author (established, novice or other) is to do what suits you best and to approach it deliberately. Decide on your target audience and speak to them. This, of course, bears a good bit of thought. You'll be targeting a broad spectrum of people; parents, carers, teachers, librarians, booksellers, publishers, agents but should always bear in mind the original intended audience of your books and your brand as a children's author.

BOUNDARIES

Set your boundaries: remember, your time is valuable and posting or creating videos takes time so set yourself a realistic schedule. Have a look at time saving tools such as Hootsuite which allow you to publish and schedule content across social media platforms. Also set boundaries on what you intend to feature; privacy concerns have never been more valid. You can still create engaging videos and posts without showing your face, your home, or your family. You can also limit the ways in which people interact with you online. You can turn off your comment section, or prevent people from 'stitching' or 'dueting' your video content on platforms such as TikTok. This highlights the importance of playing around and getting familiar with the settings and features of these platforms. Also set yourself some hard rules: that video idea you think was amazing at 2am can wait for the morning and a clear head.

INTERACTIONS

Remember that social media is a conversation, the content you make will not exist in a vacuum— being an author, you might be better suited than most for this. That said, people can be a lot braver online than they might be in real life. Everybody's approach is different when faced with sometimes tricky situations, perhaps unwelcome engagement which can range from mild to hostile—but the block and delete buttons were invented for a reason: don't hesitate to use them. The flip side of this is that authors need to respect reader's spaces. People online are entitled to talk about your book and what they thought of it. It's more important than ever to know when not to engage and to allow readers their say.

HAVE FUN

Not to sound too much like an anxious mammy dropping off her child at their first summer camp, but do remember to have fun. As an author of books for children and young people, you'll know that fun is infectious. Don't be afraid to throw on a silly filter and embrace 'the cringe' as the kids say. With influencer culture infiltrating society in so many different ways, it's easy to get caught up in follower counts, engagement statistics and the almost Arthurian quest of going viral but your mental health will not thank you and you will lose sight of the many advantages of using social media. Social media is a useful tool, it should not dominate your life or creative practice as an author. At its best though, it can open you up to opportunities, connections and community. So start small, be deliberate, be comfortable and build up.

MARRIAGE OF TRUE MINDS:

GETTING A CHILDREN'S BOOK PUBLISHED

Siobhán Parkinson

G etting published is not a competition that sep-arates fabulous writers from mediocre ones: it's a slow, meticulous process whereby manuscripts get turned into books – which hopefully enough people will buy to cover the costs of publication. Not a fun thought, but that's the truth.

Here's a more romantic idea: getting published is a bit like getting married – to make a success of it, you need to find the best possible publisher for your work, one whose list you admire and where your book will be at home. There needs to be a lot of trust in a publishing relationship, and the court-ship may be long and arduous. So, let's go dating.

CHOOSING A PUBLISHER

Not many Irish publishers publish for children, but the ones that do usually accept unsolicited manuscripts – though only from time to time. Watch their websites or social media, and pounce when they say they are open to submissions. If you submit out of turn, you are likely to be ignored. UK publishers usually accept submissions from agents only, which is a whole other ball-game.

Do your research, and don't send an adult book to a children's editor, or vice versa. (It happens.) A company that has published a single sci-fi book, let's say, may or may not want another. Don't guess: read their submission guidelines – and if in doubt, ask.

There is no rule that says you must only send your manuscript to one publisher, but if you are submitting simultaneously to more than one, it is polite to say so.

SUBMITTING YOUR WORK

Your first reader outside your own circle is going to be a harried editor, who has hundreds of submissions to read; most of these they will reject, because they can only publish a handful of books a year – and most of those will be by authors they already publish, or books they have commissioned. If your book is going to be among what amounts to a fraction of a handful, you'll need to engage that harried editor, and fast. They won't read beyond a few pages if they are not absolutely fascinated. So fascinate them. Don't submit your book until you have polished it to within an inch of its (your) life and it absolutely sparkles. The editor can't take the time to read a rough draft.

The biggest barrier between you and your prospective publisher is the limited time the editor has to spend on each submission, so when you interact make everything as easy as possible for them, and follow the submission guidelines.

Some publishers prefer to receive three chapters of a manuscript – not your favourite ones, the *first* three, so the editor can see how you draw your reader in from page one. If you like, and the publisher has expressed no preference, you can send the whole lot, just in case the editor is totally hooked. (Yay!)

Most publishers also like to see a succinct but complete synopsis (not necessary for picturebooks). Don't worry about spoilers. The editor needs to know what happens, so tell them.

Send a *short* covering letter/email. Keep this letter crisp and stick with information the editor needs and can't know unless you tell them. We take it as read that you are an avid reader and have always wanted to be a writer and that your (grand)children absolutely love your book. What you *can* mention is your extensive experience in schools or how you love working with kids and giving writing workshops.

It's useful to give a rough indication of the target age group: young children, 'middle grade' (8-12), teens (12+), YA (15+). Children always want to read 'up', so if your protagonist is 12, you should be writing for 10-year-olds.

A word on picturebooks. It might look easy, but it is *extremely* difficult to write a picturebook, and even more difficult to get one published. Think in terms of fourteen double-page spreads, and keep the text very short. Do not submit artwork, unless you yourself are the illustrator, as publishers prefer to source their own illustrations.

WHAT TO EXPECT

You are unlikely to hear within a few weeks. That's because the editor is unreasonably busy with other people's submissions; also, they may ask colleagues or an external reader for a second opinion, and that takes time. Give it three months before you prod the editor.

If your book is accepted, or if the editor is seriously considering accepting it, you will probably get extensive feedback to help you with revising the text. Very occasionally, if the editor really likes a book but can't offer to publish it for reasons of their own, they may pass on some helpful comments. But in general a rejection will consist of only a line or two: I know, this seems mean, but the editor needs to spend most of their time on the books they *are* publishing. If you would like advice on your work, a creative writing class may be your best option.

If your book is accepted, you will get a contract, and once signed, an advance (typically quite modest, when it comes to independent Irish publishers) against expected royalties. Contracts are generally pretty standard and, in the case of reputable publishers, they are usually fair. But do take advice. A contract is a legal document and signing one brings obligations as well as benefits.

IF YOU DON'T GET PUBLISHED

The sad fact is that there are more writers than published authors. Which means that, pending publication, the most important thing when you sit down to write is that you write what you like and you enjoy the process. Bonus: that will show in your work.

INSIGHTS INTO PICTURE BOOKS
AND CHAPTER BOOKS

Patricia Forde

For me, the easiest part of the whole writing process is the initial idea – but one thing I have learned about ideas is that they don't automatically develop into a book.

Picture books are like poems: they are short and intense. For a strong picture book you need an idea that will withstand being read and re-read. It needs to read well *aloud,* as most of the audience depend on an adult to read the book to them. Therefore, every word counts – the sound of the word, the meaning of the word, the emotional pull of the word. As with every rule, there are exceptions, but in general the story needs to be told in five hundred words or fewer.

Writing picture books requires a lot of patience, and for me, the attrition rate is high. For every twenty or so ideas I come up with, only one might become a published picture book. The market is fiercely competitive and the cost of producing the books is high; therefore, publishers are cautious.

Despite the challenges, I love working in this area, especially as I get to collaborate with illustrators – something which brings a whole other dimension to the process. Nothing beats the thrill of seeing your words brought to life by a gifted artist.

Writing chapter books for older children is a totally different experience. Firstly, it's a huge commitment. When I start a chapter book, I know that it will take me a year or maybe two to complete. My head will be colonised by that one idea, those characters, that setting, and I won't rest until the book is finished. So, I need to love it.

Writing a novel is a marathon and, like running, is best trained for every day. I aim to write 1,000 words a day, but there are days when I have other commitments and don't write anything at all. There are days when I am totally in the zone and might write 3,000 words. It is relentless, but I tell myself that each word counts. I keep a chart showing what I've done and what I have still to do. I tell myself to get to the finish line, and then I can fix everything.

In reality, I edit as I go. I'm not a great planner, so I'm usually making it up as I go along. That involves a lot of rewriting as I meander down byroads and dead ends, doubling back to the path and trying a different direction.

Finally, when I've done the best I can, I send the manuscript to my agent to hear her thoughts. This always involves more rewriting, more difficult questions to answer, more time at my desk. It then goes to the editor and the whole process starts again.

I enjoy writing both forms; writing a picture book can be a respite from the exertion of writing a novel – but equally sometimes I yearn for the space to really develop an idea, unrestrained by a 500 word yoke.

One thing I am certain of, neither form gets written unless I show up! So I try to be at my desk most days, or scribbling in my notebook anywhere I find myself.

Illustration by Elina Braslina from *Bumpfizzle* (Little Island), by Patricia Forde. Reproduced by kind permission of the illustrator.

INSIGHTS INTO ILLUSTRATION

Paddy Donnelly

WHAT BROUGHT YOU TO ILLUSTRATION?

My background is actually in web and graphic design. I never studied art or illustration at all. I worked for years as a web designer, and then transitioned into designing mobile apps. I created a few iPhone and iPad apps for kids, which I really enjoyed. That mix of illustration and design, and the fact that each project was quite different really appealed to me. That's what spurred me into the world of picture books, and I'm loving it!

WHAT IS THE MOST MISUNDERSTOOD THING ABOUT AN ILLUSTRATOR'S ROLE?

A lot of people think that an illustrator's job is really easy to do and that it's just fun all the time. Don't get me wrong, it's a TONNE of fun being an illustrator, but it's also a lot of work. There are deadlines, there are frustrations, just like in any job. Bringing that creativity to a book each time, establishing a strong look and feel, discovering the characters and creating all of the detailed illustrations does take a lot of effort. But holding that finished book in your hands is worth it.

WHAT GIVES YOU A BUZZ ABOUT YOUR WORK?

Sharing my books with children and hearing from them that they liked it. Listening to them telling me that they spotted something hidden in an illustration, or hearing what they think happens to the characters after the story ends. That feedback and interaction really is the best reward.

HOW DO YOU APPROACH ILLUSTRATING SOMEONE ELSE'S STORY, AS OPPOSED TO YOUR OWN?

When I'm illustrating another author's text, that story has already gone through rewrite after rewrite – it's already quite finalised. So I don't really want to change anything in the text; my illustrations are 'phase two' of the process. Together with the art director we make an effort to blend both parts together seamlessly.

When I'm working on a story I've written myself, then I can be a lot more ruthless when it comes to chopping and changing words to fit with the illustrations, and vice versa. For one of my own books, like *The Vanishing Lake*, it's a very back and forth process, pruning text and illustration together up until the last moment.

WHAT DO YOU KEEP IN MIND WHEN ILLUSTRATING FOR CHILDREN?

When illustrating for children, I try to include lots of animals and little background elements in the illustrations that children can pore over on their second, third, and tenth reading of the book. But the thing about creating picture books is that they are for both adults and children. Usually a parent is reading it to a child, so you're creating something for that special moment between both adult and child. There always has to be something in the illustrations and text for the adults too.

WHAT'S BEEN THE MOST CHALLENGING PART OF BEING AN ILLUSTRATOR?

Definitely getting your foot in the door is tough. It's a very competitive industry to work in; however once you've made a connection with a publisher and they know you can deliver the work, they're much more likely to return to you for a second project.

So in the beginning you're creating a lot of artwork for your portfolio, sending it out there, showing it off to publishers and sometimes not hearing much back. That can be disheartening, but eventually with enough persistence you start to make little dents into the industry and eventually the projects get better and better, as does your work.

WHAT ADVICE WOULD YOU GIVE TO SOMEONE WHO IS CONSIDERING BECOMING AN ILLUSTRATOR?

You need to keep drawing, drawing, drawing. There aren't any real shortcuts. It's so vital to keep up the practice and eventually things will fall into place if you stay committed. Creating children's books really is a dream job, but there is so much work that goes into it that nobody sees. If it really is your dream to become an illustrator, you need to dedicate so much time and effort into it. As well as writing a lot, you need to read, read, read. Read lots of picture books and figure out what works especially well in them. Take notes on how the book is structured, how the story grabs you, what details the illustrator has woven into the artwork. It's important to get really familiar with the picture book world before you can start creating your own stories.

KNOWING YOUR WHY, WHAT AND HOW:

LESSONS FOR THE ASPIRING CHILDREN'S BOOK ILLUSTRATOR

Ashwin Chacko

The children's book industry can seem like a daunting place to break into – here, I hope to share with you some lessons that might encourage you on your journey.

THINK LIKE A BUSINESS

I think as creators we often approach publishing as a means to an end, and we forget that first and foremost publishing is a business – so we need to start thinking like them. Put yourself in their shoes and consider what you might do if you were in charge.

I've found with publishing it's all about perceived value – because in truth it's an investment game: instead of stocks, publishers are betting on which authors or illustrators have the potential to bring a good profit. Sure, that is not their only objective, but it is a big part of it. They want to ensure that they're not taking too high a risk.

If I were to restart today I would ask myself: what can I do to present as a lower-risk option with high potential? Here are some steps I would take.

CLARIFY YOUR PATH

In all creative industries there are many possible roles you could play – and this is no different in the world of children's publishing. Homing in on your area of focus – whether this is children's picture books, chapter books, or exclusively covers – is an important step. I think it's essential to have a vision of where you want to go: knowing your *why* and *what* will help you map out your *how*.

JUST START

Knowing your *why* and *what* is not enough, you must now work on your *how*. We often get caught up in dreaming and never end up doing anything to manifest it; I have been guilty of this. If we want to succeed in our chosen path we need to stop waiting for opportunities and just start.

What could this look like? If you've never created or illustrated a picture book before, start by creating one. You don't have to write your own – pick a classic and reinterpret it. What would your take be on *Little Red Riding Hood* or *Little Miss Muffet*? You have to be able to draw a character consistently from many different angles. Hone your craft, develop systems, and understand what it's like to meet a deadline.

Creating a dummy book or even a self-published book

is a great way to show your ability to meet deadlines and complete a project. It will also offer an insight into what it takes to put a book into the world. In truth, I've found the making of the book the easiest part; the marketing and distribution can be tedious and challenging.

PRO TIP: Books are formatted in multiples of four pages: with board books it's usually 12 spreads or 24 pages, and with picture books it's usually 16 spreads or 32 pages.

KNOW YOUR AUDIENCE AND BUILD YOUR OWN

It's very hard to sell water to a fish, while someone in a desert might give everything for a drink. Your work isn't for everyone – because the simple fact is value is relative. When developing your approach to picture books it's important to know which area you want to focus on. Who is your key audience and what can you do to communicate with them? This could mean a variation in style, colour choice, and method of storytelling. Below are some key audience types to consider:

- Board Books (Infant to 3 years)
- Picture Books (3 to 6 years)
- Early Reader (6 to 10 years)
- Middle Grade (8 to 12 years)
- Young Adults (12 years and older)

Today more than ever we live in a world where we have direct access to our audience through social media – a powerful tool which can bypass the gatekeepers of the past. When you grow an audience around your work, you build social clout, or social currency. The larger your clout, the more negotiation power you will have.

PORTFOLIO

Your portfolio is an essential part of the illustrator's arsenal. Your portfolio is usually the second point of contact after your social media account. Outside of your craft, this is your next big investment. Here are five rules for your portfolio:

1. BANG FOR BUCK

You only have a couple of seconds to grab someone's attention so show them your best work first.

2. WHO ARE YOU?

Let me ask you this: when you have two products that for all intents and purposes are the same quality, how do you decide which to get? It comes down to personality and taste – your portfolio should give me a sense of who you are. People buy from someone they know, like, and trust. What can you do to give them that gut feeling?

3. QUALITY OVER QUANTITY

Your portfolio is only as good as your weakest piece.

4. WHAT YOU SHOW, YOU GET

Curate your portfolio for the work you want to get – not the work you have. Or inevitably you will be hired for the work in your portfolio. For instance, if you don't like creating covers don't put covers in your portfolio, or you will be hired to create more covers. It doesn't have to be a real project or a real client – what the publisher or agent wants to see is your ability to draw a character consistently and tell a visual story.

5. CONSISTENCY IS KEY

Your work should show a consistent style and have a consistent quality. The more constant you are with results, the better able you are to position yourself in the market as low-risk and charge a premium rate.

PRO TIP: Invest in a domain name and hire or develop a professional-looking website. There are lots of options out there; do your research and choose what works for you. In Ireland, there are grants available from your Local Enterprise Office specifically for small businesses and freelancers to develop their online presence.

COMMUNITY

Publishing is a team sport. Being a part of and contributing to the children's literature world is integral to a thriving career. Community plays a vital role in our ability to grow, and gives you access to experience and knowledge. I've found that the publishing world is smaller than you think – and it's not what you know but who you know that could make the difference in the opportunities that come your way. When you make yourself available and show your genuine enthusiasm for the industry, people notice, and word gets around. Your work alone won't speak for you – it's the people in the community who will champion you.

I want to leave you with this quote from the movie *Field of Dreams* as I think it encapsulates the creator's journey perfectly: 'If you build it, they will come.'

This Writing Life

ON BEING PUBLISHED:

NOTES ON THE DEBUT EXPERIENCE

Olivia Fitzsimons

———————————————

Publishing a debut is hard; even when you have a brilliant experience, it costs something. It can make you feel lonely, because it's full of less than straightforward expectations: those you might put on yourself; what your agent wants for your book; your publisher's vision. So many factors that contribute to a book's success are beyond your control – here are some practical things that might help you survive the process. All or some or none of this advice might resonate. Use what works and ignore the rest.

Cherish your friends and family – the ones who knew you before the book came out, and who still love you whether your debut is a bestseller, gets reviewed or doesn't. They will listen, laugh and console you when you bore them senseless about your author highs and lows – and then tell you about their cat, aunt Margaret at the wedding or their horrible boss. They won't mind if they haven't seen you for months while you edited the book. They will buy copies and are your best resource.

Have some way of getting out of your own head. Writing – even not writing – takes up a lot of mental space, so it's great to run around a football pitch, swim or hike – or whatever works for you – and even better to do it with the friends mentioned above. I'm starting to realise you need to be fit to sit at the desk, and writing about running won't do it (believe me I've tried). This is especially helpful right after paperback publication when everyone is asking what the second book is about, and when it's coming out.

Like voice, your publishing journey is unique and, while on paper your debut might resemble other writers in the same imprint, with the same agent and editor, every writer will have different experiences: comparison is the thief of joy. You are now part of a creative industry, which includes the business side of things; most of this – marketing budget, reviews, events, and so on – is completely out of your control. Be happy for peers doing well, but focus on your own experience and try to enjoy it.

It can be difficult to write after your book comes out. You're busy with the launch, press, events, readings, and book signings. The intensity of public interaction can be overwhelming for people who like to sit in a room and write. It can be great fun and *still* become overwhelming. The opposite is also true: some debut authors find that they have very little attention. The effect of this – a feeling of lack, or something not playing out like you imagined – can be paralysing in a completely different way. The change from unpublished to published overnight should not be underestimated. It takes time to adjust. It might be several months or more until you get back to the page – but it will happen eventually. It might feel like you've forgotten how to write, but each book is different, *you* are different – and you are now a more accomplished writer: embrace it.

Remember this book is only your debut. Think about your writing career in the long term. Almost all writers have another job, or are otherwise financially supported. Unless you are one of the few writers who survives on advances alone, writing is not the way to make money. Be understanding of your peers; while everything might look rosy on social media, it doesn't mean there aren't problems and difficult life circumstances behind the glossy, happy images associated with publication.

When press and events die down after publication, you might experience a low. So many writers feel this way – it's natural after all the excitement. You might have had long-held expectations about how your debut experience would go; some parts might have exceeded your wildest dreams but others might have left you feeling flat. Talk to other writers you trust. You are not alone.

All writers get rejected, it's part of the job – and having a book out doesn't change that – so if it works for you, set goals, big and small. Keep submitting to the journal you'd like to appear in. Build a skill set in essays. Find out how to write better applications. Apply for the residency. There will be so many unexpected experiences that are going to happen, like befriending other writers along the way who will become your comrades and champions, or meeting your literary heroes. There are future collaborations and opportunities that you can't imagine in this moment which are on the horizon. This is what being published brings – welcome it.

TIPS

Publishing seems to have two speeds: slow-not-happening-at-all or breakneck-writing-emergency. Find your own pace and remember it takes as long as it takes (best advice stolen from Tom Morris).

Writing a book is the very least of what some authors are expected to do. Choose wisely where you spend your energy, and seek advice from other writers.

A simple author website with a mini press-pack (bio, headshots, event listings, press release and contact details) can be a great investment.

Check out Match In The Dark, Words Ireland, and The Irish Writers Centre for recommendations on what fees to expect for festival appearances, workshops and so on.

If things aren't working, speak up. If you are unsure of something check with your agent or editor; if you don't have an agent, bring a friend to meetings if you can – it really helps if you get tongue-tied. Make lists of questions for when you speak to marketing and publicity professionals. Publishers sometimes forget that authors have no experience of the industry and don't understand the terminology. You need to inform yourself or make sure someone is advocating for you. The Society of Authors are a brilliant resource with sympathetic and objective staff who can advise on tricky problems.

Ask about author aftercare. Don't sign with a publisher who isn't committed to this. Kids? Caring responsibilities? Mental-health needs? Whatever it is, let people know how each of these might affect your publishing journey. Burnout is very real. Check out Minding Creative Minds for free help and advice.

Tell your local Arts Office, Council, Library Service, Arts Centre and regional festivals about your debut. Ditto Literature Ireland, embassies, EFACIS. Ask your publisher to send them a proof.

Sign up for ACLS and PLR.

Organise headshots well in advance.

Don't agree to do anything that you are uncomfortable with just to sell a few books. If there is a subject that you don't want to discuss – don't. Media training should be mandatory but isn't; if you need support, ask.

Sketch out some essay ideas about themes in your work in advance, and start writing these if you have a publication in mind (a great tip from Jan Carson). Some authors won't have worked on essays since school or college and there is an often unspoken expectation to have journalistic writing skills. Take a course or ask your editor/agent for help.

If your book launch isn't on the same day as your publication date, mark it somehow (thanks to Sarah Webb for this glorious advice). Have coffee with a friend, arrange a dinner, eat cake, take your book out for a pint, but do something to celebrate your achievement.

Send thank you cards.

Read widely. Poetry helps.

Be yourself.

TOP TEN TIPS FOR
SURVIVING AS A WRITER

Jan Carson

PUT YOUR OWN WRITING FIRST

Give the best of yourself to your words. Spend some time thinking about the conditions which have facilitated your best writing sessions and do your best to replicate these conditions as often as possible. Think about where, when and how you write. It's a physical act as much as a cerebral one. Don't be afraid to schedule writing sessions in your diary and take these as seriously as other appointments. It's ok to say no to things which will distract you from your writing.

TAKE YOUR WORK SERIOUSLY

There's a difference between developing an enormous ego and understanding the value of what you do. Don't talk yourself down. Don't accept jobs or commissions which don't resonate with your own creative goals. Don't take on unpaid work. The Match in the Dark guidelines are extremely helpful for outlining what writers should be paid. Politely turning down unpaid work helps to create better working conditions for other writers, shows that you value your time and frees you up for other more beneficial projects.

KNOW WHAT YOU WANT FROM YOUR WRITING

It's good to think about why you're writing. What do you want to achieve from your writing? This could be a tangible goal, like publishing a book or acquiring an agent. It might be something more difficult to define such as finding a healthy outlet for expressing your feelings. Setting goals helps you to realise what you've achieved and how you're progressing. It'll also help you to keep motivated. I'd recommend regularly reassessing your writing goals as your career progresses. Keep a record of all these achievements. They'll form the basis of your History of Artistic Practice which you'll need when applying for funding applications.

DON'T COMPARE YOURSELF TO OTHER WRITERS

You're the only person who can write the story/poem/novel you're writing. It's good to remember you have a unique voice when you're tempted to compare yourself to others or find yourself jealous of their successes. Comparison frequently leads to frustration and substandard, derivative work. It's better to channel the energy into developing your own distinctive writing and working out what interests you creatively.

KEEP THE ADMIN IN ITS PLACE

There's an enormous amount of admin associated with freelance writing practice. It can quickly take over your creative space. I suggest allocating slots of time for working on invoices, finances, press etc. I usually set aside two hours in the afternoon and a day a month to keep track of receipts, invoices and tax requirements. Keep good records. Put systems in place early on. Spreadsheets are a great way to keep all the relevant information under control and to hand.

READ LIKE YOUR LIFE DEPENDS UPON IT

If you're not feeding your creative curiosity you'll soon run out of ideas. Try to allocate at least as much time to reading as writing. Read instinctively, don't get swayed by the trendy books. Read with a pen in hand, taking note of what other writers are doing with words. Read to target weaknesses in your writing practice, focusing in on writers who excel in areas where you're struggling. Read in community. Find other writers who want to have robust conversations about the books they're reading. Always be ready to learn.

INVEST IN COMMUNITY

We're lucky to have a strong writing community here in Ireland. If you want to make the most of the support, encouragement and practical advice that's out there, make sure you're contributing to the community. Attend other writers' readings, buy their books, mentor, encourage, offer helpful critique. In short, model the kind of support you'd like to receive and you'll get the most out of community.

USE SOCIAL MEDIA, DON'T LET IT USE YOU

Social media can be a great asset when it comes to promoting your work and making contacts. However, it can also take up a lot of time and expose you to some really negative forces. Set your boundaries early on. Only do what you feel comfortable with, sharing as little or as much as feels useful. Protect yourself by keeping your personal contact details private. Don't get drawn into online squabbles. Social media's rarely the place for a nuanced conversation about a complex topic. Personally, I rarely post anything which isn't positive as it's not the ideal platform for critique or debate.

WORK WITH GOOD PEOPLE

Surround yourself with a team of people who you trust and respect and who have your best interests at heart. Don't sign with the first agent or publisher who expresses an interest. Do some research. Talk to other writers they represent. Ask difficult questions about their plans and hopes for your career. Remember agents and publishers are making money from you. If you feel they're not representing you correctly, it's ok to hold them to account and ask difficult questions. Publishers and agents are great but they're not your friends. Keep the working relationship professional. Remember that no one will work as hard for your writing as you will. Have realistic expectations. Acquiring an agent won't take all the pressure off you but it definitely should help a little.

ENJOY EVERY STEP ALONG THE ROAD

Sometimes writers can be too future focused. Celebrate every little milestone along the road. Your first published piece of work. Your first live reading. Your first shortlisting. You'll never get these experiences back so make sure you don't miss the opportunity to enjoy them. Relish the freedom of early career writing. No one has any expectations of your writing. You can experiment with language, grow into your voice and take as long as you like to finish your book without a publisher breathing down your neck. This is the freest you'll ever be as a writer. Savour it. Remember that whatever issues a career in writing throws at you, you still have words. The actual writing's the very best part of being a writer and no one can take this from you.

To be Unburdened:

WRITING FOR WELL-BEING

Daragh Fleming

E ach day I return here. It's not pressure or a mandatory word count that drags me to the chair; I'm hardly ever here to work on the project I ought to be chipping away at. No, I come here each day, armed with a mug of tea and something to get off of my chest, because this is how I cope. This is how I manage. Each word that lands upon the page reduces any weight I find myself carrying. This is why I come: to be unburdened.

Writing is a solitary undertaking: so many hours are spent alone trying to think, comprehend, and understand. The road inward can be a frightening one. Yet writers are drawn to it, fixated on what we might uncover, addicted to the sensation of articulating a feeling. In some ways, there's a yearning for this; we want to uncover pain because it might lead to some beautiful, universal realisation. Paradoxically, the thing that can harm us – this aloneness – is also what brings us peace.

And so it makes sense that we writers, more so than anyone else, should use this skill set, this calling, to fortify our well-being, to ensure that we are not slipping too far into our own minds without a way back out.

Writing about how we feel can allow us to process our experience in ways that contemplation alone cannot. When we write out the words, we naturally become more honest. We're objective and direct when we write, because anything less than this feels superficial. Whereas our thoughts can feel like a swirling wind, our minds circling a truth they may never touch upon, writing feels more like rain – certain and grounding – gravity doing most of the heavy lifting, forcing us to see things our thoughts have obscured.

Whenever I find time to sit and write about my experiences, and about the emotions that come with them, I feel lighter. But it's more than that, too. Writing about such subjects allows us to uncover self-knowledge. Since writing *Lonely Boy*, I've told people that writing that book was worthwhile whether it was published or not – because it allowed me to get to know myself on a deeper level, to understand my flaws, and to accept myself in spite of them. The relationship I have with myself now is far better for having written about these difficult and complex things.

In this sense, writing about our pain can help to alleviate it. When we write, we let go. We accept. We understand. And in the end, we come out the other end more whole.

On a more practical note, there are ways we writers can (and should) look after our well-being. Doing these simple tasks can give us a baseline of wellness, but they can also enhance our writing, both our ability and the quality of the work.

DEVELOP A MENTAL HEALTH ROUTINE

A mental health routine is a simple checklist of things we know enhance our well-being. Getting enough sleep, exercising, staying hydrated, seeing friends. Whatever you know will make your day a little brighter, put it on the list and try to make time for it every day. Consistency, just like in writing, is key here.

WRITE THE EMOTIONS

Whatever your genre, when the emotions are running high write them down. This may lead to an idea emerging, but more importantly, it'll allow you to get something off your chest in a meaningful and personal way. My best poetry has come from doing this, because the writing is raw and unrestricted.

LIVE YOUR LIFE

If you're anything like me, you feel guilty any time you're not working. This productivity guilt can lead to writer's block and make the work feel like more of a chore than something you enjoy. Remember that while we are writers, we're also people with complicated and wonderful lives to live. Don't beat yourself up for stepping away from the work. In fact, the work will more than likely benefit from you leading a full and adventurous life.

ANTICIPATE REJECTION

Ah, rejection. The constant in a writer's life that no one talks about. Rejection can be painful, and it can feel personal. We have to remember that it's par for the course. All writers experience rejection far more than acceptance. This is the way it goes, and being aware of this makes the rejection more palatable.

BE SOUND TO YOURSELF

No one will be as harsh on you as you. We're a sensitive bunch, and we often beat ourselves up when things don't go our way. The fact that you're writing and putting yourself out there is a feat in itself. Be sound to yourself and try not to take yourself too seriously. To paraphrase an Oscar Wilde line, life is far too important to be taken seriously. Remembering this can go a long way.

ALWAYS ON MY MIND:

YOUR RELATIONSHIP WITH WRITING

Anne Tannam

O ne of the exercises I sometimes do with writers is to ask them, without overthinking it, what song represents their relationship with their writing life. The answers are often poignant (*Home Again*), sometimes hilarious (*Pump up the Volume*), and nearly always on the button (Joni Mitchell's *River*). A writing life is, to quote Walt Whitman, a song of myself.

I didn't start humming my song until I turned forty. Up to then, I didn't believe I had anything worthwhile to say. Peel back the layers of that statement, and underneath lies the simple truth: I didn't believe in myself and hardly knew who I was. Like many, I'd been too busy in the nitty gritty of living to draw breath and ask myself what I wanted beyond the many roles I juggled. When I finally did slow down, the quiet answer came. I wanted to meet myself, to reclaim the parts I'd left behind.

Committing to a writing life was one way of demonstrating how serious I was about reclaiming this intimacy with myself. Unlike other activities in my life, writing was just for me and in the beginning anyway, of no obvious use to anyone else. The time I committed to writing was less time for family, work and friends. Hard to justify until I realised that writing filled me up, so when I returned from it, I was more fully present. Seventeen years later and counting, it's the number one reason why I continue to write (sometimes more sporadically than I'll admit to!).

- What is your writing *why*, the *why* that depends on no one else's opinion or go ahead? It might be 'to set the darkness echoing', capture an alternative universe lodged inside your brain or for the sweet pleasure of playing with language. Take the time to discover your unique *why* (write yourself slowly into the answer), and whatever it is, that's your North Star, guiding and sustaining you through the dry or fallow periods.

Turning up on Valentine's Day with a shitload of gifts, hoping that might make up for a year of unanswered texts and no-shows. Sometimes, that's what we do; apart from the occasional workshop or writers retreat, we ignore or push aside our deep desire to write, feel guilty about it, making it even less likely that we'll turn up to the page any day soon. Why? Because when we think about writing, the first thought is negative and our binary brains are programmed to avoid the negative (perceived as a threat) and seek the positive (perceived as a reward). So, we avoid thinking about writing and feel more guilty, and the negative loop continues.

Here are some tips or strategies that may help us get out of the negative loop, and create a positive one instead:

- What small action feels possible? Whatever that action is, no matter how tiny or inconsequential it may seem, commit fully to doing it (it could be to look over what you wrote last month, complete ten minutes of research, write 100 words, find that missing folder on your computer, or have a nap if you know that exhaustion is feeding into the negative feelings). Then when you've done that and have the reward of having accomplished something, you repeat the question and commit again to whatever action feels possible. You are building a new habit with what the sociologist Christine Carter calls 'wildly unambitious goals'.

- Having identified your why, make writing the priority that other activities accommodate rather than the other way around. Trust your circadian rhythm and when you're creatively at your best. Then, fight tooth and nail with everyone, including yourself, to claim time for the writing, just like you would make sure you had time for those you love most.

- Many of us believe we don't have time to write. For some people, that's actually true. For the rest of us, it's a belief rather than a fact. If you believe you don't have any time to write, track your activities over a week. Note, without judgement, what you're spending time on. If there is an hour or two or ten that you're spending on any activity you have control over that isn't adding satisfaction or value to your life, swoop in and claim it for your writing. My time wasters include scrolling, surfing and people-pleasing, to name a few!

Most days and weeks, I fall short of being a great partner, but I've put a ring on it and there's no going back to the single life. Yes, there's risk involved and the possibility of heartbreak when the world rejects the work, but it's worth it for those revelatory moments of intimacy and connection that every writing life offers.

The Ghost in the Machine

Chandrika Narayanan-Mohan

I arrived in Ireland in 2012 after leaving the UK due to restrictive immigration policies. I had studied Art History and English Literature, and worked mostly in sales and business development for the fine arts in London. In Ireland I completed an MA in Arts Management and Cultural Policy, and began working in fundraising and marketing for arts organisations, with a three-year detour into hospitality due to more immigration issues, before returning to the arts, and eventually going freelance as a full-time creative and strategic consultant for arts organisations. Over the years Dublin also introduced me to storytelling and spoken word events; I performed at open mics, eventually becoming confident at reading my work and public speaking. In 2019 I had my first poems published, and since then I've focused on building a writing career.

As an Indian citizen, and therefore a non-EU national, I often didn't choose the paths I ended up on: they happened out of necessity, and I tried to make the most of them, even when they broke me. And trust me, they did. The above sounds like a fantastic resumé, but it was achieved at the expense of my mental, physical, and emotional health.

I also had great privilege in many respects which enabled me to get so far (most importantly financial stability and English as a first language), but I also dealt with institutional barriers of immigration instability and unconscious bias. So instead of giving you 'I did it and so can you!' platitudes, I will instead identify a few things that helped me navigate my creative career, and hope you can find what resonates for you within my story.

CULTURAL CAPITAL

Ireland is small, and cultural capital is king; people trust who they know. When I was applying for arts jobs during my time in the drinks industry, despite an excellent CV, I had no viable job offers for three years. After eventually being hired by a theatre company that backed my work permit, I became a familiar face in the sector, and the same people who refused to even interview me were trying to poach me. The sector is frustrating and deeply biased. Being visible and making connections earned trust, and got me opportunities – activities based on extroversion.

As an autistic introvert with ADHD, socialising exhausts me. Someone once told me that I'm in the wrong job because of this. They were wrong; I excel at the mechanics of conversation, and when chatting to fellow arts people, it's enjoyable. But it's still draining. In order to manage my energy, I am picky about social events, making sure they are ones where the people I want to meet will be, like festival events, opening nights, and book launches. Attending events is a great a way of getting to know people, which leads to new connections and opportunities; it feels important to turn up and be present to support others. I also just like experiencing the art!

However, many of us are not able for socialising or networking – for personal reasons, disability reasons, all of them valid. The system is deeply ableist and often superficial. A silver lining of Covid-19 is that there are more online events and workshops, where I have connected with excellent people and been welcomed into new communities. Finding these accessible spaces will take research on your part, but it will pay off. There are ways to make yourself known in a sector in a way that suits you, but they don't come easy (even though they should).

BEING STRATEGIC ABOUT MONEY

At the time of writing, I could earn €50 for a published poem (if I'm lucky). According to the Words Ireland Pay Scale survey in 2021, established writers might earn only €2000 a year from their writing.[3] With rates like this, I could publish extensively and still earn next to nothing. But if I'm asked to read at the launch of the publication, I might

3   The median for mid-career and established writers and illustrators who might be expected to earn a substantial portion of their annual income from their creative work was €2,000.
Source: www.wordsireland.ie/surveys

be paid €100. If I'm asked to read at a festival, or be on a panel, that's maybe €250 per event.[4]

The actual writing may pay the least, but provides the initial pathway to more income. More often than not I'm rewarded for public speaking, not necessarily the writing. This system stacks the odds unfairly against people who aren't able for public speaking. However, the published work is what mattered the most when I applied for Arts Council funding, leading to thousands of euros worth of support.

RESEARCH AND TRAINING

As an arts fundraiser, I am trained to speak concisely and impactfully about art in order to secure investment. As a writer, I had to turn that skill to myself. This was hard in the beginning, but by researching, practising, and actively seeking information, I improved. I kept myself informed about the sector and other writers, paid close attention to criteria, attended workshops, noted how others spoke of/wrote about their work, and asked for help from other writers doing what I wanted to do. This applied to both developing business-wise and also to my own artistic development: at the end of the day, art is at the core of it, so it has to be good, and open to improvement.

---

4   Match in the Dark has done vital work for our sector, ensuring writers get paid properly, ideally earning more than the amounts I mentioned above. Please use their Writers Pay Guide to advocate for better fees for yourself and others when you can, available at www.matchinthedark.com.

COMMUNITY

I am strategic, but that doesn't mean I'm inauthentic: I love our writing community, my friends in arts organisations, and the amazing ways I have been supported and been lucky to support others. I genuinely enjoy doing a lot of the work above. And when there is a gap in my skill set, whether its grant writing, confidence-building, networking, or artistic development, the community has been there for me through workshops, mentorships, or just people generous with their time. I vibe best with neurodivergent and/or migrant artists and arts workers: those are my people who have my back, and I have theirs. But finding these groups took research, trial and error, and vulnerability, for over a decade. It wasn't easy, but it was worth it.

CHAMPIONING OTHERS

To really embed yourself in a sector and community, it has to be a two-way street. I ask people for support, but in turn I support them. I love connecting people to opportunities, especially if they are new to the scene, and from minoritised demographics in the arts – and now that I'm in decision-making roles, I can work to dismantle the barriers that impede the progression of artists like me. For me, it's empowering and fun. Now this is just how I feel: I can't tell you how to feel, or make you care. But if you want to be part of the literary ecosystem, it's vital to both give and take.

I wish you well on your writing journey. May your art propel you, your community guide you, and hard work lift you.

Don't Think You Don't Belong:

HOW DO WE HAVE FAITH THAT WE HAVE A STORY WORTH TELLING AND THAT WE CAN TELL IT WELL?

Kit de Waal

S ome of us don't think we have what it takes to be a writer. Some of us think we don't come from the right kind of family or background, or we didn't have the right kind of education, or we don't have the right accent or look or language or connections. Some of us think writing is for other people, it happens somewhere else, in other homes and better places.

We get this message from history and what we learned at school, from social media and how glamorous some writers' lives look and we get it from society and what kinds of people we see being successful and getting on in life. Not all of us are born with confidence and self-belief – and even if we had it once, time and circumstance have a way of eroding our sense of hope and possibilities.

So how do we turn that around – and how do we have faith that we have a story worth telling, and that we can tell it well?

First of all, everyone starts off by learning the craft. Just like a chef or a plumber or a carpenter, you have to learn how to write well, either by formal apprenticeship, education, or by trial and error, but you're not just going to write perfectly and beautifully the first time you try. That goes for James Joyce, Molly Keane or Toni Morrison; they all started with mistakes. And they didn't let it put them off.

If you can't afford a university course – and many can't – don't let that be a disadvantage. There are short courses, free courses (see MOOCs), writing groups, online courses, and the very best education of all which is to read.

Read the books you know and love and ask yourself why you love it: what has the writer done to make you cry or laugh or turn the page? Interrogate the words and the lines and paragraphs; write on the pages – yes, write on the pages – underline the places where you learn stuff. Before ever there were MAs in creative writing, there were men and women who talked about writing with one another. They'd discuss what they had learned and what worked and what didn't. You can do the same. Read new books by modern writers, read the books that everyone raves about and if you don't like them, ask yourself why and what you would have changed. Read the writers that come from your background, that speak to you about a life you recognise. Read about other worlds and other lives, always asking 'how have they put this together?' and 'how can I write like this?'

The more you work at the craft the better you will be. It really is no different to sewing or driving or making bread.

But what about finding a story? All writing starts with a seed of 'what if'. What if that woman killed that man, what if I stole a thousand euro, what if he took poison, what if they were lost. Start there and let the 'what ifs' guide you right to the end of the story.

You might be working two jobs and writing in between them. What if you never got to work today but ran off with the next-door neighbour. You might have to write with pen and paper because you haven't got a laptop. What if the pen was magic and wrote in a secret language. Your spelling and grammar might let you down because you never went to school? What if you were telling stories around a campfire in the Middle Ages. Dictate them into your phone.

Lastly, the glamorous life of the writer is very over-rated. The photos of the literary festivals and book signings, launches and shindigs hide hours and hours of hard work, alone with the blank page, pulling words left and right to try and make them work.

All writers have self-doubt and we worry that we can't do it, that we're not as good as we were or we wanted to be, and we are all comparing ourselves to one another endlessly. Don't fall for the hype. Don't think you don't belong. Have a go. You will be welcomed.

CHOP WOOD, CARRY WATER

Danielle McLaughlin

(This piece was first published in
The Stinging Fly, *July 2022)*

I was in the audience at Cork International Short Story Festival in 2011, sitting with a new friend from one of the festival workshops. In the same row was the acclaimed US writer Valerie Trueblood, shortlisted for that year's Frank O'Connor Award. She leaned over and asked: 'Are you writers?'

I didn't know how to answer that question back then, but my friend replied that, yes, we were.

Trueblood looked at us. 'Keep going,' she said.

She went on to tell us how she'd stopped sending her work out for 30 years, thinking that she wasn't any good. That was in the 1970s. Her first published story was in 2004. I would later read an interview where she said that it was the rejections that had stopped her sending her work out, even though she described them as kindly by today's standards.

It's tough to keep going when the messages we're receiving seem to suggest that we should do the opposite. The publishing world can be cruel. A friend who used to read the slush pile for a New York literary agency once told me about a template rejection referred to in their office as the 'Stop Writing' letter. Nobody has ever told me to stop writing, though I suppose it's possible that they couched it in such polite language that it went over my head. Even so, rejection, when I first started sending out stories, felt crushing. It sat upon me like a physical thing, squat and heavy. It sapped creative energy. Rejection – or more accurately, the sense of pointlessness it triggered – wasted so much precious time. Back then, if someone had told me to stop writing, I very well might have.

Alongside the disappointment of rejection was the shame. How had I ever thought that story was good enough to send out when, clearly, it was pathetically bad? And now someone had read it. Someone I might bump into at a festival or book launch. The thought was humiliating. I'd yet to learn that the writing life is populated by myriad small humiliations, with, now and again, a larger one. We make ourselves vulnerable every time we write honestly, every time we bring a piece of ourselves to the page.

There's a Buddhist saying (isn't there always?): 'Before Enlightenment: chop wood, carry water. After Enlightenment: chop wood, carry water.' It feels like an apt analogy for rejection in the life of the writer – constant, ever present, necessary. It's our perspective on rejection that can change. Easier said than done, of course. One day while tidying my desk, in among the detritus of broken paperclips, receipts, and all those scraps of paper (you know the ones) with scribbles that must have meant something once but now made no sense, I found a sheet of paper whose sentiment, at least, was in no doubt. Over and over, like a schoolchild doing punitive lines, I'd scrawled in green ink: 'They can all just fuck off.' Most un-Buddhist. I have no recollection now of which particular writing misery prompted that hissy fit. It was a moment in time. Alright, maybe more than a moment. Maybe it was one of those bad writing days, or even weeks. Sometimes, if a writer is unlucky (more about luck later), the bad writing moments can last months. Occasionally, years. The thing is, it passed, I kept going.

'All of writing is a huge lake,' Jean Rhys said. 'There are great rivers that feed the lake, like Tolstoy or Dostoyevsky. And then there are mere trickles, like Jean Rhys. All that matters is feeding the lake. I don't matter. The lake matters. You must keep feeding the lake.' This quote is something I find myself coming back to on days when I'm wondering: why bother? There already exists an abundance of books in the world, multitudes of them better than anything I will ever produce. Why keep going? I would never categorise Jean Rhys as a 'mere trickle', but I like her lake analogy. When we send our stories out into the world, when we feed that lake, they become, if I may be permitted a cliché, part of something bigger. I see writing as a way of going – or getting – through life, what a Buddhist might call a practice. It's a practice that's focused on creating, as opposed to destroying. Our stories might be mere dots, but they're engaged in a sort of literary pointillism. And since we're on the subject of rejection, it's worth remembering that while the word 'pointillism' would in time come to denote an art movement, it was initially a pejorative term coined by critics to ridicule its practitioners.

But back to the thorny question of luck. I feel it would be dishonest of me to write a piece on rejection without acknowledging that I've been lucky. And yes, luck is most definitely a thing. Many writers put in the hours and years and produce good work; only some of those writers receive recognition early, if at all. I'd like to be able to say that the external validation didn't matter, but it did. The journal acceptances, the prizes and short-listings, even though I knew they were subjective, all helped counteract the doubt. I had so little belief in my abilities that without the external validation I might have stopped writing. I have immense admiration for those writers who keep going in its absence. Jean Rhys withdrew from public life in the 1940s and was only tracked down when advertisements were placed in the *New Statesman*, looking for her. Few writers will receive such a public call to keep going. When recognition did eventually arrive for Rhys, she declared: 'It has come too late.' The world is very fortunate that she kept writing.

Now that I've been writing for some years, any suggestion that I should stop would bounce right off me. Being published helps, of course. If it happened once, it can happen again, right? But I think it's more than that. These days my decision to write, and to keep writing, is no longer tied to a need that someone should like my stories. Yes, it would be nice if they did. But I'm currently finishing a novel at peace with the fact that ultimately nobody may want it. Rejection never goes away, it just shape-shifts. I'm loving writing this novel that may never be published. Age has something to do with it, I think. I'm older now and may even be a little bit wiser. I'm slightly thicker-skinned.

But it's more that writing is now embedded deeper in my life as a practice. I can't claim enlightenment, but I'm happy to keep on chopping the wood, carrying the water.

The
Directory

Book Publishers

21st Century Renaissance
Dublin
History, medical, science, art, education, illustration, poetry
Contact: Alison Hackett
Email: alison.hackett@21cr.ie
www.21cr.ie

Ambassador International
Belfast
Religious, non-fiction, fiction
Email: info@emeraldhouse.com
www.ambassador-international.com

Appletree Press
Belfast
Non-fiction, humour, travel, lifestyle
Note: No submissions without prior email.
Email: murphyj@appletree.ie
Email: reception@appletree.ie
www.appletree.ie

Arlen House
Dublin
Fiction, poetry and drama

Contact: Alan Hayes
Email: contact@arlenhouse.ie
www.arlenhouse.ie

BARZAZ
Galway
Irish language contemporary fiction and poetry
Contact: Breda Ní Chonghaile
Email: eolas@barzaz.ie
www.barzaz.ie

BEEHIVE BOOKS
Dublin
Adult and children's non-fiction
Contact: Síne Quinn
Email: sine.quinn@veritas.ie / info@beehive.ie
www.veritasbooksonline.com

BEREANS PUBLISHING
Down
Religious
Email: info@the-bereans.com
www.the-bereans.com

BETIMES BOOKS
Dublin
Fiction
Email: contact@betimesbooks.com
www.betimesbooks.com

BEYOND THE PALE BOOKS
Belfast
Non-fiction
Email: info@beyondthepalebooks.com
www.beyondthepalebooks.com

BLACKHALL PUBLISHING
Dublin
Legal
Email: info@blackhallpublishing.com
www.blackhallpublishing.com

BLACKSTAFF PRESS
Down
Biography & memoir, fiction, history & politics, humour, sports
Email: sales@colourpoint.co.uk
www.blackstaffpress.com

BRANDON
Dublin
Biography & memoir, crime fiction, fiction, history, poetry, politics, travel
Note: an imprint of O'Brien Press
Email: ivan@obrien.ie / books@obrien.ie
www.obrien.ie/brandon

BULLAUN PRESS
Sligo
Cultural literature in translation
Contact: Bridget Farrell

Email: info@bullaunpress.com
wwwbullaunpress.com

BULLFINCH BOOKS
Belfast
Children's fiction and non-fiction
www.bullfinchbooks.co.uk

CHURCH OF EVANGELICAL FELLOWSHIP
Antrim
Religious
www.cief.co.uk/publications.html

CHURCH OF IRELAND PUBLISHING
Dublin & Belfast
Religous
www.cip.ireland.anglican.org

CLACHAN PUBLISHING
Antrim
Non-fiction
Contact: Seán O'Halloran
Email: clachanpublishing@outlook.com
www.clachan-publishing.co.uk

CLARUS PRESS
Dublin/Monaghan
Legal
Contact: David McCartney
Email: davidmccartney@claruspress.ie / info@claruspress.ie
www.claruspress.ie

Cló

Dublin
Irish language
Email: clo@comhar.ie
www.clo.ie/en/fuinn/scribhneoiri

Cló Iar-Chonnacht

Galway
Irish language, children's, fiction, non-fiction, poetry
Email: poibliocht@cic.ie
www.cic.ie

Coiscéim

Dublin
Irish language, fiction, non-fiction, drama
www.coisceim.ie

Colmcille Press | Cló Cholmcille

Derry
History, sport, fiction, poetry and biography in English and
Irish
Contact: Garbhán Downey
Email: info@colmcillepress.com
www.colmcillepress.com

Columba Books

Dublin
Religious
Email: info@columba.ie
www.columbabooks.com

Cork University Press
Cork
Academic/scholarly
Contact: Maria O'Donovan
Email: corkuniversitypress@ucc.ie
www.corkuniversitypress.com

Dalen Éireann
Cork & Wales
Graphic novels in translation
Contact: Alun Ceri Jones
Emali: acj@daleneireann.com / dalen@daleneireann.com
www.daleneireann.com

DCU Press
Dublin
Academic/scholarly & open access
Contact: Ellen Breen
Email: ellen.breen@dcu.ie / DCUPress@dcu.ie
www.dcupress.dcu.ie

Dedalus Press
Dublin
Poetry
Contact: Raffaela Tranchino
Email: manager@dedaluspress.com
Email: office@dedaluspress.com
www.dedaluspress.com

DOIRE PRESS
Galway
Poetry and short stories
Contact: Lisa Frank/John Walsh
Email: doirepress@gmail.com
www.doirepress.com

DUBLIN INSTITUTE FOR ADVANCED STUDIES (DIAS)
Irish and Celtic Studies
Contact: Margaret Irons
Email: margaret@celt.dias.ie / contact@dias.ie
www.dias.ie

DUBLIN UNIVERSITY PRESS
Dublin
Academic/scholarly
Contact: Niamh Brennan
Email: nbrenn@tcd.ie
www.tcd.ie

ÉABHLÓID
Donegal
Irish language, fiction, poetry and children's
Contact: Eoghan Mac Giolla Bhríde
Email: eoghan@eabhloid.com
www.eolas@eabhloid.com

EASTWOOD BOOKS
Dublin
Academic/scholarly, history and general non-fiction
Contact: Ronan Colgan

Note: An imprint of the Wordwell Group
Email: ronan@wordwell.ie / office@wordwellbooks.com
www.eastwoodbooks.com

ELY'S ARCH
Dublin
Fiction
Note: An imprint of Liberties Press
Email: info@libertiespress.com
www.elysarch.com

ERIÚ
Dublin
Fiction & Non-fiction, adult & children's
Contact: Deirdre Nolan
Email: hello@bonnierbooks.com
www.bonnierbooks.co.uk/imprints/eriu

FISH PUBLISHING
Cork
Short anthology pieces
Email: info@fishpublishing.com
www.fishpublishing.com

FLYLEAF PRESS
Dublin
Family history & genealogy
Email: books@flyleaf.ie
www.flyleaf.ie

Four Courts Press
Dublin
Academic/scholarly, history, art, literature, law, Celtic studies
Contact: Martin Fanning
Email: info@fourcourtspress.ie
www.fourcourtspress.ie

Futa Fata
Galway
Irish language, children's
Contact: Breda Ní Chonghaile
Email: breda@futafata.ie
www.futafata.ie

Gallery Press
Meath
Poetry, drama, prose
Contact: Jean Fallon
Email: jean@gallerypress.com / books@gallerypress.com
www.gallerypress.com

Gill Books
Dublin
Trade non-fiction, sport, lifestyle
Email: info@gill.ie
www.gillbooks.ie

Guildhall Press
Derry
Local history, general non-fiction, fiction
Contact: Paul Hippsley

Email: info@ghpress.com
www.ghpress.com

An Gúm / Foras na Gaeilge
Dublin
Irish language
Email: angum@forasgaeilge.ie
www.forasgaeilge.ie/about/an-gum

Hachette Ireland
Dublin
Trade fiction & non-fiction
Contact: Joanna Smyth
Email: joanna.smyth@hbgi.ie / info@hbgi.ie
www.hachettebooksireland.ie

Harper Collins
Dublin
Trade fiction & non-fiction
https://corporate.harpercollins.co.uk

Harvest Press
Carlow
Fiction & non-fiction
Contact: Angela Keogh
Email: editor@theharvestpress.ie
www.theharvestpress.ie

Institute of Public Administration
Dublin
Academic/scholarly, government and politics

Contact: John Paul Owens
Email: jpowens@ipa.ie / information@ipa.ie
www.ipa.ie

IRELANDIA PRESS
Dublin
Trade non-fiction, business
Contact: Ellen James
Email: ellenjames@irelandia.ie
www.irelandiapress.ie

IRISH ACADEMIC PRESS | MERRION PRESS
Kildare
Academic/scholarly & trade non-fiction, history, current
affairs, fiction
Contact: Síne Quinn
Email: sine.quinn@iap.ie / info@iap.ie
www.irishacademicpress.ie

IRISH MANUSCRIPTS COMMISSION
Dublin
Academic/scholarly
Contact: Cathy Hayes
Email: support@irishmanuscripts.ie
www.irishmanuscripts.ie

LAPWING PUBLICATIONS
Belfast
Poetry
Email: lapwing.poetry@ntlworld.com

Laurel Cottage

Down
Local history
Email: info@cottage-publications.com
www.cottage-publications.com

Leabhar Breac

Galway
Irish language, fiction, non-fiction, poetry, childrens
eolas@leabharbreac.com
www.leabharbreac.com

LeabhairCOMHAR

Dublin
Irish language, fiction, history, poetry, childrens, biography
Contact: Jennifer Gorissen
Email: leabhaircomhar@comhar.ie
https://comhar.ie/leabhair/

Liberties Press

Dublin
Non-fiction, fiction, poetry
Email: info@libertiespress.com
https://libertiespress.com

The Lifeboat

Belfast
Poetry
https://lifeboatpress.com

The Liffey Press
Dublin
Non-fiction, short stories
Contact: David Givens
Email: theliffeypress@gmail.com
https://theliffeypress.com

Lilliput Press
Dublin
Biography, historical non-fiction and memoir, fiction
Contact: Antony Farrell
Email: editorial@lilliputpress.ie / contact@lilliputpress.ie
www.lilliputpress.ie

Little Island
Dublin
Children's
Contact: Matthew Parkinson-Bennett
Email: matthew.pb@littleisland.ie / info@littleisland.ie
www.littleisland.ie

Marino Institute of Education Library
Dublin
Academic/scholarly
Contact: Genevieve Larkin
Email: genevieve.larkin@mie.ie
Email: librarydesk@mie.ie
www.mie.ie/en/library

MAURICE WYLIE MEDIA
Belfast
Religious
Email: info@mauricewyliemedia.com
https://mauricewyliemedia.com

MAVERICK HOUSE
Dublin
Non-fiction
Email: info@maverickhouse.com
www.maverickhouse.com

MERCIER PRESS
Cork
Non-fiction, history, sports, biography
Email: info@mercierpress.ie
www.mercierpress.ie

MESSENGER PUBLICATIONS
Dublin
Religious
Contact: Cecilia West
Email: c.west@messenger.ie / info@messenger.ie
www.messenger.ie

NATURAL WORLD PUBLISHING
Dublin
Illustrated nature & Natural history
submissions@naturalworldpublishing.ie
https://naturalworldpublishing.ie

New Island
Dublin
Non-fiction, fiction, poety, drama, adult literacy
Contact: Mariel Deegan
Email: mariel.deegan@newisland.ie / info@newisland.ie
www.newisland.ie

Nine Bean Rows
Dublin
Cookery
Contact: Kristin Jensen
Email: kjensen@ninebeanrowsbooks.com
Email: info@ninebeanrowsbooks.com
https://ninebeanrowsbooks.com/

No Alibis Press
Belfast
Fiction
Email: info@noalibispress.com
www.noalibispress.com

Oak Tree Press
Cork
Business non-fiction
Contact: Brian O'Kane
Email: info@oaktreepress.com
https://oaktreepress.eu

O'Brien Press
Dublin
Non-fiction, fiction, childrens, biography, cookery, sport

Contact: Ivan O'Brien
Email: ivan@obrien.ie / books@obrien.ie
https://obrien.ie

OILEAN PRESS
Galway
Poetry and prose, Irish language & bilingual (Irish/English)
Contact: Dara Ó Coola
Email: arauthor@gmail.com

ORPEN PRESS
Dublin
Non-fiction
Contact: Eileen O'Brien
Email: eileen@orpenpress.com / info@orpenpress.com
www.orpenpress.com

PENGUIN / SANDYCOVE
Dublin
Trade non-fiction and fiction
Note: Sandycove is the Irish imprint of Penguin Random House
Email: submissions@penguinrandomhouse.ie
www.penguin.co.uk

PHAETON PUBLISHING
Dublin
Literary Fiction and non-fiction
Email: phaeton@iol.ie
www.phaeton.ie

Poetry Ireland
Dublin
Poetry
Contact: Paul Lenehan
Email: publications@poetryireland.ie
www.poetryireland.ie/publications

Poolbeg
Dublin
Fiction, non-fiction
Contact: Paula Campbell
Email: paula@poolbeg.com / info@poolbeg.com
https://poolbeg.com/

Red Stripe Press
Dublin
Non-fiction
Note: Red Stripe Press is an imprint of Orpen Press
Contact: Eileen O'Brien
Email: eileen@orpenpress.com / info@redstripepress.com
www.redstripepress.com

Royal Irish Academy
Dublin
Academic/scholarly
Contact: Ruth Hegarty
Email: publications@ria.ie
www.ria.ie

Salmon Poetry
Clare

Poetry
Contact: Siobhán Hutson
Email: siobhan@salmonpoetry.com
Email: info@salmonpoetry.com
www.salmonpoetry.com

SHANWAY PRESS
Belfast
Fiction, non-fiction
Email: info@shanway.com
www.shanway.com

SKEIN PRESS
Dublin
Fiction
Note: Focus on under-represented writers
Contact: Gráinne O'Toole
Email: grainne@skeinpress.com
Email: info@skeinpress.com
https://skeinpress.com

SOMERVILLE PRESS
Cork
Fiction, non-fiction
Email: somervillepress@gmail.com
https://somervillepress.company.site/

THE STINGING FLY PRESS
Dublin
Literary fiction and non-fiction

Note: The Stinging Fly Press is the book imprint of
The Stinging Fly literary journal.
Email: info@stingingfly.org
www.stingingfly.org

TEMPLE DARK BOOKS
Dublin
Speculative fiction
Email: thegatekeeper@templedarkbooks.com
www.templedarkbooks.com/

TIMELESS THEOLOGICAL ACADEMY
Antrim
Religious
Email: admin@timelesstheologicalacademy.com
https://books.timelesstheologicalacademy.com

TIRGEARR PUBLISHING
Meath
Fiction, romance, mystery
Email: info@tirgearrpublishing.com
www.tirgearrpublishing.com

TRAMP PRESS
Dublin
Literary fiction and non-fiction
Contact: Sarah Davis-Goff
Email: info@tramppress.com
https://tramppress.com

AN TSNÁTHAID MHÓR
Belfast
Irish language, children's
Contact: Caitríona Nic Sheáin
Email: eolas@antsnathaidmhor.com
www.antsnathaidmhor.com

TURAS PRESS
Dublin
Poetry & fiction
https://turaspress.ie

TURNPIKE BOOKS
Belfast
New editions of Northern Irish fiction and non-fiction
http://turnpikebooks.co.uk/

UCD PRESS
Dublin
Academic/scholarly, non-fiction
Email: ucdpress@ucd.ie
www.ucdpress.ie

ULSTER ARCHITECTURAL HERITAGE
Belfast
Local architecture
Email: info@uahs.org.uk
www.ulsterarchitecturalheritage.org.uk

ULSTER HISTORICAL FOUNDATION
Down

Local history, genealogy
Email: enquiry@uhf.org.uk
www.ancestryireland.com

WHITE ROW PRESS
Belfast
Non-fiction
Contact: Peter Carr
Email: info@whiterow.net
www.whiterow.net

THE WOODFIELD PRESS
Dublin
Non-fiction, history
Email: woodfield-press@mail.com
www.woodfield-press.com

WORDS ON THE STREET
Fiction, poetry
Email: publisher@wordsonthestreet.com
www.wordsonthestreet.com

WORDWELL BOOKS
Dublin
Archaeology, history, academic & trade non-fiction
Note: Also the publishers of *History Ireland* and
Archaeology Ireland magazines
Contact: Ronan Colgan
Email: office@wordwellbooks.com
www.wordwellbooks.com

JOURNALS

A NEW ULSTER
Poetry & Prose
anuanewulster.wixsite.com

ABRIDGED
Poetry & Art
www.abridged.zone

ANEAS
Irish literature
https://munsterlit.ie/aneas

BANSHEE
Fiction, non-fiction & poetry
www.bansheepress.org

BOOKS IRELAND MAGAZINE
Flash fiction
https://booksirelandmagazine.com

CATFLAP
Queer writing, essays & poetry
https://channelmag.org

CHANNEL
Environmental fiction, non-fiction & poetry
https://channelmag.org

CRANNÓG MAGAZINE
Fiction, non-fiction & poetry
https://crannogmagazine.com

CYPHERS
Fiction, reviews & poetry
www.cyphers.ie

DODGING THE RAIN
Poetry
https://dodgingtherain.com

DRAWN TO THE LIGHT PRESS
Poetry
https://drawntothelightpress.com

DUBLIN REVIEW OF BOOKS
Essays and reflections on literature
www.drb.ie

FRAZLED LIT
Prose, flash fiction, poetry and CNF
www.frazzledlit.com

GORSE
Fiction & creative non-fiction
www.gorse.ie

HOLY SHOW
Non-fiction
https://holyshow.ie

HOWL
Fiction, poetry & Irish language
www.howlwriting.ie

IMPOSSIBLE ARCHETYPE
LGBTQ+ poetry
https://impossiblearchetype.wordpress.com

IRISH PAGES
Fiction, non-fiction, poetry & translated work
https://irishpages.org

NEW ISLES PRESS
Short fiction, poetry
www.yellowhousepublishing.com

PAPER LANTERNS
Short stories, poetry, flash fiction, features, book reviews for
teen and young adult audience
www.paperlanternslit.com

POETRY IRELAND REVIEW
Articles, reviews, poetry & translated work
www.poetryireland.ie

PROFILES
Fiction, non-fiction & translated work
www.profilesjournal.com

PÚCA MAGAZINE
Fiction, creative non-fiction & poetry
https://pucalit.com

ROPES LITERARY JOURNAL
Short fiction, flash fiction, creative non-fiction & poetry
www.ropesliteraryjournal.com

SKYLIGHT 47
Poetry
https://skylight47poetry.wordpress.com

SONDER MAGAZINE
Fiction & creative non-fiction
https://sonderlit.com

SOUTHWORD JOURNAL
Fiction & poetry
https://munsterlit.ie/southword

SPLONK
Flash fiction & translated flash fiction
https://splonk.ie

SPONTANEITY JOURNAL
Fiction & poetry
www.spontaneity.org

The Bangor Literary Journal
Flash fiction & poetry
https://thebangorliteraryjournal.com

The Dublin Review
Fiction & non-fiction
https://thedublinreview.com

The Four Faced Liar
Fiction, creative non-fiction, poetry & translated work
www.the4facedliar.com

The Honest Ulsterman
Fiction, creative non-fiction & poetry
https://humag.co

The Galway Review
Fiction, creative non-fiction, poetry & translated work
https://thegalwayreview.com

The Madrigal
Poetry
www.themadrigalpress.com

The Martello
Fiction, non-fiction & poetry
https://themartello.squarespace.com

The Ogham Stone
Fiction, creative non-fiction & poetry
https://www.ul.ie/artsoc

THE PIG'S BACK
Fiction & non-fiction
www.thepigsback.ie

THE POETRY BUS
Poetry
www.thepoetrybuspress.onlineweb.shop

THE STINGING FLY
Fiction, creative non-fiction & poetry
https://stingingfly.org

THE STORMS
Fiction & poetry
https://eatthestorms.com

THE TANGERINE
Fiction, non-fiction & poetry
https://thetangerinemagazine.com

THE WAXED LEMON
Fiction & poetry
www.thewaxedlemon.com

THE WILD UMBRELLA
Short stories, non-fiction
www.thewildumbrella.com

TÍR NA NÓG
Fiction & poetry
https://tirnanoglit.com

Tolka

Non-fiction, autofiction, travel writing & reportage
www.tolkajournal.org

Trasna

Short stories, poetry, essays
www.trasna.online

Winter Pages

Fiction, creative non-fiction & poetry
https://winterpapers.com

AGENTS

Agents based in Ireland

Jonathan Williams Literary Agency

Jonathan Williams
Represents literary fiction, general fiction & non-fiction
Telephone: +353 (0)1 2803482

Marianne Gunn O'Connor Literary Agency

Represents fiction, non-fiction & children's books
www.mariannegunnoconnor.com

PaperCuts Literary Agency & Consultancy Ltd

Polly Nolan
Represents children's and middle grade fiction & novels
for all ages
www.papercutsltd.com

Storyline Literary Agency

Brian Langan
Represents literary fiction, crime fiction & non-fiction
www.storylineagency.com

The Book Bureau Literary Agency

Ger Nichol

Represents literary fiction, commercial fiction & crime fiction

Email: thebookbureau@oceanfree.net

The Feldstein Agency

Represents literary fiction, commercial fiction, non-fiction
& children's books

www.thefeldsteinagency.co.uk

The Inkwell Group

Literary talent scouts working with agents and publishers
to spot new authors

www.inkwellwriters.ie

The Lisa Richards Agency

Faith O'Grady

Represents fiction, non-fiction & children's literature

www.lisarichards.ie

The Nagle Agency

Conor Nagle

Represents across the publishing spectrum
(except poetry and academic)

www.thenagleagency.com

Agents overseas representing Irish authors

Aitken Alexander Associates

Represents fiction, non-fiction, screenwriting

www.aitkenalexander.co.uk

Alan Brodie Representation
Represents writers for the stage
www.alanbrodie.com

Andrew Nurnberg Associates
Sara O'Keeffe
Represents literary and commercial fiction
www. andrewnurnberg.com

C &W Agency
Represents fiction, non-fiction & children's books
www.cwagency.co.uk

Clare Wallace
Represents picture books right through to YA and a boutique list
of adult fiction
www.darleyandersonchildrens.com

Curtis Brown
Represents fiction, non-fiction, YA and children's books
www.curtisbrown.co.uk

Grainne Fox
Fletcher and Company
Represents literary fiction, upmarket commercial fiction &
narrative non-fiction
www.fletcherandco.com

Janklow & Nesbitt
Commercial & literary fiction, non-fiction, children's & YA
www.janklowandnesbitt.co.uk

Johnson & Alcock
Represents commercial & literary fiction, general non-fiction, children's & YA
www.johnsonandalcok.co.uk

Kate Nash Literary Agency
Represents commercial fiction & non-fiction for adults, young adults and children
www.katenashlit.co.uk

Pew Literary
Represents literary fiction, memoir & non-fiction
www.pewliterary.com

Rachel Mills Literary
Nelle Andrew
Represents best-selling fiction and non-fiction
www.rachelmillsliterary.co.uk

Rogers, Coleridge & White Ltd Literary Agency
Literary and commercial fiction, crime and thrillers, children's and YA & non-fiction
www.rcwlitagency.com

Sallyanne Sweeney
MMB Creative
Represents fiction, non-fiction & children's books
www.mmbcreative.com

Simon Trewin
Simon Trewin Creative
Fiction and non-fiction, art, culture, digital & live events
www.simontrewin.co.uk

Sophie Hicks Agency

Represents fiction, non-fiction, children's (9+) and YA
www.sophiehicksagency.com

The Bent Agency

Nicola Barr
Represents commercial fiction, crime, literary fiction, non-fiction
& YA
www.thebentagency.com

The Soho Agency

Philippa Milnes-Smith
Represents children's literature, including picture books, middle
grade fiction, illustrated books (including graphic novels) and
non-fiction
www.thesohoagency.co.uk

COMPETITIONS

*For ongoing information, the Irish Writers Centre, Poetry Ireland,
and Writing.ie regularly update their competition listings.*

AESTHETICA CREATIVE WRITING AWARD

Poetry & short fiction
https://aestheticamagazine.com

ALLINGHAM FESTIVAL WRITING COMPETITIONS

Poetry (Adults)
Flash fiction (Adults)
www.allinghamfestival.com

AN POST IRISH BOOK AWARDS

Novel of the Year
Crime Fiction Book of the Year
Sports Book of the Year
Newcomer of the Year
Non-fiction Book of the Year
Cookbook of the Year
Popular Fiction Book of the Year
Lifestyle Book of the Year
RTÉ Audience Choice Awards
Best Irish-Published Book
Children's Book of the Year (Senior)

Children's Book of the Year (Junior)
Irish Language Book of the Year
Teen and Young Adult Book of the Year
Poem of the Year
Short Story of the Year
Library Association of Ireland Author of the Year
Biography of the Year
An Post Bookshop of the Year
www.irishbookawards.ie

BALLYDONOGHUE BARDIC FESTIVAL
WRITING COMPETITIONS

The James Award
The Jer Lynch Poetry Award
Quiet Man Maurice Walsh Award
Duais Phádraig Liath Ó Conchubhair
The Chrissie Nolan Creative Writing Award
Dán
https://ballydbardfest.com

BATH SHORT STORY AWARD

Short fiction
www.bathshortstoryaward.org

BRIDPORT INTERNATIONAL CREATIVE
WRITING COMPETITION

Poetry
Fiction
Flash fiction
Novels
Memoir
https://bridportprize.org.uk

Caledonia Novel Award 2025
Novel writing
www.thecaledonianovelaward.com

Carlow Little Theatre One Act Playwriting Competition
Playwriting
www.carlowlittletheatre.com

Creative Writing Ink Poetry Prize
Poetry
https://creativewriting.ie

Cúirt New Writing Prize
Short fiction, poetry & prose & poetry in Irish
www.cuirt.ie

Date with an Agent
Novels
www.inkwellwriters.ie

Fiction Factory Poetry Competition
Poetry
www.fiction-factory.biz/poetry-competition

Fingal Poetry Prize and An Fiach Dubh Competitions
Irish and English poetry
https://fingalpoetryfestival.com

First Chapters Contest
First chapter of a novel
www.craftliterary.com

Fish Publishing Prize

Poetry, flash fiction, short fiction, short memoir

www.fishpublishing.com

Fool for Poetry International Chapbook Competition

Poetry collection

www.munsterlit.ie

Frances Browne Poetry Competition

Poetry (English, Irish, Ulster-Scots)

www.francesbrowneliteraryfestival.com

Hour of Writes – Weekly Writing Competition

Fiction

www.hourofwrites.com/index/welcome

Irish Writers Centre Novel Fair

Introduces up-and-coming writers to top publishers and literary agents.

https://irishwriterscentre.ie

Ledbury Poetry Competition 2024

Poetry

ledburypoetry.org.uk/home/ledbury-poetry-competition-2024

Letterkenny Cathedral Quarter 2024 Flash Fiction Competition

Flash fiction

www.lkcqlitfest.weebly.com

Listowel Writers' Week Writing Competitions
Kerry Group Novel of the Year Award 2023
Pigott Poetry Prize Award 2023
Bryan MacMahon Short Story Award
Poetry Collection
Duais Foras na Gaeilge
Nilsson Local Heritage Award
Creative Writing for Adults with Learning Difficulties and, or,
Disabilities, Award
https://writersweek.ie

Manchester Writing Competition
Poetry & short fiction
www.mmu.ac.uk/writingcompetition

Mslexia Women's Flash Fiction Competition
Flash fiction
https://mslexia.co.uk

Ó'Bhéal Five Words Competition
Poetry
www.obheal.ie

Ó Faoláin Short Story Competition Open
Short fiction
www.munsterlit.ie

Oxford Poetry Prize
Poetry
www.oxfordpoetry.com

Paper Lanterns Teen Short Story Competition
Short fiction
https://paperlanternslit.com/short-story-competition

Patrick Kavanagh Poetry Award
Poetry
https://patrickkavanaghcentre.com

Red Line Festival Poetry Competition
Poetry
https://redlinefestival.ie

Searchlight Writing for Children Awards
Children's picture book or novel
www.searchlightawards.co.uk

The Anthology Short Story Competition
Short fiction
https://anthology-magazine.com

The Bath Novel Awards
Not-yet-published and independently published novels
The Bath Children's Novel Award
The Bath Novel Award
https://bathnovelaward.co.uk

The Benedict Kiely Short Story Competition
Short fiction
https://kielyweekend.wordpress.com

The Caledonia Novel Award
Unpublished and self-published novels
https://thecaledonianovelaward.com

The Gregory O'Donoghue International Poetry Competition
Poetry
www.munsterlit.ie

The Irish Writers' Centre Novel Fair
Novels
https://irishwriterscentre.ie

The John McGahern Award
Short fiction
www.ironmountainfestival.ie/john-mcgahern-award

The Mairtín Crawford Awards
Short fiction and poetry from entrants who have not yet
published a full collection of poetry, short fiction, or a novel
https://belfastbookfestival.com/mairtin-crawford-award

The Masters Review Short Story Award for New Writers
Short fiction
https://mastersreview.com

The Moth Writing Prizes
The Moth Short Story Prize
The Moth Nature Writing Prize
The Moth Poetry Prize
https://themothmagazine.com

The Rooney Prize for Irish Literature

Body of work by an Irish writer under 40

www.tcd.ie/OWC/rooney-prize

The RTÉ Short Story Competition

Short fiction

www.rte.ie/radio/radio1/francis-macmanus-short-story

The Seamus Heaney First Collection Poetry Prize

Poetry

www.qub.ac.uk/schools/seamus-heaney-centre/poetry-prize

Wild Atlantic Words Short Story Competitions

Short fiction, flash fiction and creative non-fiction

www.wildatlanticwords.ie

Winchester Poetry Prize

Poetry

www.winchesterpoetryfestival.org/prize

Witcraft Annual Humour Competition

Short fiction, Non-fiction and Poetry

www.witcraft.org/witcraft-annual-humour-competition

Write By the Sea Literary Festival Writing Competitions

Short fiction, Flash fiction, Poetry & Memoir/Personal essay

https://writebythesea.ie

Writer's Digest Annual Writing Competition

Short fiction, Non-fiction & Poetry

www.writersdigest.com/writers-digest-competitions

Yeats Thoor Ballylee International Poetry Prize

Poetry

https://yeatsthoorballylee.org

Radio & Podcasts

All About Books
Katy Conneely, Dublin City FM
www.dublincityfm.ie

Arena
Seán Rocks
RTÉ Radio 1
www.rte.ie

AskALLi Podcasts
www.allianceindependentauthors.org

Books on One
www.rte.ie/radio/radio1/book-on-one

Book Review podcast
Clonmel Library
www.tipperarylibraries.ie

Bookline
Teresa Quinn
Liffey FM
www.mixcloud.com/liffeysoundfm/bookline

Books for Breakfast
Peter Sirr and Enda Wyley
https://booksforbreakfast.buzzsprout.com

Burning Books
Ruth McKee
Books Ireland
www.booksirelandmagazine.com

Censored
Aoife Bhreatnach
http://censored.ie

City of Books
Martina Devlin
https://radio.moli.ie

Dublin Book Festival Podcast
https://dublinbookfestival.com

Eat the Storms
www.eatthestorms.com

Inside Books
Breda Brown
https://soundcloud.com/insidebooks

Natter
Michelle McDonagh/ Kate Durrant
www.shows.acast.com/natter

New Books in Irish Studies
https://newbooksnetwork.com

Poetry File
www.rte.ie/radio/podcasts

Poetry Unbound
https://onbeing.org

RadioMoLI
https://moli.ie

Southword Poetry Podcast
Munster Lit Centre
https://munsterlit.ie/podcasts

Story-shaped Pod
Susan Cahill and Sinead O'Hart
www.susancahill.co.uk/podcast

Sunday Miscellany
RTÉ Radio 1
www.rte.ie/radio/radio1/sunday-miscellany

Talking Translations
Literature Ireland
www.literatureireland.com/talking-translations

The Bookshelf
Ryan Tubridy
www.easons.com

The Irish Itinerary Podcast
EFACIS – the European Federation of Associations and Centres of Irish Studies
www.efacis.eu/podcast

The Poetry Programme
RTÉ Radio 1
www.rte.ie/radio/radio1/the-poetry-programme

The Salmon Poetry Podcast
https://salmonpoetry.podbean.com

The Shaking Bog
www.shakingbog.ie

The Stinging Fly Podcast
https://stingingfly.org/podcast

Words Lightly Spoken
Poetry Ireland
https://radio.moli.ie

FESTIVALS

ALLINGHAM ARTS FESTIVAL (INCLUDES LITERARY EVENTS)
November
Ballyshannon, Co. Donegal
www.allinghamfestival.com

AN FHÉILE BEAG FILÍOCHTA
October
Ballyferriter, Dingle, Co. Kerry
http://feilebheagfiliochta.com

ASPECTS FESTIVAL
October
Ards Peninsula, Bangor, Co. Down
https://aspectsfestival.com

BALLYDONOGHUE BARDIC FESTIVAL
March
Ballydonoghue, Co. Kerry
https://ballydbardfest.com/blog/

BELFAST BOOK FESTIVAL
June
Belfast City
https://belfastbookfestival.com

Belfast International Arts Festival (includes literary events)
October
Belfast City
https://belfastinternationalartsfestival.com

Belfast Children's Festival
March
Belfast City
https://youngatart.co.uk/festival/

Bloomsday Festival
Ulysses-related literature and study
June
Dublin City
www.bloomsdayfestival.ie

Blueway Poetry Festival
August
Lismore, Co Waterford
www.facebook.com/BluewayPoetry/

Bookville Festival Kilkenny
October
Kilkenny City
www.bookvillekilkenny.com

Borris House Festival of Writing and Ideas
June
Borris, Co Carlow
https://festivalofwritingandideas.com

Boyle Arts Festival (includes literary events)
July
Boyle, Co. Roscommon
www.boylearts.com

Bray Literary Festival
September-October
Bray, Co. Wicklow
brayliteraryfestival.com

Cashel Arts Festival
September
Cashel, Co. Tipperary
https://cashelartsfest.com

**Cathedral Quarter Arts Festival
(includes literary events)**
April
Cathedral Quarter, Belfast
https://cqaf.com

**Children's Books Ireland International
Conference**
September
Dublin City
https://childrensbooksireland.ie

Classics Now
January
Dublin City
www.classicsnow.ie

Clifden Community Arts Festival
(includes literary events)
September
Clifden. Co. Galway
https://clifdenartsfestival.ie

Clonmel Junction Arts Festival
July
Clonmel, Co. Tipperary
www.junctionfestival.com

Cork International Poetry Fest
May
Cork City
https://corkpoetryfest.net

Cork International Short Story Fest
October
Cork City
https://corkshortstory.net

Cork World Book Fest
April
Cork City
https://corkworldbookfest.com

Cúirt International Festival of Literature
April
Galway City
www.cuirt.ie

Dalkey Book Festival
June
Dalkey, County Dublin
www.dalkeybookfestival.org

Drogheda Arts Festival (includes literary events)
April
Drogheda, Co. Louth
https://droghedaartsfestival.ie

Dromineer Nenagh Literary Festival
October
Dromineer, Nenagh, Co. Tipperary
http://dnlf.ie

Dublin Book Festival
November
Dublin City
https://dublinbookfestival.com

Dublin: One City One Book
April
Dublin City
www.onedublinonebook.ie

Dublin International Literary Festival
May
Dublin City
https://ilfdublin.com

Earagail Arts Festival
(includes literary events)
July
Letterkenny, Co. Donegal
https://eaf.ie

Echoes Maeve Binchy & Irish Writers Festival
October
Dalkey, Co. Dublin
www.echoes.ie

Éigse Michael Hartnett Literary and Arts Festival
October
Newcastle West, Co. Limerick
https://eigsemichaelhartnett.ie

Ennis Book Club Festival
March
Ennis, Co. Clare
https://ennisbookclubfestival.com

Ennistymon Book Town Festival
August
Ennistymon, Co. Clare
https://ennistymonbooktown.ie

Féile na Bealtaine (includes literary events)
April-May
Dingle, Co. Kerry
https://feilenabealtaine.ie

Five Lamps Arts Festival (includes literary events)
March-April
Dublin City North
https://fivelampsarts.ie

Franco-Irish Literary Festival
March
Dublin City
http://francoirishliteraryfestival.com

Gerard Manley Hopkins International Literary Festival
July
Newbridge, Co. Kildare
https://gerardmanleyhopkins.org

Goldsmith International Literary Festival
June
Ballymahon, Co. Louth
https://olivergoldsmithfestival.com

Graiguenamanagh Town of Books Festival
August
Graiguenamanagh, Co. Kilkenny
https://graiguenamanaghtownofbooks.ie

Hinterland Festival (includes literary events)
June
Kells, Co. Meath
www.hinterland.ie

Imagine Arts Festival/Waterford Writers Weekend
October
Waterford City
www.imagineartsfestival.com

Immrama Children's Festival
June
Lismore, County Waterford
https://lismore-immrama.com

IMRAM (Irish Language Literature Festival)
May
Dublin City
https://imram.ie

Independent bookshop week
June
www.booksaremybag.com/IndependentBookshopWeek

Inishbofin Arts Festival
April-May
Inishbofin, Co. Galway
www.inishbofin.com

International Literature Festival Dublin
May
Dublin City
https://ilfdublin.com

International Dublin Writers Festival
September

Dublin City
https://internationaldublinwritersfestival.com

Irish Book Week
October
www.booksaremybag.com/IrishBookWeek/About

Iron Mountain Literature Festival
October
Carrick on Shannon, Co. Leitrim
www.ironmountainfestival.ie

Kanturk Arts Festival
March
Kanturk, Co. Cork
https://www.kanturkarts.ie

K- Fest- Killorglin Arts Festival
June
Killorglin, Co. Kerry
www.kfest.ie

Kildare Readers Festival
October
Newbridge, Co. Kildare
https://kildarecoco.ie/library/KildareReadersFestival

Kilkenny Arts Festival (includes literary events)
August
Kilkenny City
www.kilkennyarts.ie

Leaves Festival of Writing & Music
November
Laois (various locations)
https://leavesfestival.ie

Limerick Literary Festival
February
Limerick City
https://limerickliteraryfestival.com

Lismore Immrama Festival of Travel writing
June
https://lismore-immrama.com

Listowel Writers' Week
June
https://writersweek.ie

Look North! The North Belfast Festival
February
Belfast City
https://northbelfastfestival.com/

Ó Bhéal and the Winter Warmer Festival
November
Cork City
www.obheal.ie

Octocon, the National Irish Science-Fiction Convention
October
Dublin City
https://2023.octocon.com

Omagh Literary festival / Benedict Kiely
October
Omagh, Co. Tyrone
https://Kielyweekend.wordpress.com

Red Line Book Festival
October
Dublin City
https://redlinefestival.ie

Shorelines Arts Festival
September
Portumna, Co. Galway
www.shorelinesartsfestival.com

Spike Island Literary Festival
September
Spike Island, Co. Cork
www.spikeislandcork.ie/literary-festival

Strokestown International Poetry Festival
April
Strokestown, County Roscommon
https://strokestownpoetryfest.ie

The Maria Edgeworth Literary Festival
May
Edgeworthstown, Co. Longford
https://mariaedgeworthcenter.com

The Rolling Sun Book Festival
November

Westport, County Mayo
https://rollingsunbookfestival.com

The Write Time Festival
September
Fingal, Co. Dublin
https://www.fingal.ie/write-time-2022-creative-writing-festival

Towers & Tales Lismore Story Festival
April
Lismore Castle, Co. Waterford
https://www.towersandtalesfestival.ie

West Cork Literary Festival
July
Bantry, Co. Cork
https://westcorkmusic.ie/literary-festival/

Westival
October
Westport, Co. Mayo
https://westival.ie

Wexford Literary Festival
July
Enniscorthy, Co. Wexford
https://wexfordliteraryartsfestival.com

Wild Atlantic Words Literary Festival
October
Castlebar, Co. Mayo
hwww.wildatlanticwords.ie

Words by Water: Kinsale Literary Festival
October
Kinsale, Co. Cork
www.wordsbywater.ie

Write by the Sea Literary Festival
September
Kilmore, Co. Wexford
https://writebythesea.ie

AFEPI

ASSOCIATION OF FREELANCE EDITORS,

PROOFREADERS & INDEXERS OF IRELAND

www.afepi-ireland.com

BRENDAN O'BRIEN
brendan@brendanedits.com
Services: Copyediting, proofreading
Specialities: All areas of non-fiction
https://afepi-ireland.com/member/obrien-brendan/

NEIL BURKEY EDITORIAL SERVICES
neilburkey.com
Services: Copyediting, project management, proofreading,
writing
Specialities: Arts, humanities, history, educational, fiction

DJINN VON NOORDEN
djinnvn@gmail.com
Services: Copyediting and proofreading
Specialities: Literary fiction, biography, history
https://afepi-ireland.com/member/noorden-djinn-von/

Dermott Barrett

barrettdermott@gmail.com
Services: Copy-editing, fiction and non-fiction, business editing, copywriting, ESL editing, plain English, proofreading, research

Niamh Hatton

niamh_hatton@hotmail.com
Services: Copy-editing, proofreading, manuscript assessment, developmental editing.
Specialities: Fiction, non-fiction (including cookery, history, biography/memoir, mind-body-spirit, business), children's literature.

Siobhán Prendergast
Dingle Publishing Services

Dinglepublishing.com
Services: editing, design
Specialities: All genres
https://afepi-ireland.com/member/prendergast-siobhan

Robert Holden

www.draftproofediting.com
Services: Non-fiction developmental edits, line edits, copyediting and proofreading
Specialities: Humanities and social sciences, reports, memoir

Emma Dunne

emma.dunne.edits@gmail.com
Services: Reader's reports, structural editing, copy-editing, proofreading
Specialities: Fiction, children's, young adult, cookery, general non-fiction
https://afepi-ireland.com/member/dunne-emma

Jennifer Armstrong

jarmstrong@edit365.com
Services: Proofreading, copyediting
Specialities: Theatre, history, travel, public administration
https://afepi-ireland.com/member/armstrong-jennifer

Amanda Bell

www.clearasabellwritingservices.ie
Specialities: Poetry, creative non-fiction, literary fiction
https://afepi-ireland.com/member/bell-amanda

Alicia McAuley Publishing Services

aliciamcauley.com
Services: Editing, proofreading, book design, indexing
Specialities: Arts, history, education, Irish language
https://afepi-ireland.com/member/mcauley-alicia

Siobhán Denham

sedenham@gmail.com
Services: Editing and proofreading services for multilingual
authors writing for research institutes, government organisations
and HEIs in the Humanities, Education and Social Sciences
fields
https://afepi-ireland.com/member/denham-siobhan

Maria Mulrooney

maria.phd.editing@outlook.ie
Services: Academic editing
Specialities: Education, Humanities and Social Sciences
https://afepi-ireland.com/member/mulrooneia

Natasha Mac a'Bháird

natashamaca@gmail.com
Services: Proofreading, copy-editing
Specialities: Fiction, children's books, history
https://afepi-ireland.com/member/mac-a-bhaird-natasha

Gráinne Treanor

grainnetreanor.editor@gmail.com
Services: Copyediting and proofreading
Specialities: Non-fiction, education (theory, methodology, philosophy, textbooks), humanities, academic, religion, well-being, general interest
https://afepi-ireland.com/member/treanor-grainne

Michelle Griffin

Michellegriffineditor.com
Services: Developmental and copyediting, manuscript assessments and proofreading
Specialities: Fiction (literary, commercial and speculative), non-fiction (creative non-fiction, Irish history)

Amanda Gray

acgray226@gmail.com
Services: Copyediting, proofreading
Specialities: Academic (defence/security, history/politics), general non-fiction
https://afepi-ireland.com/member/gray-amanda

Perfectly Write Editing & Training

perfectlywrite.eu
editor@perfectlywrite.eu
Services: Copywriting, plain English writing, copyediting,

structural editing, proofreading
Specialities: Law, IT, public sector, history, arts & culture, human rights
https://afepi-ireland.com/member/odwyer-maire

Paula Elmore
paula.elmore@outlook.com
Services: Copy-editing, developmental/structural editing
Specialities: General non-fiction, fiction (YA, children's)
https://afepi-ireland.com/member/elmore-paula

Book Nanny Writing and Editing Services
Booknannyfictioneditor.com
Services: Developmental and structural editing, manuscript assessments, copy-editing
Specialities: Literary fiction, commercial fiction, historical fiction, crime and mystery, fantasy

Geraldine Begley
gpbegley@gmail.com
Services: Indexing and proofreading
https://afepi-ireland.com/member/begley-geraldine

Robert Doran
www.robert-edits.com
Services: Developmental editing and copy-editing
Specialities: Literary fiction, commercial fiction, narrative non-fiction

Meg Walker – The Perfect Word
megwalker@theperfectword.ie
www.theperfectword.ie

Services: Copyediting, proofreading, ghostwriting
Specialities: Non-fiction, creative non-fiction, fiction
https://afepi-ireland.com/member/walker-meg

Liz Beasley

parish.hall.editing@gmail.com
Services: Copy-editing, proofreading, substantive editing
Specialities: Non-fiction, literary fiction, religion, cookbooks, music
https://afepi-ireland.com/member/beasley-liz

Therese Caherty

tcaherty@yahoo.com
Services: Writing, proofreading, editing
Specialties: Education, women's issues, social justice
https://afepi-ireland.com/member/caherty-therese

Dr Rachel Finnegan

rachelfinnegan@gmail.com
Services: Academic proofreading, academic copyediting
Specialties: Art, history, archaeology, official reports

Simon Coury

simoncoury@gmail.com
Services: Developmental editing, editorial assessment, copy-editing
Specialities: Fiction, historical fiction, creative non-fiction, academic editing
https://afepi-ireland.com/member/coury-simon

Elizabeth Mayes

mayese@gofree.indigo.ie
Services: Proofreading and copy editing
Specialties: Art and architecture, especially Irish art; history and heritage subjects

Liza Costello
www.thefictionshed.com
Services: Developmental editing and mentoring services for fiction writers.
Specialities: Standard copy-editing and proofreading for trade publishers.

Richard Bradburn
editor@editorial.ie
editorial.ie
Services: Developmental editing, manuscript assessment, copyediting
Specialties: Literary fiction, commercial fiction, non-fiction, memoir

Aoife Barrett
Barrett Editing
aoife@barrettediting.ie
barrettediting.com
Services: Project Management, developmental and structural editing, copyediting
Specialities: Educational, non-fiction (true crime, biography), children's fiction

Antoinette Walker Editorial Services
amwalker@eircom.net
Services: Writing, ghostwriting, editing, copyediting, proofreading
Specialities: Medicine/healthcare, education, current affairs, history, memoir
https://afepi-ireland.com/member/walker-antoinette

Tom Dwyer
dwyertomj65@gmail.com
Services: Structural editing, copy editing, proofreading

Specialities: Arts and humanities, literature and literary criticism, history, aesthetics and art theory, philosophy, government and politics
https://afepi-ireland.com/member/dwyer-tom

Donna McCormack

donnamccormackedits@gmail.com
Services: Developmental and structural editing, Copyediting, Proofreading, Editorial Project Management
Specialities: Educational textbooks, non-fiction, health and wellness
https://afepi-ireland.com/member/mccormack-donna

Silver View Editing

silverviewediting.com
Services: Copyediting, Proofreading
Specialities: History, historical fiction, politics, sociology, criminology, gender, faith
https://afepi-ireland.com/member/reidy-conor

Rosemary Dawson

Rosemarydawsoned@gmail.com
Services: Project management, copy-editing, commissioning, ghost-writing, publicity
Specialities: Education (post-primary), dyslexia, non-fiction, biography, politics, children's and adult fiction

Brian Langan

Storyline Editing and Storyline Literary Agency

brian@storylineediting.com or brian@storylineagency.com
www.storylineediting.com
Services: Developmental and structural editing, manuscript assessments

Specialties: Literary fiction, commercial fiction,
creative non-fiction

Writing Matters
www.writingmatters.ie
Services: Proofreading, copyediting
Specialities: Non-fiction, academic, health and social sciences

Bríd Nowlan
www.bridnowlan.com
Services: Copyediting, proofreading.
Specialities: Academic books/articles, science, politics, history.

Jane Rogers
janerogersedit@gmail.com
Services: Copy editing, proofreading, indexing.
Specialities: Humanities, education, current affairs, biography/
memoirs, gardening, natural history, cookery, reference, general
non-fiction.

RESOURCES & ORGANISATIONS

ARTS AND DISABILITY IRELAND (ADI)
WWW.ADIARTS.IE

ASSOCIATION OF FREELANCE EDITORS, PROOFREADERS AND INDEXERS OF IRELAND (AFEPI IRELAND)
www.afepi-ireland.com

ALLIANCE OF INDEPENDENT AUTHORS (ALLI)
www.allianceindependentauthors.org

AONTAS NA SCRÍBHNEOIRÍ GAEILGE
www.aontasnascribhneoiri.ie

BOOKS IRELAND
www.booksirelandmagazine.com

BUY THE BOOK
www.buythebook.ie

BOOKSELLING IRELAND
www.booksellers.org.uk

Catherine Gough Editorial
www.catherinegough.ie

Children's Books Ireland
www.childrensbooksireland.ie

CREATE
WWW.CREATE-IRELAND.IE

Creative Commons
www.creativecommons.org

Crescent Arts Centre
www.crescentarts.org

Culture Ireland
www.cultureireland.ie

Dublin UNESCO
www.dublincityofliterature.ie

Duotrope
www.duotrope.com

Editors' and Proofreaders' Alliance of Northern Ireland (EPANI)
www.epani.org.uk

Fighting Words
www.fightingwords.ie

Foras na Gaeilge
www.forasnagaeilge.ie

Illustrators Ireland
www.illustratorsireland.com

Irish Copyright Licensing Agency
www.icla.ie

Irish Pen
www.irishpen.com

Libraries Ireland
www.librariesireland.ie

Literature Ireland
www.literatureireland.com

Match in the Dark
www.matchinthedark.com

Minding Creative Minds
www.mindingcreativeminds.ie

National Adult Literacy
www.nala.ie

National Library of Ireland
www.nli.ie

National Museum Archives
www.museum.ie

Playography Ireland
www.irishplayography.com

Poetry Ireland
www.poetryireland.ie

Publishing Ireland
www.publishingireland.com

Publish OA (Open Access)
www.publishoa.ie

Safe to Create
www.safetocreate.ie

Smashing Times International Centre for the Arts & Equality
www.smashingtimes.ie

The Arts Council of Ireland
www.artscouncil.ie

The Arts Council of Northern Ireland
www.artscouncil-ni.org

The Irish Writers Centre
www.irishwriterscentre.ie

The Irish Writers Union
www.irishwritersunion.org

The Irish Literary Society
www.irishlitsoc.org

The Munster Literature Centre
www.munsterlit.ie

The Oral History Network Ireland
www.oralhistorynetworkireland.ie

The Publishing Training Centre
www.publishingtrainingcentre.co.uk

The Seamus Heaney Centre
www.qub.ac.uk/schools/seamus-heaney-centre

The Society of Young Publishers
www.thesyp.org.uk

The Society of Authors
www.societyofauthors.org

The Stinging Fly
www.stingingfly.org

Verbal
www.theverbal.co

VISUAL ARTISTS IRELAND
www.visualartists.ie

WORDS IRELAND
www.wordsireland.ie

WRITERS GUILD OF IRELAND
www.script.ie

WRITING HQ
www.writershq.co.uk

WRITING.IE
www.writing.ie